THE SIERRAVILLE EXPERIENCE
A Quantum Publication

Quantum T.G.
PO BOX 12103
Reno, Nevada 89510-2103

© 1995 by Thomas
All Rights Reserved
First Publication 1993

Manuscript Printed by Professional Press
Printed in the United States of America
Second Printing 1996

Library of Congress Card Number 95-72522
ISBN 1-57087-212-0

AUTHORS COMMENT

Guidance for the creation of this special work came from various spiritual circumstances and multiple associated events. I make no specific claims as to the narrative's content, verifiability or implied reality. These are meant for you dear ones, to contemplate, process and decide upon. Further, I make no claims to the information contained herein and take no particular credit for the development of this publication. I was only an instrument who was guided and urged to recount or convert the various experiences, messages and Higher Thought input into the written word. I consider my involvement a blessing and fulfillment of one of my many prayers... to be of service to others.

A vast portion of the cosmos, our Earth being part of that sector, is in vibratory transition at this time. A completed transformation will occur in the coming years. Most of us here now, will experience it. The time remaining is precious, if not critical. We are approaching the flashpoint where there can be no turning back. Some of the accompanying events have a possibility of being tumultuous. First delivered to me in 1972, I was uncomfortable about having *any* knowledge of these particular issues, but have since been shown what is actually taking place. The net result of these extraordinary modifications of vibration, will be positive. It will leave its' mark, chronicled with a wonderfully enhanced world, and illuminated humanity.

The diverse and insightful messages found throughout this volume, are not provided nor intended as merely subjective. They illustrate important and tangible concepts of spiritual thinking and application. We pray they will promote for you, a more complete spiritual understanding, elevate within you a higher state of consciousness, personal awareness, and comprehension; and urge from within you a desire to seek, discover and experience self-realization while there is still an opportunity to do so in this changing plane. My friends, we are instrumental in this process of transformation... *we*, hold the key!

CONTENTS

A TRUTH

Spiritual interpretation of life experience,
is the key to divine knowledge

Interwoven in this knowledge, lies divine wisdom.
With wisdom revealed then, comes divine understanding.

How we embrace and apply this understanding,
is that which will hold back, or allow us personal freedom.

Personal freedom does precipitate from spiritual growth,
which in turn, promotes even more experience.

This, is a truth.

ACKNOWLEDGMENTS

To my parents, for their wonderful support and especially just being who they are. I consider myself very fortunate to be a part of you, and of this family.

To Mary, with whom I began my greater and expanded spiritual education and growth. I shall cherish you forever.

To Ron, with whom I received the opportunity in answer to a special prayer, to find spiritual camaraderie, and who assisted in my exploration of further attributes of BEing. You are a very caring and special person, Thank you.

To Maxine, the most significant mentor in my physical life as it concerns spiritual development. You first introduced me to a greater personal knowledge about life and presented a clearer understanding of infinite mind. God bless you and your work.

To Lucille, for showing me my auric self. You have helped so many to understand more about themselves through your special talents and love. Thank you so much.

To Vinnie and Terri, who allowed other understandings about myself, past and present. Thank you.

To Mac, Gator, Floyd, Rubin, Ray and the many others whom I became one with through an extraordinary and special spiritual gathering. Never cease in the sharing of your valuable knowledge, so many good things have and will come from your continued efforts.

To Sal, who allowed me the means and the time to initially produce this work. Thank you.

To the unnamed others who crossed my path for one or more purposes. I now understand.

To No-Eyes, Reya and others, most specifically, to my predominate teacher and guide whose identity came to me during the onset of this creation as Wantanka (seemingly pronounced 'Won-Tonka'), for their wonderful spiritual input, direction, sensitivity and patience. Without the varied experiences and their gentle urging, this manuscript would truly not have been possible.

♥   ♥   ♥

I send *much* Love and Light to you all. I feel blessed with having had the opportunity to share my life with yours, and I am grateful beyond any words.

Thank you all, very much.

V

FORWARD

Dear reader,

Within each of us, there exists an ethereal glow of cosmic thought. That part of us which shares a foundation in Divine Love and is referred to as our soul. This Great Cosmic Light represents our *true* life-form, our Spiritual Self. When we learn that our greater and God granted capabilities lie therein, and then seek to use Universal Laws properly, we will find that we can more fully utilize the fantastic and divine gifts bestowed us. You see, each and every one of us was, and continues to be blessed with absolutely unlimited capabilities.

Creation or the ability to manifest by thought, matter (a 'thing' or end-result) into the physical from the etheric, is but *one* of these precious gifts. Many of us however, can not or will not acknowledge this Cosmic Truth for ourselves, and for a variety of reasons. Yet we do it all the time whether or not we are aware of it, or familiar with *how* it is accomplished. When unique or unexplainable, especially wondrous situations happen in our lives, we usually conclude that they are simply coincidental or happenstance. With this material, you may come to appreciate why they are not.

Desire to experience all of the divine gifts we were given. *Self-realization* is a good first step in developing a working comprehension of a Higher Source of power within yourself. Seek to understand more information on this subject from any positively structured reference. Pursue *only* those concepts which solicit a sincere feeling of spiritual direction and insight. Utilize those which advance knowledge you feel you can accept without reservation. Your heart will know what is right, even if your mind questions. Should you aspire to embrace such concepts, then you may well have taken significant steps toward *your* individual path of awakening, enlightenment, truth and fulfilling yourself as the unique and divine BEing you truly are.

Precious ones, what we have, and will experience in this life as our reality, is actually molded *only* by our perceptions, beliefs and the *kinds* of energy we put forth. Particularly, it is how we utilize such knowledge which will determine each of our destiny's. Collectively inclusive, *we* are the forgers of our terrestrial realm and conditions. Independently however, we are the creator of *our* personal environments and experiences... What then, with increased perception, do we render with *this* knowledge? Our individual and positive efforts will absolutely contribute toward affecting the existing planetary condition for the better, and we *can* impact the conditions previously set up in the ether to experience. These efforts need not be monumental, only pure of heart and of the right intention(s).

And they must begin *within* us. Further, there are no extended costs to bear. No expense but desire and application on our part to make it so. Accordingly, the information in this book is intended to stimulate your mind, offer growth opportunities for yourself that perhaps you haven't considered, possibly answer some complex questions, and hopefully inspire a *basic* life philosophy as it concerns your outlook on personal experience and spiritual awakening.

Our third-dimensional world, as we tend to interpret it, can hold many obstacles for us *IF* we permit it to. In the body of this manuscript, there exist concepts for allowing one to evaluate the constraints of old and accepted dogma's of life, while presenting a foundational direction for the attainment of a higher state of consciousness. Generally speaking, we contest change in our lives. Especially if it involves controversial topics or themes, or goes against our prior and personally embraced teachings. We unknowingly tend to shelter all our beliefs within neat and tidy frameworks of typically rigid and *patterned* thought. It is exactly this particular process which impedes our development.

Expanded thought, allows room for *possibilities* which might otherwise elude human explanation, understanding or possibly, experience. Without it we face unknowns with partial, if not total skepticism and/or fear. We might have no point of reference, no comfort factor from which to interpret what is presented to us. We typically listen to, adopt and apply only that knowledge which feels tangible and is readily understood by us; And even though many may not necessarily be content with how their lives seem to ebb and flow, too often we then choose to accept our lives as they are; or rather, as they *seem* to be.

With this in mind, more of us are beginning to ask profound and sincere questions about the nature of reality, and the meaning of our lives. About *who* we are, *why* our lives are as they are and, is *this* all there is? There is a serious desire and longing to know and understand more, and it is sweeping across the entire planet.

If this material, compiled as an aid for those in search of truth, can motivate us to examine, or at least urge *exploration* of our inner belief systems, then we will have at least given ourselves the option to *have* options in our lives. What we then do with them, is as always, up to us...

May each of you awake to all that you are, in the name of Love,

Thomas

This material is dedicated to all Mankind

PROLOGUE

"A NEW PATH"

Without doubt, our sojourn on this life plane is one of profuse and mixed experiences. Some are planned for, some perhaps not, some placed on our paths purposely to see what we would do with them, others are requested, and still others may occur for reasons not (*yet*) made clear to us. I've heard it said, that all *substantial* life experiences are created. Some could probably debate this perhaps, rhetorical statement forever. I am not here to postulate the merit of any particular response. However, I do believe the bulk of the experiences we encounter are intended for our spiritual growth; as *we* had priorly determined for ourselves before choosing this incarnation. One thing is certain for me as a person, mine have been made manifest for me to grow and learn from. This, I recognize and accept as absolute truth.

I wish I could say that through my life I have made all the proper choices and decisions along my journey, but I clearly didn't. I did the best I knew how or thought I could, now realizing that I had a very limited set of interpretations from which to work with at the time. These limitations clouded many of my views of adult life and played havoc with my purpose for being here. I can say, without reservation that it is easier for me to appreciate those experiences which brought or bring me closer to the truth for myself, including those I once viewed as what one might call "negative" reality.

I am grateful to have come across information allowing for higher understandings and for the positive changes which have occurred within me; But, I *asked* and searched for them! Sure there are things I would do differently if I were to do them now, but that is why our life span is the length it is.

1

THE SIERRAVILLE EXPERIENCE

It allows for perceived personal failure(s) to be replaced by action(s) bearing the fruit of wisdom and knowledge. A perhaps unnoticed continuum of second chances. I am trying to take advantage of these (each existing or new experience) in that I am seeking the worth behind the experience which allows me to incorporate those interpretations which were missing for so long... the Spiritual aspect of Self. To that end, I am still growing, still learning... I ardently persist in seeking and fine tuning the proper "eyes and ears" to better see and hear the world around me. I feel even now, that I have an infinitely grander understanding of that world. Of how situations come into being, hidden purposes behind the physical form, of why there is anguish and why there is joy, and how all of the pieces of our individual puzzles fit neatly together when we really understand what the bigger picture is.

In discussions with others, common questions are repeatedly raised: "Why can't we go through life without encountering the pitfalls we do?" "What prevents us from traversing through our life from Point-A to Point-Z in a straight unencumbered line?" "Why is life, at times, so damn difficult?" These wonderfully in-depth questions allude to several things...

Firstly, we are not yet perfect in all aspects of BEing. Man in general, has imbalances in his multifaceted essence. Only now do we openly and more intimately begin to discuss the <u>four</u> primary natures of Man: the Mental, the Emotional, the Physical and the *Spiritual* as being intertwined parts of the whole. Each of these attributes has a need to be realized. One or more of these, for reasons unique to each of us, has a need to be healed and/or expanded from within before aggregate spiritual growth can continue. If we have imbalances within our overall 'system', we hinder our ability to accomplish and attain. We can literally waste our entire existence and purpose on this plane if we are too engrossed with the physical or get too side-tracked by earthly influences. In consideration of this, certain events may occur at times in our lives in order that we get purposefully steered back to our specific task(s) at hand... to rise *beyond* the focus of just ourselves!

Secondly, should one already possess completed growth, there would be no absolute mandate for retaining our third-dimensional existence. Therein lies the evidence for the variations experienced in any given physical life. Many of our experiences come into being to attempt to get us to recognize that perhaps we might (or could) have take a different approach to certain experiences, and thusly have altered the result or effect. If truly understood, they bring to our attention deficiencies (not given as a negative term) in our interpretation of life. "Ask, and you shall receive"... Direction, information, guidance. Not for trivial pursuit, but for earnest desire to bring extended comprehension, balance and harmony into our life.

Lastly, due to the fact that we normally overlook various pearls of knowledge when they do manifest consciously (or empirically), we find ourselves repeating experiences which may (on the outside) look different due to circumstances, but retain an underlying premise of wisdom which we have failed to grasp. We are, without doubt, our own worst adversary of personal progress. All too often this is unrecognizable, even to those *seeking* growth.

As was pointed out to me: An evergreen tree has many branches and they do all connect to the upward bound trunk. So it is in our own life. We find *ourselves* branching out, taking an infinite number of side roads as we travel through life. All of these roads lead to experiences. Once encountered, we return to our main path hopefully centering ourselves with what we've learned. Sometimes however, lack of knowledge, understanding, stress or frustration blocks our growth or obscures the lessons. Yet when we do come to understand and as we grow from within, the side roads become fewer just as the branches of the evergreen become fewer and smaller near the top. Above which is the apex, or that part which is closest to the Light.

Indeed I have traveled many a side road and many times asked the question, "Why can't I seem to get it right?" The answer (I learned) was *always*: because I was not listening. I do not speak of our physical senses. I refer to the heart, mind and soul communication which lights the path of decision and guides us with absolute cognition. That aspect ignored for the millennium, the fantastic connection to our Source. Therein lies our higher dimension of Self.

Feeling that this attribute was seemingly absent from my active consciousness, I sought to "find" it and incorporate it into my BEing. Of course it had always been there, I just didn't recognize it for what it was. My efforts and persistence have been, and continue to be rewarded. If only by a token experience I find new meaning and understanding, then I can say I'm headed in the right direction. But even this direction, I find, has multiple courses transcending accepted reality and experience. Not long ago I found myself on one such path. A unique path, and one I believe to be an outgrowth of my expanding consciousness. It began in 1991, as what I unwittingly at the time interpreted as a rather intense and peculiar dream...

So acute were my senses and so real and tangible were the surroundings, that I awoke and sat straight up in my bed... It was about four in the morning. I tried to logically discount the images I had been witness to, as at the time they made no sense, being scattered 'live film shorts' of another place and time totally unfamiliar to me. They began with finding myself far out in a body of water *slowing* turning from left to right, taking in all of the scenery. I had no flotation device(s), no boat, nothing; yet I was standing upright with most of my body out of the water.

THE SIERRAVILLE EXPERIENCE

How was this physically possible? As I turned in the water under the warm rays of the sun, I perceived the vastness of a shoreline and a deep forest of trees... but nary a soul was seen. It seemed that I was completely alone, but I didn't feel apprehensive, nor necessarily isolated. Other 'scenes' followed this one. Taken collectively I felt they must mean something significant, I was sure of it... but what exactly? Then this stop and go 'movie' ended... and *much* more dramatically than it had started.

I found myself standing in front of an old graying tree stump about two feet in diameter and solarplexus high. The top was weathered and fairly flat. Upon this and centered, were seven river stones of three sizes. There was nothing unusual about the stones, except how they were placed... They formed a pyramid. The three larger stones were placed side-to-side forming a triangle. On these were similarly placed, three smaller stones rotated by sixty degrees so that they laid in the upper crevices formed by the bottom three stones. Centrally placed on top of this second row of stones was a single and yet smaller stone. What where these doing sitting on a stump next to a meadow I wondered. I was so intrigued with this formation of rock, I spent what seemed like minutes examining it. I then recalled from my scouting days that such a formation was an American Indian sign indicating "You're on the right path", or "Continue on this path".

As this moment sank in, my attention was drawn such that I looked up from the stack of rocks before me. There, immediately on the other side of the stump, were two male Indians. *Maidu.* Together we formed a triangle around the base of the stump. I don't know how they got there and I wasn't shaken by their sudden appearance. I was as calm as one would be meeting old friends. However, I can not say that I knew *who* they were, only that I was very comfortable with them. I looked them over as they stood before me.

They were not ceremonially dressed, although they were in full length skins. These clothes bore some very modest bead work around the upper chest area. Unseen and distanced behind these two I sensed many more standing about, including more males, women and children. What's more, I sensed an established community, and I felt them all to be family. The two in front of me looked solemnly into my eyes as if that was all they saw of me. They neither smiled or frowned. They made no sound, nor did they move in any way except for their long black hair which gently moved in the light breeze. They simply, *were*. It was then that I awoke.

I had never (consciously anyway) remembered having a dream about water, forests or Native Americans, so in that regard I found the data extraordinarily odd. I passed off the vivid experience as an overworked mind and imagination and attempted to forget it... but I just couldn't shake the absolute realness of what I had experienced.

Approximately thirty days later however, I was to find substantiation to this dream which precluded any logical explanation I could have come up with on my own. My dream was in fact, a vision.

I love to camp, I always have. When I say camp, I mean no RV, no radios, TV or other distractions of 20th century life. Me, my tent and the wilderness, whenever and wherever possible. My significant other and I had decided to find a nice place to relax for the weekend in the mountains surrounding Sierraville, preferably near water and in the pines. We had been in this area many times for day trips, so we were pretty familiar with what was available.

The day was overcast and a tad bit chilly. For some reason we just couldn't locate a satisfactory place to bivouac. Nothing we found really 'felt' right. This had *never* been a problem for us; we'd eagerly make almost any place do. Today though, we couldn't mutually agree on any location... *this* was very odd. We'd been searching for hours and the weather was intermittently sprinkling us with light snow and most often, rain showers. To our chagrin, we decided to drive to one of the more popular lakes in the area as time and light were now running out. When we got there, people were packed in together tighter than sardines in a can. Radios blaring, wild children and dogs running everywhere. This was definitely not our idea of camping. Where was the 'space'... And where was the *tranquillity*? That *one* thing demanded most by serious campers.

We decided to return home, very disappointed. On the way we became aware that a turn off to another secluded lake was available to us. As we reached the crossroad, we stopped and debated whether or not to proceed. It was an unknown to us both, and a dirt passage beside. There would be no markings to indicate how to get there, we didn't have a map and the 'road' was more than probably intersected by a multitude of forestry, fire and other 'roads'... Should we? Instinct told us no. Surely the weather had muddied the route, and we knew the risks of going into unmapped mountain areas exploring at approaching dusk, leaving no message as to our whereabouts in case we were to get lost or stuck. Not a wise thing to do. Then, as if we were urged by an interceding force, we abruptly and jointly decided to turn off the highway *in spite* of what was felt to be well founded trepidation.

The wind appeared to calm down and the setting sun shined on and off through the broken cloud mass. The road became curiously dry and we experienced no more soggy weather. We passed several turnoffs, eventually taking a several mile detour which we had to retrace. Had we not seen a *tiny* faded hand made sign that read "Lake 5 miles" (the arrow pointed back, the way we came... *what*!?...) approximately twenty feet off the ground nailed to a well enshrouded pine tree, we'd probably still be looking.

THE SIERRAVILLE EXPERIENCE

From that point on something lead us toward the lake through all the turns we could have wrongly taken, but didn't. It became quite obvious to us that only someone who was meant to find the lake, was suppose to. These mountain roads were always laid out like labyrinths and often difficult to traverse when dry. As we made our approach not having a clue to how much further it was, a broken assembly of water appeared through the trees. This had to be the lake! We drove to, and then along the shore area finding a wonderfully sheltered place to stop. I got out of our vehicle and felt an overwhelming warmness and closeness. Somehow I *knew* this place... My exact, relaxed and first words were: "I'm home". It actually felt closer to me than anywhere in the continental states that I had ever been or camped.

This was a holiday weekend, so where were all the other campers? Why should, or how could a place this beautiful be so empty? There wasn't a soul around, we were isolated - all to ourselves. Certainly others would soon arrive... We unpacked our supplies and made camp. The trees around our site made a cozy shelter from the wind coming off the lake, as well as providing for overhead protection from what looked like impending rain.

Traces of which were visible since the ground was damp, but thankfully, at least it wasn't wet. Evening came and we made dinner after having explored the area for a while. It seemed like the entire place was alive with electrical energy; but it was neither storm nor mechanically generated. We definitely felt a strong and magnificent presence here. Later on we walked the shoreline with a flashlight since there was no moon this evening to light our path, eventually returning to our campsite.

Earlier we had prepared for having a fire and decided to light it while making some coffee to warm up with. We talked of how special the atmosphere was here in this hidden paradise, how absolutely beautiful and comforting it was. This lead to us meditating for a while prior to putting out the fire and heading for the zip-together sleeping bags. My confidant, Mary, fell asleep quickly while I laid there contemplating the day. Then there was the cry of a nighthawk. A shrill sound, which utters the emotions of security and warning in the same breath. This cry is special to Native Americans. It means among other things, that the all-knowing night spirits were present and offering their unseen protection. It's cry gave me a special feeling.

The forest was so absolutely quiet after the wind had stopped, that it seemed if a leaf or pine needle should fall it would certainly awaken its' local inhabitants. I was beginning to drift off now, warm and pleasantly tired from this days exercise and adventure. I then heard in the distance what sounded like a dog's bark. It was definitely annoyed. I got the impression it was restrained, but wanted release very badly. Moments later it became quiet again.

PROLOGUE

Not quite asleep, I had been jerked wide awake wondering about the presence of a dog, but slowly found myself drifting toward the land of nod once again. Mary, already there, never moved a muscle since entering the sleeping bag. *Then*, came the footsteps from the darkness... bearing in from the remote far front-left, toward us and our vehicle parked directly fifteen feet from our heads. *Not* your ordinary bipedal footsteps mind you, these literally shook the very forest ground we were sleeping on. There was no softness in these well spaced two-legged movements. My heart began to pound furiously, my throat seemed to instantaneously dry out and I found myself unable, or perhaps unwilling, to move. I discovered I could however and attempted to quietly waken my better half, who in normal circumstances would have no problem in doing so, but could not keep her awake.

Each time I got her attention, the footsteps and any associated noises would cease and she would black out, falling immediately back to deep sleep. When she *would* reply, it would be with a trance-like incoherency. Every time her head hit the pillow, the movements would start up again. It was like that 'thing' out there knew! After four or five attempts to fully waken her, I gave up. Obviously she just was not going to respond. 'Odd... Why can't I get her attention?' I thought. To me, this situation seemed to approach absolute seriousness! I felt alone and totally vulnerable. These sounds were most unsettling and I was very uneasy. I had to face this experience by myself for some reason and I didn't want to. I knew there were no bears up here, but still, I desperately wanted to be anywhere but here. My logical mind began to produce negative what-if's.

The footsteps then ceased and I heard what sounded like large, heavy, definitely hair laden extremities of an unknown creature "feeling" our vehicle. It began its exploration on the hood, slowly walking around the entire frame, then stopped directly between us and our transportation. I wanted to yell out to it, but didn't dare. "IT", now stood still. I suddenly picked up a stray thought that IT was simply investigating, but this gave me *very* little comfort. If my muscles could have moved more I probably would have found myself shaking uncontrollably. Our visitor then walked directly *at* the tent. IT took two steps to do so, with one shortened step as it halted within inches of the side of the tent. IT had to have weighed 700 or 800 pounds to shake the ground like that! Our heads were only ten inches on the other side and I was wondering what was going to happen next.

Mentally, I anxiously prayed for 'him' to leave. 'Please go away... Leave us alone, we don't want any trouble.' It seemed that I repeated this thought twenty times. I've slept with bears and mountain lions coming into camp, no big deal, but *this* was neither of those! Not taken to fright easily I have never been so unnerved in my life. IT just stood there, making no sound what-so-ever. I couldn't even hear IT breathing!

THE SIERRAVILLE EXPERIENCE

I was literally waiting for a gigantic hand and arm to come ripping through the side of the tent. I know IT must have heard my heart pounding away and sensed my fear. The ground shook again as IT turned to it's right and walked ever so slowly and carefully around our tent, making sure not to disturb the long guy ropes. IT seemed to go purposely 'out of it's way' to avoid interfering any further with our campsite; totally ignoring our separate kitchen/cooking area which contained all manner of eats, both exposed and contained. With all those wonderful smells, a bear would have stopped at nothing to get at a snack, and they can be quite noisy doing so. This area (covered and enclosed on two sides by tarps) was also shorn up by long guy ropes, which *we* tripped over in broad daylight *knowing* that they were there! We also had various ropes tied to surrounding trees as clothes lines cutting off the entire back portion of our campsite. How could IT have possibly avoided all of them, it was pitch black outside?! Moments later it became discontentingly quiet.

Was IT contemplating returning to investigate more? I then heard distant trash cans being tossed around like they were play toys. Then again, silence. I soon sensed 'he' was leaving the area and felt comfortable enough to go to sleep.

Morning came and as I so often do when camping, I slept in. Sleeping in a forest environment is so relaxing and special to me. I love to take advantage of those moments. I'm not sure what time it was when I opened my eyes, but I must have needed the extra rest. I turned over to Mary, but she wasn't there! I panicked. Rapidly dressing I called out to her... No response. Zipping down the tent doorway, I scanned the area for her still calling out. What the blazes had happened here? Where was she? Had I slept through her abduction? How would this be possible? I am a very light sleeper... I found absolutely no clues necessary for an intelligent mind to make any sense out of this situation. Worry was overtaking me.

I decided to look for footprints in the morning dampness, in the grasses and sandy soil around the campsite. Not only did I not find hers, I found nothing of our late night visitor. Surely nothing that weighed that much could have left not a single impression in the sandy earth, nor not bent the grasses under it's bulk. After walking much of the close forest boundaries, I ended up waiting anxiously for hours not having any idea where she might be. Then I heard the snapping of twigs as *she* walked toward camp from the Northeast. I felt agitated and relieved at the same time. Why didn't she at least leave me a note? What if something had happened to her, she could have been anywhere in a ten mile radius... (I tell you this, her sudden appearance was more comforting to me than she'll ever know; especially in light of what had occurred during the night.)

She informed me she had simply gone for a walk, finding a small fire road for most of her trek. A *walk*, that took her half way around the lake! She said she had to make her own way and trails for some of the journey, laying out signs that she would hopefully recognize as she returned. This effort proved successful. As she shared her adventure, she spoke of things which more than grabbed my attention. She said she felt as if she had been observed from the forest for almost all of her hike. At one juncture this sensation unnerved her to the point that she opted to return to camp; and anyway, she reasoned, it was getting late and she thought she should get back.

Returning, she caught a breeze that brought a tremendously heavy and foul odor with it. What was *this* doing amidst the sweetness of the pines, herbs and wild flowers? Being the inquisitive type, she investigated the smell by walking off the fire road and into the forest. So strong was the emanation, that she was sure she was going to find a large dead body of some nature. The smell was nauseating, but she continued to walk deeper into the brush. Instead she found only a flat and dried out corpse of a rabbit.

Picking it up, she cautiously sniffed the air around it to see if this was the source... it wasn't. Then in an instant she noticed the ever present and overwhelming scent had *moved*, it was gone. And so was she! She also recounted her find of a huge portion of a tree trunk. It had probably been sectioned from a large pine by the forestry service along time before her arriving upon it. What made it stand out, was the fact that there were no other sections of the tree to be found anywhere near this piece, AND it was stuck firmly into the ground on the single eight to ten inch diameter stub of a limb protruding from it's side. Showing it to me later, I was amazed to see the stump standing several feet above the ground on that limb, *like a marker*. I estimated the weight to have been several hundred pounds.

In repacing her trek she also showed me several trees that had had some of their bark ripped off in a downward motion, not laterally. These were oddities to us as we'd never encountered anything like this in all of our outdoor experiences. These pieces were typically removed at the twelve to fifteen foot or higher level and were two to three foot in length. No claw marks were indicated or found. Bears would typically mark the bottom portion of a tree leaving tell-tale nail marks etched into the trunk. It was like these had been simply peeled like a banana. We reasoned from the perceivable data, especially in light of my sharing about our strange visitor, that these must also be markers... but for what purpose or for whom? Or better yet, *what*? We later came up with a very strong suspicion.

It was a beautifully warm day and we explored much of the surrounding country, spying small groups of deer here and there.

THE SIERRAVILLE EXPERIENCE

Several ospreys flew over the lake while various other foul bobbed on top of it, all looking for lunch. We thought that a good idea and returned to camp for some munchies. Still finding ourselves alone, we later explored the shoreline finding many osprey feathers. We then ventured into other areas of the forest finding red-tail hawk feathers and to our astonishment, an unbroken osprey egg in a small tributary. We collected these things, I suppose out of their uniqueness, and carefully packed them away. In the afternoon of the next day I decided to go for a swim. To my amazement, the incline of the lake bottom was extremely shallow. I walked straight out into the brisk water. Approximately forty or fifty yards from the shore I stopped. The water was only up to my waist, with gentle shore bound waves occasionally mating with my chest.

As I began to turn to my right to view the shoreline, I felt as if I were suddenly in *extreme* slow motion. I can not really say I felt dizzy, but something awfully close to it. It was the strangest sensation. 'Had I been in a similar situation like this one before?' That wasn't possible... *Was it*? Not to my conscious knowledge. Soon the blanketing affect and feeling left me and I actively began to enjoy the water, swimming about for quite awhile. I later reached the shore and laid in the warm sand to relax and dry off.

It was approaching the time for us to pack up and head for home. I longed to stay another day but other obligations called us both back in the morning. We ate lunch, broke down the camping gear stowing most of it away, and took in some last views before we were to head out. Mary bent down to examine a forest flower growing at the base of a tree. During these last moments I realized that I had had several occasions of what I felt was paramnesia, or what we all commonly call deja vue. Experiences that alluded to my having already had them, the details of which felt too familiar to discount. This wasn't possible, as we had never been here before; nor as we found out later, is there any information published about where we were. What exactly, had drawn us here?

We finished the packing and started out the way we had come, mentioning between ourselves that we want to spend a lot more time at this special place. Not far from the ingress to the lake I saw something that caught my breath. I absolutely *had* to stop and get out. There on my left side was the meadow and the stump in my dream, exact in *every* detail right down to the seven stones setting upon it! Now it all came back... All of my recent experiences were exact replicas of the film shorts in that past dream... but to what end? What purpose? What was I to learn? Questions filled my head as I got back into the vehicle and continued toward home. I knew then I had to return, nothing could possibly keep me from coming back. There was more for me to experience here and I knew it!

A week or so afterward, I contacted a clairvoyant friend of mine to share our trip and what had occurred. She asked me to bring the feathers and the egg to my office, telling me that she wanted to see them and that she would bring a friend over to hear the narrative and view the items found. I met a most wonderful person that night. He was a Native American, a Choctaw. Mild mannered and soft spoken. You could just feel the love and warmth extending out of this man. Never have I met anyone quite like him. I cherish the moments and times shared with him until he moved on. I will never forget him.

He laid the feathers out on the carpet in a manner and arrangement with reasons known only to him. He touched and handled the plumage as if they were newborn infants, gently placing each item so as to configure a silent but purposeful form. Then he asked for the egg, and placed it among the feathers. He was quiet for some moments, intently focused on the pattern before him. He picked up a crooked feather and was moved to place it next to two others. The three feathers then slowly straightened out, as if by unseen hands! I shall not reveal the comments he made over the next minutes as he considered what was being shown to him and occurring to us, sacred. He went on to share with me that it was important for humanity that I take these things back to the lake and ceremonially bury them, saying a prayer over them when I was finished. I was instructed: 'To bury them in such a manner that they faced a certain direction, being laid out as was before us now, and to a depth that none could disturb it, nor even recognize its placement thereto.'

Needless to say, I was anxious for another trip "home". Very little time passed before we placed ourselves once more in the depths of nature. Taking off right after work, we arrived in late afternoon for the weekend. We again found ourselves to be alone in the wilderness. The dusking sky was overcast with a rather fierce wind blowing in off the lake, making it hard to stand unprotected. I prepared the burial site and smudged us off as the sky began its transformation into night, mentally asking permission to continue within the confines of a prayer. When I was finished, I topped off the site with an extremely large rock and removed any traces of our being there. As we stood back, the winds instantly stopped! At first, we made no association... A wonderful calmness now permeated the entire area, remaining with us throughout the evening.

The next day brought in a few day-trippers and a couple of overnighters, but not until the early afternoon. We made breakfast and took off to do some further exploring. Again, an unseen presence was all around us. That being the concealed and unique life-force energies, not particularly the unusual night visitor's energy... at least at that time we didn't presume they were one in the same. In fact, we still aren't sure. I do suspect that the visitor's energy could actually be a part of the overall vibration in this region.

11

THE SIERRAVILLE EXPERIENCE

We really feel that there is an abundance of various spiritual energies permeating the area. One of our travels took us along the near side of the lake. It gave us the impression at times that we were walking the Black Forest. The old, sometimes overgrown path we were traveling was shrouded overhead by branches so thick in places it many times blocked out all light from the sun. It (this entire area) was alive... well beyond the life forms of the deer, little critters and birds we came across. We felt that if we were to speak out, 'someone' would have surely answered us from the underbrush and ferns. The sensation was fantastic. As we progressed we intermittently talked between ourselves in soft tones so as not to disturb the nature we were feeling and witnessing. We did this instinctively.

At one point we stopped in our tracks, recognizing that we more than several times had heard voices while we were talking to each other. Yet we were the only ones (physically speaking) up here. We began to walk again and the voices manifested once more. We both heard them and immediately looked at each other in silence as we smiled at each other. They came from our right, up the slopes back into the forest. It was as if you were just able to hear a large group of people busy doing daily activities and communicating between themselves. We could make out voices of both genders, as well as those of the mature and the young, but couldn't understand the verbiage. Sometimes they would seem to suddenly stop and then later and just as suddenly, start up again. They occurred whether we were standing still, moving, talking or being quiet.

The voices never seemed to get closer, nor did they ever fade. They maintained the same level of intensity over several miles of our hike. When we came back down the path they would again occur, but stayed to our left. The strong impression it left us both with, was that of an active Indian village going about their lives and business. I use the word *impression*, because both of us are 'sensitive' in certain ways to the unseen world of vibration and energy, albeit not always in the same manner, at the same time nor at the same intensities.

Unusual experiences can often happen to a group of people and only certain ones will sense anything out of the (physically) normal; or perhaps several will, or they might all sense different and individual things unique to that particular occurrence. Perhaps only one person will sense anything out of the ordinary. This is due to several reasons: Sometimes the message(s) are meant for only one individual, as they continue their spiritual awakening and growth. Yet most often to what degree we might have an experience, depends on how fortified are our walls of security are and how open our mind is to the unknown and unseen. In some mixed groups, the individuals will tend to vacillate somewhere between acceptance and fear of such unknowns. Then there is the especially interesting and acute matter of: "*Are we ready*?"

One can have the bejesus scared out of them if they experience something that is foreign to their comprehension, beliefs, understandings or interpretations of (third-dimensional) life. And sometimes this very thing happens. Initially (the first time) occurring to get our attention, but many times it leaves an unfavorable impression on the witness. This is indeed unfortunate. Especially if one fails to TRY to understand what has happened, or simply refuses to acknowledge that it did. We create reasoning based in so much question that the experience becomes 'un-real'. Many of us will push such experiences into the depths of our minds. We call this repression. An act of consciousness which puts frightening, unexplainable or intangible data to rest. It hides it behind our active capacities for confrontation. This act can also keep us 'in the dark' as it were, by not allowing us to pursue, evaluate or explore. It can hold us back and keep us confused by not allowing knowledge to become manifest, through desire to resolve. How can one possibly come to appreciate such a situation if they refuse to seek out, accept or use tools or information which are readily available to accomplish that task?

As Mary and I walked, we talked about what people are missing out on recalling part of the statement used in the Star Trek series... "The last frontier". To us it has an entirely different meaning. It isn't space, the stars or even the bottom of the ocean, as some present day scholars claim. It is the spiritual aspect of Man. In this search, one need not be a rocket scientist nor even have an education. Each voyage is unique to each individual, yet all are predicated on the same spiritual truths. One need only seek these truths and attempt to incorporate them into their lives to experience new dimensions of Self and Life. As we neared the campsite, the first rural visitors came rolling in. We made lunch and gathered some wood for that evening's fire.

Afterward we decided to go exploring, this time in a new direction. On occasion we would hear a voice, or perhaps two in conversation. Like before, they were just enough out of range to be able to understand the words clearly. It's like a person tightly cupping a hand over their mouth and attempting to speak. Standing right next to them you can not understand what they're saying, but you clearly know they are speaking. Sometimes these voices would sound male, sometimes female. At other infrequent times, they almost sounded like early 1900's American English. Voices can travel quite a distance over water, this is a fact, but in thick underbrush and forest environments a voice is baffled and subdued within multiple tens of yards of the speaker. On this particular hike we were well into the woods, crossed many a hill, and at times were no closer than a mile to the lake. Yet most of the time the voices sounded as close to us as ten or twenty feet away. Again, they didn't fade or get louder as we moved about. The voices simply either were, or were not with us.

THE SIERRAVILLE EXPERIENCE

Occasionally we would hear what sounded like a large piece of wood solidly bashed into tree, perhaps ten feet or so off the ground. Usually there would only be one strike, but sometimes we might hear two, or even several spaced out in unusual time increments. Even with the night of our visitor (speaking for myself) we have never felt threatened in this place, and we don't feel like we are intruders. We do however, 'feel' occasional odd etheric vibrations. Odd because they're undefined, or new to us. Mary and I agreed that we had to tell our association of 'sensitive' friends about this inspiring site. We've since concluded and truly feel this place to be one of learning, healing and consolation.

There have been many trips made to this forest wonderland since our first locating it. Multiple times alone, and multiple times with our friends. We have located an ancient medicine wheel, and what we call the Medicine Rock. This monolith has seven trees growing around it, with one growing out of the top center. It is quite large and flat on the top and sits all by itself. One particular weekend, we had a special ceremony here. It was a perfect day, not a cloud anywhere. Just as we were ending, a huge heart shaped cloud formed overhead as if in recognition of why we were there.

Some of our other experiences have been incredible. Between those of us who venture up on a regular basis, we have individually seen small forest stick people (for lack of better words) and fully formed and various sized shadow people that appear and disappear; heard footsteps following us closely with no visible entity attached to them; seen parts of the near-forest actually undulate by what looks like thick heat waves; at night we've experienced a sudden upright elongated ball of silent light, perhaps three by four feet in size, appearing three dimensional to us, which after several moments just as suddenly disappeared (it never moved); had sounds manifest that can't be linked to known wild creatures, and taken some unusual pictures.

There were sightings of large undulating lights across the lake where no-one in their right mind would try to camp. The terrain there is rough, rocky and not conducive to level habitation. Exploring it later gave no hint of any recent people or fires. In several cases it seemed a night voice would communicate to only one individual, and *always*, we feel a presence. One morning through the trees not far from the lake, two of us saw a large bright silvery 'object' moving near the ground. We never did locate it.

These experiences for the most part, have been witnessed by almost two dozen of us... And with every new trip, there are new experiences. We do not all experience the same things, nor at the same times and some things seem to manifest only to certain parties. On one journey, four of us were hiking far back from the lake and came into a small elongated meadow.

PROLOGUE

On the far side of the meadow came our familiar knocking, but this time it was different. It produced *sets* of knocks, some shorter than others, yet continued in its unusual rhythms as we stood there and listened. We decided to approach the cluster of pines from which the emanations were occurring. It did not cease as we approached. We eventually encircled this cluster as a group, and later separately, while the knocking continued. It seemed to say "We are *here*". After listening for about fifteen minutes, two of us decided to enter the cluster. As we did, the sounds ceased. Inside of the cluster was a large circular area. It was entirely surrounded by pines so thick you couldn't see out, but you could see straight up to the sky. It was peaceful inside of that circle of trees, yet the knocking was gone and remained silent even after we had gone back outside of the cluster. We waited for sometime to hear more, but to no avail.

That night brought more wonders. As we had just finished dinner, we were star gazing. Flying what looked like right over the area, were three bright lights. They were in the formation of a triangle, very geometrical but widely spaced. You could see many stars between them. You could also see them independently waver out of line a bit as they passed. No sound was heard. They were several miles up into the clear night sky and flew in a straight line until they were out of sight. We have seen jets and planes at various altitudes fly over head there, and always one can hear the engines and see the safety lights.

These vehicles had no visible strobes, or any other lights associated with them, they were each only a solid light perhaps slightly golden in color, with misty edges. Then, as if out of one of the scenes from Close Encounters, the night sky filled with moving lights. None of us had never seen anything like *this* before! They came from several different directions. Most however approached from the same direction as the triangular three. Two came *from* where the three in formation had gone, using the same path, playing what looked like tag with each other. Flying side-by-side, then racing around each other, giving the appearance of a cat-n'-mouse game. Then the show was over. Overall, we counted at least eighteen objects. Satisfied at having been given a special opportunity, the others left and retired their binoculars for the night, for coffee and more conversation. I sat alone in the open darkness awhile before joining the rest, contemplating what I strongly feel will soon be a unique visitation.

For many years, I have felt that when the time was right, I would have a personal close encounter experience 'of the third kind'. Three years ago I had an intense dream (?) of being invited aboard one especially large craft commandeered by an actual *family* of beautiful individuals. A man, a woman and a young boy, and they all seemed to glow with a beautiful, but faint aura of golden light. It was the woman who had approached me first...

15

THE SIERRAVILLE EXPERIENCE

I was offered an opportunity to travel with them with full knowledge that it would be many (earthly) lifetimes before they returned. They even gave me permission to document the fact that they were here with our video camera, so I could leave this data behind if I chose to go with them so my family would know exactly what had occurred. I was permitted to view an internal section of the craft, which seemed to be as large as several stadiums. It appeared several hundred feet tall.

I saw countless items from various worlds stored (apparently locked and suspended in mid air) upon acres of massive metal structures looking much like I-beams. My first thought at seeing familiar items, including aircraft, was that they were abducting them. A mental impression quickly came to me that this wasn't the case at all. The items weren't stolen, and they *never* tampered with humans or other lifeforms, but did take various opportunities to 'pick up' lost, abandoned or crashed items of technology.

These items represented where various forms of 'Man' was, as far as his technology was concerned, and mirrored his level of achievement and echoed purposes of such knowledge. Yes, we too, were being studied... but in a remote 'hands-off' sense. I asked to see and was shown the flight controls, and 'knew' that anything else I wanted to know would be just as easily disclosed to me. Communication was always telepathic and they were extremely warm and friendly.

If I decided to go with them, everything I would need for my comfort would be made available at my request. I later found myself back in my room again with Mary, apparently having decided not to go at that time. Well, so much for getting too personally side-tracked...

Up to now, the closest I've physically been to actual daylight crafts is about fifteen hundred feet away. Personally, I am looking forward to meeting other forms of Man (Universal interpretation). Although acknowledging potential awkwardness, and possible nervousness, I have absolutely no *fear* of such a rendezvous. Day or night, I believe I am ready to learn and to experience.

Our 'group' believes this forest vortex to be not only an awakening area for us as individuals, but more importantly, a classroom environment where we have an opportunity to become comfortable enough with these strange and significant experiences by repeated exposure so that full disclosure of one kind or another may ultimately be obtained. Independently and/or collectively. What, when or how it occurs is not important to us; nor to, or for whom. We all feel strongly however, that further enlightening event(s) will eventually occur in expanded detail.

- - - - - - -

All of the foregoing which I have just shared, has been accurate and of a true re-accounting. There have been absolutely *no* embellishments. To have modified any detail would have been counter-productive and misleading. This very special place in the mountain woods is real. The experiences had, were real. The people who shared in these experiences are real and come from many walks of life, and are not taken to delusional manifestations, nor any impedance of mental capacities. All are 'sensitives' and each is continuing to explore their own growth from within; seeking to understand the awesome and beneficial spiritual aspects of multi-dimensional reality... *Suprareality*. The exact word 'given' me to share.

Our fundamental purpose in such exploration has nothing whatever to do with entertainment, frivolity, notoriety, materialistic gain, theatrics, cultism, 'show' or passive experimentation. It is to re-awaken, study and use those extraordinary capabilities and specialized pieces of knowledge locked away in the recesses of our individual higher essence and consciousness. Held there by the threads of social suppression, structure and teachings. It is to gain information and or direction which can best be utilized for our individual and spiritual growth. It is to strengthen the direct link to our Source so that we may best use God's gifts. We wish to utilize these abilities in ourselves not only to continue our growth, but so that we may better help others if called upon, in their search of themselves and the true purpose of Life... in the name of brotherly love. Nothing more, nothing less.

Love is the greatest and most absolute power in the cosmos. So many will tell you that this is true, yet so few really understand what it actually implies. The time has come to break the stifling and restrictive bonds of the materialistic third-dimensional thinking of Mankind if we are to continue our habitation of this wonderful and magnificent blue space marble. To do so means that we must all come to understand the infinite word: Love.

- - - - - - -

For our and other groups of like minded souls, I personally ask: Are you also willing to explore the possibilities? To go where few upon this plane as yet have ever ventured... To experience dimensions of suprareality?

If you are so inclined, then what follows is information permitted for me to share, beginning after one particular visit to our special place in the mountains and close communion with a very special entity. I have recaptured for you, the events exactly as I participated in them, or was shown. It was an amazing set of experiences which left me with a simple concluding impression... That at the very *least*, some of these details were made available to illustrate substantial information which we as humankind should give careful, if not full consideration to.

THE SIERRAVILLE EXPERIENCE

Should even one concept of enlightenment pull on your heart strings, then perhaps you are ready to explore. If one idea urges inquisitiveness from you, then perhaps you should follow that lead. If one principle becomes even a little clearer, attempting to use it may provide wonderful benefits for you.

Listen to your inner heart and consciousness. You may or may not hear a voice, but you will however sense a direction, a rightness, a knowing... a new path to walk upon.

With that in mind, let's meander down a most intriguing footpath together...

JOURNAL 1

✵

"MANY QUESTIONS"

Late one uneventful evening after everyone had decided to turn in for the night, I felt motivated to take an unaccompanied walk through the trees down to the lake's edge. Having sat around our campfire attempting once again to extract why it could be that we stumbled into this extraordinary area of vibrations and energies, I had decided to meditate under the starlit sky and ponder further. I relaxed against a large rock by the shore and gazed into the twinkling diamonds of the heavens.

After a moment I thought to myself 'I want to know more'; 'If there is but a single purpose to finding this place, please let me know what it is.' I shut my eyes and began to meditate. Soon thereafter, came the sound of someone or some 'thing' walking in the sand, breaking my concentration. I opened my eyes and sat so I had a better view of the immediate area. Approaching me from the right was what appeared to be a man, apparently taking an evening walk to relax. As he came nearer I offered "Beautiful night isn't it?" He responded pleasantly and asked me if I was enjoying my stay. "More than one might ever guess" I answered. This led to further conversation while I invited him into my 'sphere'. Our talk began with simple discussions and moved rather rapidly into the realm of the unexplained. As he continued, I felt as if he were probing me with his kind words in an attempt to locate my personal convictions on the diverse subject of metaphysics.

Even though it wasn't possible, I soon felt like I had known this man from somewhere... or perhaps it was just the vibrations he was giving off. They were very comfortable and warm. As we talked, I found myself becoming more energized than I thought possible at this late hour.

THE SIERRAVILLE EXPERIENCE

He later presented me with not so odd a question: "How serious are you in your seeking of substantiation?" I got the strong mental impression that he knew many things he wasn't able to disclose, at least at this moment. Without hesitation I said "I'm a literal sponge; I'm searching for any spiritual truths which will allow me to comprehend more. I want the understanding to be able evaluate any potential thought concept I come across, and the awareness to pursue the reality of any such impression."

He then asked me "Why?" I replied that I wanted to be able to help others in their search of the deeper meaning of life, but realized that I had to comprehend more myself before I could be of any assistance to others. He just quietly nodded back. Our discussions progressed for probably an hour or so more. Eventually he asked me if I had any latitude, as to time, to meet with him the next week. I said sure.

We rose to our feet and he instructed me to meet him at a cafe in Sierraville the following Friday night. We shook hands, I told him I'd be there and then we parted company. As he melted into the darkness back the way he'd come, I realized that we hadn't even introduced ourselves. Further, I wasn't even sure I'd be able to recognize him again because it was rather dark and I didn't get a real good look at him. 'That, was an interesting man... Wonder who he is' I thought to myself as I walked back to camp after finishing my meditating.

Morning came and I shared my unusual story during breakfast. Instead of the usual rib-elbowing one might get with others of lessor beliefs, it was met with great interest. We broke camp a few hours later. Not knowing what to expect, I prepared my gear, note pads and other provisions throughout the next week. As Friday turned into late afternoon I headed off alone to the mountains. I tried not to generate any unrealistic expectations within myself, but just couldn't help sensing something special was in store for me.

It was about eight o'clock this moderate summer night, when I found myself on Lincoln drive. The heavens were becoming alive and several lone stars were transitioning into full brightness. The air was fresh and the light breeze brought occasional whiffs of moist field grasses and hay. An elderly woman was methodically walking her dog and I noticed several couples were out for a relaxing after-dinner stroll as I drove deeper into their quiet mountain town.

I parked my car and walked through the rustic access to the cafe. As I did I noticed a man at a corner table. His face said 'Over here.' I walked toward him and he smiled, standing to shake my hand. "They call me Mr. B around here" he offered. I introduced myself and we sat down, then being met by the waitress. He asked me if I was hungry and said I was starving, so we perused the menu as we exchanged small talk.

As we ate, the conversation grew to probing various aspects of the paranormal. I shared many of my experiences with him and told him how I felt about each one. He listened intently, and often would add to my thoughts with various input of his own. He told me a little about the town and asked if I had ever been to the hot springs. I said I had and really enjoyed those times. He asked me if I was aware that they lie on ancient Indian soil. I replied that I didn't, but felt that there was a tremendously peaceful and positive vibration in that area, and that I had walked many of the hills surrounding the springs sensing the same. He continued to talk of many things. Of particular interest to me, were his brief elaboration's on multiple extraterrestrial visitations in the area. He mentioned that they had mostly been observer craft.

He informed me that they'd come here for centuries and on many occasions had directly communed with this valley's ancient inhabitants. They had brought only peace and guidance with them he said. That, and during one latter visitation, Tablets of Light. Before I could get him to clarify what he meant, we were interrupted by our friendly waitress wanting to know if we desired any dessert. I shook my head no. "Not tonight" Mr. B said, asking for the check. We split it and then he asked if I'd be interested in going up the road for an Irish Coffee. "Fine with me" I responded.

We had just settled into our bars stools when several young men wearing tank-tops and jeans came bursting through the door. The bartender was pouring a drink for one of his customers when the three slid onto the worn stools at the far end of the bar. "You guy's look kind'a sun burned..." say the barkeep. "What a day! We found what we think is a old Indian settlement with a medicine wheel, up in the woods" one of them says. "Yeah, we did a lot of exploring and just at dusk as we left the area, we saw a craft we're sure was a saucer!" the taller of them exclaims. That last statement seemed to grab most peoples attention in the room. Mr. B quietly said "That's Tom. The one on his right is Billy and the other is Greg." "Wha'd it look like?" asks the bartender. "It wasn't *real* big" says Billy, "But it sure was sleek." "Yeah" Greg enters, "It looked like it was about thirty feet in diameter, maybe about twelve foot thick at the center. Silvery colored, but not a shiny silver."

Tom follows "There weren't any lights that we could see except for a glow around the bottom, kind of an orange-ish tinge." "There weren't any windows or openings, engines, nothing" says Greg. The bartender asks if it made any noises. Billy replies "Nope, none." Tom clarifies, "We were prob'ly too far away to hear anything anyway." "What did it do?" inquires one of the customers. "It just seemed to hang there, right on top the hill" he says pointing East. "If you weren't paying attention, you'd miss it. Then it just took off" he adds. "You mean it *disappeared* straight up, and so fast it was unbelievable!" comments Greg. "True enough" Tom agrees.

THE SIERRAVILLE EXPERIENCE

One of older customers sitting at a table with several others disgruntedly adds "You just probably saw Mac in his duster [crop duster] with the sun reflecting off his wings!" without even turning his head. "That's some story" the apparently interested barkeep responds, "What'll you guys have?" "A couple of sodas" says Tom as he pulls out his wallet. The semi-interested portion of the crowd now goes back about their business. Billy is served first and takes a brief swallow. Tom and Greg follow suit while the jukebox starts playing something about 'all my rowdy friends'...

Sitting isolated at the far end of the bar, I'd been soaking up their story. Mr. B looks at me and says "I forgot to mention earlier that our 'visitors' continue to keep coming around, even after all this time. They're seen fairly frequently, but there's *a lot* of folks around here that will deny it, don't believe in such things, or are too afraid to talk about it." "Fascinating" I replied. Mr. B is a dark skinned and weathered looking man appearing to be in his 60's, give or take, and sports an old beat up black hat with a tattered eagle feather. He dresses extremely casual and fits right in with everyone else. At least that's the impression I got until John came in, a local sheriff. A tall and well-built man who seemed to tower over everyone.

I was introduced to him and later asked by him if I wanted to play a game of pool. "You bet, eight-ball?" I inquired. "Sure... Set 'em up." he said. As we played he asked me how long I'd known Mr. B. "About three hours" I responded. John said that many locals consider him an odd-ball. He's heard some of them say he was a prospector many years ago. Others just mention, or know *of* him as the town recluse and therefore keep their distance... I then took what I thought was a sure corner pocket shot, but missed. He continued that he'd known him many years now and felt he still didn't know all there was to know about him.

Mr. B was quietly sipping his coffee, looking up occasionally to study the trio. "He's known of them since they were just children" John says. "They're pretty good kids but Tom can get a little rowdy once in awhile, especially around Mr. B, so we might want to keep an eye on him. His life hasn't been particularly easy because of his heritage and he is *very* susceptible to 'perceived' attitudes." He mentioned that Tom was a descendant of some remote Indian Nation from the Northwest. As we were playing, the three pulled up to the other table and began to rack the balls.

The trio made minor spectacles of themselves as they offered amusement to those of us witnessing their simple charades. Together they seemed a harmonious and cheerful bunch. We had previously returned to Mr. B's side and he and I were in conversation when John excused himself for the restroom. Within moments, Mr. B suddenly but quietly says "Stay clear of what is about to happen." He didn't elaborate...

I looked around, then unknowingly walked across the room for a fresh pack of smokes. Apparently, Tom waiting his turn at the pool table uneasily catches Mr. B eyeing him and saunters over to find out why. "What are you lookin' at, ol' man?" I heard as I dropped in my quarters.

Mr. B slowly turning from his coffee to Tom, looks softly but directly into his eyes... as if he was peering straight through them. There was no verbal response from Mr. B. "*You*, I'm talkin' to *you!*" Everything seems to go quiet. Mr. B is facing him, but says nothing. I cautiously begin moving toward them, keeping my eye on Tom's friends who appear quite embarrassed at his disruptive actions. Tom continues, "*Look*, who are you anyway!?" "Hold on a minute!" I interject. "Who are *you*?! This is between the ol' man and me" insists Tom, as he turns back to Mr. B.

"There's *something* different about you ol' man. I don't know what it is, but it *really* bothers me." Tom's keys, which were hanging from his front jean pocket then fall loose, hitting the floor. Mr. B bends down to pick them up, loosing his hat. As he rights himself, his open shirt briefly exposes a small golden emblem hanging around his neck. He offers the keys to Tom, who rudely and quickly snaps them from Mr. B's open hand. I then notice John returning. He'd apparently heard some of the commotion. His broad form moved intensely toward the two as Tom was in the beginning throws of another verbal assault. A large, heavy hand crashes down on the base of Toms neck and right shoulder, stunning him and followed by "I think that's enough for one night; Why don't you guys take it on home now."

Tom grudgingly backs away while Greg moves in to escort Tom back toward their table. "You okay Mr. B?" John gently pry's. "Yup" comes his soft reply. The rank and file go back to their drinking and pick up on their conversations as if they had never stopped. The aging jukebox has played throughout the entire incident. John had told me, that in the past Mr. B has been the focus point for several altercations and sometimes found himself in protective custody, for safekeeping, since he *appears* not able to defend himself. However incorrect local scuttlebutt over the years had suggested he went there to 'sleep it off'. "Give you a ride out to your place?" asks John, "Or would you rather stay with us awhile?"

John had informed me that he has a fairly close rapport with Mr. B and knows him to be a private, quiet, and mild mannered man not apt to provoke anyone, and that he watches out for him as best he can. "Just take me home, John. I've got some company comin' over later tonight." Frowning under the wide brim of his trooper hat John booms, "I *said* **Outta' Here!**" to the boys. Greg whines back "But..." John glares sideways and continues "Go home, or I'll lock tha' bunch of ya' up. I *mean* it Tom... Get out of here before I change my mind."

THE SIERRAVILLE EXPERIENCE

Mr. B bends over, picks up his hat and places it back on his head while the boys shuffle toward the door. Heads low from total embarrassment and all of the air gone from their bubble. Tom casually glances back to Mr. B as they move toward the door.

A faint, strange memory lays like a heavy fog in his mind...

"Guys...", we overhear Billy say, "I don't feel real good." Tom then motions for Greg. We decide to leave at this point as well, and I place a tip on the bar as we do. Billy is in the process of being helped to the cab of their truck when John, Mr. B and I step over the threshold and onto the boardwalk. "G'night boys" John says pleasantly but sternly as we walk toward his late-model cruiser. John unlocks the right front passenger door to the patrol car, "Hop on in Mr. B." Mr. B asks if I can go along, and I get thusly invited. He then walks around the vehicle and positions himself behind the wheel. Picking up the mic he says "Central, this is Car 5, I'm 10-8"; letting the station know that he is back into service.

Meanwhile, the three have loaded themselves into the Ford pickup and will soon head home. John pulls the cruiser out of the parking lot and turns South leaving a small cloud of dust behind him. "Thanks for the ride, John." "No problem Mr. B." There is some general small talk taking place between us for a while, then minutes seem to go by in silence. I'm quietly sitting centered behind the two facing the front, and to me, it appears like Mr. B has a look of anticipation on his face. John on the other hand looks puzzled, like he's trying to figure something out in his head. Both men continue to face only forward. I decide to watch out the window.

Suddenly John is taken back by "Whud ya' say?" creaked by Mr. B. The radio then abruptly blasts **"Car 5, 10-63, come in!"** Almost without hesitation, **"Car 5, Car 5, John... are you *there*, OVER?!"** "Yes Central, keep your britches on, What the sam-hill is it?" **"John ya' got to get over to tha' lake"** the voice stressed. Calmly, John returns "You mind just slowing down a bit, an' telling me what this is all about?" **"People are callin' in from all over... They say there's something weird happening by tha' lake! Strange lights and high-pitched sorta' noises... I musta' got 8 calls on tha' phone and Channel 9** [the Citizen's Band emergency radio channel] **Jim drove his truck clean inta' a tree and..."**

"*Steve... Calm down.* I *swear*, you've gotta' get another brand of coffee. I'm approximately 10-20 at highway 89 and Henness Pass, I'm only a few minutes away. I have a stop to make, so I'll get back to you in a few, over and out." "10-4."

A warm, almost-crafty smile grows over Mr. B's weathered face. "What do ya' make of *that*, Mr. B?"

"It's Friday night John, you know some of the hard workin' folks 'round here, 'specially the hunters... out letting off steam for the weekend. Maybe they're chasing down those darn fool pink elephants again." "You're prob'bly right Mr. B... After they've been partyin', many of 'em couldn't find their way outta' the rain... even if they *had* an umbrella." (chuckles from all of us)

• ▲ •

I find out in later discussions, that back in the Ford Tom was in deep concentrated thought. "I've *seen* that symbol before" he told Greg. "I don't know where or when, but I *know* I've seen it before." Greg, having no idea what he was talking about "a-huh'ed" him while trying to keep his focus on staying on the bumpy unlit road.

A ranch house soon loomed out of the darkness and Greg cautiously pulled into his drive. Not quite reaching the house he stopped his truck and turned off the motor. He had intentionally parked in the barn yard so as not to wake his parents. The two then helped Billy into the building where all three of them crashed for the night in the fresh, sweet smelling hay. The truck headlights however, burned on into the night...

• ▲ •

John now pulls off the main road, onto a small, rough, semi-overgrown dirt trail that winds a ways into the forest. Up ahead is Mr. B's place. A one room time-worn cabin with a small front porch and a moss covered sagging overhang soon appears. A soft glow from a kerosene lamp emanates from the small windows. "Well, here you go Mr. B; Home safe and sound." Mr. B opens the door and starts to get out as the radio comes alive again "John, I mean Car 5, ya' there yet? Car 3's already 10-7 in that area..."

Mr. B asks me in, and then tips his hat slightly to John to say thank you as we shut our doors. John turns the car around, quickly waves good-bye, picks up the mic and starts talking to it as he drives away. We stand on Mr. B's porch, while he waves back, and then watches until the tail lights fade into the darkness.

• ▲ •

Again I am later informed, that during this moment a young couple was tenderly enjoying each others company at the lake... They were apparently alone and oblivious to anything but themselves. The windows were down and the front of the car was pointed at the lake, about 30 feet away. The surroundings seemed peaceful and quiet, save that the jerry-rigged radio was playing a mid-sixties love song.

The radio apparently began to fade in and out, then went completely silent. The couple was so deeply involved with each other that they didn't even sense the initial fading of the radio.

THE SIERRAVILLE EXPERIENCE

But after it went dead quiet they took immediate notice. The young man sat up from his reclined car seat and gently slapped the top of the console in a vain attempt to activate the radio. "Probably a loose wire" he said, reaching for the dome light that wouldn't turn on. "Must be a fuse or something" he adds. Readjusting himself, he started to put his key into the ignition hoping the problem wasn't the battery. Then, without a warning or a preemptive sound of any kind, the interior of his car was filled with a powerful and blinding white light. It seemed, to them, to come from *everywhere* at the same time and felt intensely warm, but in an unusual way... not harsh. The young man had dropped his keys from the sudden unexpected shock of intrusion. He tried to find them he told me, but couldn't see anything even with squinted eyes. Moments of silence passed by.

He also said that there was a warbling high pitched sound accompanying the light that seemed to make the inside of their heads literally vibrate from the intensity. Then the light and sound vanished in an instant, and all was *too-o-o* quiet. He said he remembered asking his girlfriend "You o.k.?", but couldn't remember if she responded. Sitting stunned at the event and sensing his eyesight adjusting to the darkness again, he edgingly yelled out **"Is anybody there!?"** The forest quietness continued to pervade the area while his young lady grabbed his arm and roughly motioned him to 'Get out of here!' Just then the radio and dome light came alive, greatly startling the two. Nothing was to be seen around the area as the anxious two visually scoured the region. The young man, then with ease, started his car and sped away from the small knoll where they had been parked.

• ▲ •

While this was occurring, Mr. B and I were waiting for a small discolored aluminum pot of herb tea to get hot. Bending down to add a few more sticks of kindling to his stove, he looked over to the old clock on the mantle. It's hands displayed 10:24. Picking himself up he moved to his nearby rocker and sat on it, occasionally pressing his foot on the floor to move the creaky but apparently comfortable old rocker. Up...... then... down....... up....... down. He said that soon we must get ready. I asked for what. He just said "In due time..." then shortly followed with "I have something I want to share with you."

From out of his deep pants pocket he pulled a strange looking mineral (my conclusion) of some kind. It had a flat top which intersected five uniform and beveled sides at about thirty degrees. The bottom section of the crystal shape came to a point with five reverse sides at about sixty degrees or so. The junction of the upper and lower parts mated with a three to four inch straight, five-sided column. It was a light royal-blue color. It was beautiful and I asked what it was made of. He said that wasn't important...

"It serves as a spatiotemporal energy displacement viewer." I said, *"WHAT?!"* He continued "It allows the possessor and anyone in close proximity, if they desire it, to witness physical or other events as they occur by mental projection... focusing. It's like watching television, but your consciousness is actually *there*. It lets the viewer(s) consciously *be* at some point of focus, but no-one being viewed knows you're there. The viewers can't see or hear each other, but you all can see and hear what's occurring at the point of focus."

"Incidentally" he said, "The viewer utilizes the energy points in the hand of the possessor for overall control and operation. Here, I'll show you what I mean; Let's see what John is up to." (The way I was looking at him, I'm sure he thought I thought he was 'touched'.) He continued "Your eyes can be closed or open it won't matter, but perhaps since this is your first time you should close them so you don't have any visual distractions." If I hadn't done it myself, I would never have believed it anything like this was possible. A view just opened up in my head. I was positioned above and a little behind John's cruiser.

With his rooftop rack of blue and red lights pulsating away, he reached the far side of the lake. Turning a corner, he almost 'T-boned' a cross-parked chevy pickup with 4 men sitting close in the bed. Having barely avoided the truck, John turns on his emergency blinkers while notifying Central of his arrival. Jumping out of the patrol car he shouts "Chuck, *what* in the heck are you doin' parked across the road like this?" "Stalled out" says Chuck, "Sorry... I haven't got any flares with me."

On approaching the truck bed, John, sniffing the air asks "You boys been drinkin'?" "You damn right we have!" came an almost unison and anxious response. Puzzled, John asks "You guys sound kinda' shook up; What's the problem?" Chuck, in a nervous voice that pitches upwards says *"Well-l-l-l..."* (momentary silence) "Don't think you'd believe us John." "Try me" came the reply. **"We were being chased by a light!"** one of the other men quickly and forcefully interjects. "All right... get out of the truck and tell me about it" John warmly commanded. After jumping to the pavement Chuck continued, "Okay... We're up here next to the lake mindin' our own business and a bright light hits us. Scared the salt out of us... We were planning a hunting trip and thought we were alone."

"We've heard of strange things happening around here, *if you know what I mean*, so we piled into tha' truck and got outta' there *FAST* but the fool thing started followin' us... All of a sudden *there it was*. In front of the truck, square in the middle of the road. I braked hard, the engine died then *it* was gone and we were stuck there."

THE SIERRAVILLE EXPERIENCE

"When I couldn't restart ol' red, we jumped into the bed for a better view. We looked everywhere but we didn't see *anything*. Damn John, what do you think it was?"

(I, am amazed at what I am experiencing. I really have no appropriate words to fully describe it.) John looked into the night sky and over the lake area. He noticed a bright spot light on a boat near a ramp across the lake. "Seems to me you boys were being chased by a boat." he said kiddingly. "Probably a *R E A L mean* rascal too." "I *knew* you wouldn't believe us" rambled Chuck dejectedly. "Okay; Let's get this rig of yours started and send you boys on home, it's gettin' late." During the next few minutes the skittery men eagerly load up and are now able to leave the area.

Sitting alone now at the side of the road, John is just finishing his notes. He is pondering over the men's story. Picking up the mic about to contact Central, Mark (a deputy sheriff) pulls up along side of John's Plymouth. He has parked drivers-window to drivers-window, since the vehicles are facing opposite directions. "Evening John" he called out. John, still concentrating on the nights events replied, "What have you found out about this light and noise thing?" Mark responded, "Talked to a few folks around the lake, but can't seem to make much out of it."

"The folks are sure they've seen or heard *something*, but they've got no evidence and I haven't seen or heard *anything*. I don't know what to make of it..." He lit a cigarette and continued, "It's a nice weekend you know, there's a lot going on in the woods." Elbow on the window jamb and hand slowly rubbing his chin, John agreed "Yeah, I know." (Pause) "Well, nothin' here for us now... Let's get back to the office and file our reports, our shift ended 30 minutes ago."

All of a sudden everything went black and I raised one eye lid to peek at Mr. B. "Whoever holds the viewer controls the process... and this demonstration's over..." he said, "Time for us to go." "Where?" I asked. "To meet them." "Meet *who*?" I pressed. He smiled and said "My company." 'Elusive answer' I laughingly thought, 'You've really got me going... What next?!'

The clock on the mantle indicated that it was now 11:35. Mr. B cleared off his small but heavy wooden table and slowly poured out a strange assortment of small objects and some documents of some sort from a stocky silver tube. He picked up one of the objects, which appeared to be a couple of inches tall, and put it into his pocket. I really didn't get a good look at whatever it was. Then gently, almost lovingly, he repacked the tube and screwed the endcap back on. "Time to leave" he voiced.

Walking to the side of his bed, he knelt down and laid the tube back into the floor just under the frame. Replacing the floorboard, he straightened out the covers and walked out the door. I followed like a pup. A small lakeside cove lies about 150 feet away, slightly West of his meager home. It isn't noticeable to me from his porch, due to the trees, thick underbrush and foliage. The cove, which apparently can't be seen from the lake unless you're right on top of it, is protected by a outcropping of stones. This area is so deeply saturated by brush and trees that the cove is literally invisible by land. The water was shallow, in and around the area and according to Mr. B offers no lure for the very few fishermen who do know of its existence.

As we walk toward the lake, a soft golden light seemed to surround he and the immediate area. The light allowed me, and I assume Mr. B, good viewing yet there were *no* shadows cast from Mr. B or the plants and trees as we continued through the foliage. I didn't know what to make of this unique light, or how it came to be.

The moon was full and setting, just 40 degrees above the horizon. Mr. B continued toward the cove asking me if I sensed the tranquility of the forest as we made our approach. The frogs and crickets were singing out in varying tempos and intensities. A small semi-crescent beach now lay directly before us. Before reaching the beach however, he picked up a thin and leafless 3 foot birch branch. Breaking off all the secondary twigs, he walked out of the vegetation onto the beach. "*Come on*" he motioned to me. The beach was very clean, appearing as a white blanket. It sloped gently toward the water's edge, about twelve feet away.

Holding the thicker end of his semi-straight branch, he drew a large circle in the fine grains of quartz. Pitching the limb away, he tosses me the viewer and tells me to find a spot to sit, and I do. He then sits cross-legged in the center of the circle facing North. The soft golden light grows to envelope this entire area as he places his hands palms up on his knees. "Shut your eyes and focus on me" he uttered with closed eyes. I hear him begin to breathe slowly inward. Holding his breath for a moment, he then slowly released it through pursed lips. He repeated this pattern several times.

I notice that the small creature sounds are diminishing and am now somehow conscious that Mr. B has fully relaxed his being. I feel as though I am integral to him at this moment. The serenity of the night adds to the peace I am feeling. I cracked my eyelids and perceived that he took a translucent object out of his pocket and cupped it in his hands. He positioned his hands near and just over his solarplexes. He was intently focusing on what was a beautiful crystalline pyramid. I realized that that was the item he'd picked up from the table tonight.

THE SIERRAVILLE EXPERIENCE

The crystal started to glow softly from *deep* within. Then, it seemed to come alive... with dozens of tiny spheres of multi-colored lights dancing within it's structure. I could sense Mr. B relax his focus and I opened my eyes further.

Ribbons of brilliant, super-charged color moved to permeate the physical sides of the pyramid and sent streams of constantly moving and blending waves of "Living Light" radiating out about 6 inches in all directions from the crystal. The lightwaves formed a sphere around the crystal where they *appeared* to stop. The surface of which looked very similar to a soap bubble in bright daylight. Patterns of constantly moving color slid over, around and into one another, but differing in that the surface was connected back to the inside of the crystal by the ribbons of light. The outside world seemed to be non-existent for me as I'd never witnessed or heard of anything like this. This experience had my *full* attention.

Soft, harmonic chime-like sounds began to emanate from the center (?) of the light-sphere. Slowly, Mr. B removed his hands and again placed them palms up on his knees. The crystal with it's light-sphere *remained in place*, hovering in mid-air! I had to look twice to believe it. The very center of the crystal brightened to an absolutely brilliant silver-white color. The crystal AND the sphere of Living Light magically appeared to be *dividing*... As it separated, the two halves of the crystal mutated into small spheres about half the size of the pyramid. The crystal orbs were about four or five inches apart from one another, with the Living Light independently surrounding each of them. The spheres now moved to position themselves above Mr. B's open palms, one over each. Mr. B then raises his head as if to gaze upwards into the star lit sky.

Looking overhead, I see a small black void in the tight veil of twinkling lights. As I watch, the small void appeared to be growing. Getting larger still, more and more of the stars were overtaken by a solid black emptiness. A circular shaped object could now easily be detected. 'That must be *them*' I said to myself. Mr. B's head lowered and he faced forward again. A soothing and gentle Western breeze had been stroking our faces on and off while this was happening.

Mr. B shuddered, almost imperceptibly, and I immediately shut my eyes. He was contemplating on his 'Higher Self'. He envisioned a beam of cosmic White Light entering the top of his head. Then seeing himself being filled and surrounded by a this beautiful and energetic light, he proceeded to raise his vibrations even more. Moments drifted by....... Then........ *Separation!* I found myself floating in the ether with him, sensing a very wonderful but weightless feeling. Connected by a fine pulsating silver cord of light, he looks down on us sitting in the sand.

We are about ten feet over and above, and in back of his physical image. Astrally, he had escaped the three dimensional form known as Mr. Beckworth, and *I* got to go along for the ultimate ride of a lifetime. He is free of all encumbrances, free of gravity, free of weight... he is only 'thought' now. I feel a very special freedom at this moment.

Seeing with our minds' eyes, we soar into the vast nothingness which I know contains the all of everything. Consciously, he seeks the 'others' awaiting his arrival. He has met with a faction of them prior to his reincarnation into this life cycle. *Suddenly*, we feel a powerful presence and find ourselves centered in a large, pure chalk white (seemingly) circular room which has no discernible height, depth or width. I sense that he instinctively knows this to be one of the Halls of Knowledge, although he has never been here before.

Mr. B's cosmic form is now directly joined by three other magnificent and majestic Life Forces which appeared facing him. They seem to have developed out of the very ether. Each is shrouded in a brilliant, undulating and effervescent golden light. The three Light Beings momentarily remain motionless and silent. A deeply felt *thought* of love and welcomeness overtakes Mr. B. Even I feel this emotion. He returns the emotions and in his consciousness he (we) then hear...

"RATUMEN..."

"Brother of Light, it is we, Keepers of the Book and glad servants of the Glorious One, The I AM Presence, the ALL IN ALL."

"We bid you glad tidings."

Between the four appears a ping-pong sized ball of azure light. It grows and ultimately takes the shape of a *gigantic* and *extremely* thick book bound by what looks like mother-of-pearl, pages edged in what I believe was gold leaf. Their book holds the entire history of Man on Earth, yet it is opened only to page 9. I instantly recalled from past numerology studies, that the number nine is indicative of an ending cycle.

The gentle but determined utterances continued...

"This, you will recall, is the Book of Man on Urantia."

"This chapter is now fast drawing to a close and a new one beginning."

"The Universal vibrational changes are already in place and continuing to grow in pitch and amplitude."

THE SIERRAVILLE EXPERIENCE

*"You once offered your services, in preparation for the
Time of Transmutation."*

"As you know, <u>that</u>, is why you are among us now."

"We are the Assigners, Scribes of the White Brotherhood."

"The choice as always, remains yours. The time is come..."

"What say you?"

A holographic, symbolic and radiating royal pink heart appears over
the entity known to me as Mr. Beckworth.

"Let it be so recorded."

"The terra-form has served you well, your journey is near its' completion."
"Your path has been strong and your desire true."

*"Permission to begin the Spiritual re-awakening of Man,
is hereby granted you RATUMEN."*

The room and all of it's elements began to dissipate into an
awesome swirling golden vapor. A singular thought was 'heard' and echoed
in chorus as the room silently explodes into an aerial display of energetic
violet lights...

*"Blessed are you RATUMEN, guide to Man,
Teacher of Enlightenment."*

"Peace, Light and Love go eternally with you."

There is a slight "pulling" sensation as Mr. B now reflects on his
physical image. The next moment finds the shimmering Mr. B re-entering his
physical self, still sitting in the sand. Upon opening my eyes I detected a soft
flower-like scent in the air around us. Breathing deeply into his lungs, he fills
them with the sweet essence of the pristine forest air.

MANY QUESTIONS

We, hadn't physically moved an inch. The crystalline Light cloaked orbs float slowly back toward each other. The heavenly and harmonic chiming sounds now appeared slightly higher in pitch. As the spheres met they created a new single form. Slowly the outer sphere of Living Light decreased until only the tiny spheres of multi-colored lights undulated and drifted within this freshly created form... a crystalline cone. The sides of the cone seemed to be the same angle as the sides of the Great Pyramid. As I remember, they're roughly 51 degrees, 52 minutes.

The melodic chiming grew fainter... Mr. B cupped his hands as before, under the cone, and soon it went dark. No longer held up by unseen forces, it fell the short distance to his hands. "The changes are *indeed* activated" he said aloud. Looking up while he returned the crystal to his pocket, I noticed the night sky had returned it's hidden gems.

Whatever had been overhead, was gone now. The heavens radiated in its' full and spectacular beauty. A shooting star passed overhead toward the horizon. Silence seemed ever present around us, even the crickets had finally gone to sleep.

Mr. B stood to stretch then closed his eyes and gave a verbal blessing to Mother Earth, and Her Kingdom of assorted life-forms. He sent multiple thoughts of healing and cleansing to the Great Planet for Her winds, waters, lands and vegetation. Then he sent a blessing for the spiritual awakening of all Mankind. He gave thanks for his being, and the opportunity to take part in the greatest adventure *this* ancient world has ever known.

So Ends Journal One

THE SIERRAVILLE EXPERIENCE

THE VIEWER

JOURNAL 2

"IT BEGINS"

We left for the cabin and once inside I was asked what I thought. I'm sure I probably sounded like a babbling oaf, but I really wasn't able to contain myself. I know I've been 'out-of-body' before but have always come 'back' without any inkling of the process; no details of the actual circumstances like other 'travelers' have experienced. I shared that I thought the viewers operation must be pretty close to the operation of having an 'OOB'. He said it was similar, but not near as meaningful or expressive since the viewer doesn't allow interactive participation. Beside that, the experience is caused by vibratory alignment and activity between the possessor and the viewing device, as opposed to being a solely self initiated and disciplined function of spirit alone. This explanation made sense to me. We talked a while longer and then determined it was time to turn in. He tossed me some blankets and said to make myself comfortable. Turning out the kerosene lamp he said I had an interesting day ahead of me and should get some rest. Looking back, I believe I was 'out' as quickly as the lamp.

DAY 2: As early morning arrived, sunlight began filtering into the cabin still comfortably warm from the coals in the stove. I am very sensitive to light and therefore easily awakened by illumination from any source... There was nothing different about that annoying personal attribute this morning. Mr. B had already been up and was entering the room when I stood to stretch. He brought in some strange looking plant life and began preparing what he called Squaw Tea. As I folded up the blankets, he fueled the stove and prepared a breakfast for us. Flapjacks and canned hash. The tea wasn't bad, kind of woody tasting though. Across the mountains other activity was in progress as we delved into yet more philosophy.

THE SIERRAVILLE EXPERIENCE

I was feeling somewhat like a student again, but at least now I knew I had a strong base to work from and that made learning new material much easier for me.

• ▲ •

The morning sun was now cresting over the hills and the three young men begin to stir in the hay. They appear as broken scarecrows as they lay scattered over the floor of the barn. Peabrain, Greg's golden retriever, his tail madly wagging, is gregariously licking at his face. *"Get outta' here"* Greg says, as he attempts to push his dog away. He then slowly sits up and after rubbing his eyes, nudges Tom and Billy. "Time for breakfast" he announces, smelling the tantalizing aroma of bacon and eggs coming from his mothers kitchen. Tom yawns and says *"A l l   r i g h t!"* in anticipation.

Standing to stretch, Tom and Greg look down on the quietly sleeping Billy. "He doesn't look too hot" offers Greg. Tom lightly kicks Billy's shoe bottom... (moans from Billy) "C'mon Billy... It's time to eat." (pause) "You come'n, or not?" pursues Tom. (more moans) Billy holds his stomach, obviously in some degree of pain.

"My-y-y stomach... I... feel nauseous." Greg and Tom notice Billy's bright red face, chest and shoulders and glance at each other with understandingly concerned looks on their faces... Sun sickness! *"Well?"* Tom asks, as he turns back to Billy who hasn't even opened his eyes. "I don't think so... You go ahead, I'm gonna' lay here awhile." "S'up to you" replies Tom, "Can we bring you anything?" "NO." The two decide to leave Billy to himself and head to the house for chow while recalling similar, albeit painful experiences of their own.

• ▲ •

In Sierraville, the people are also rising and thinking about what they're going to be accomplishing today. Wonderful smells are wafting out and permeating the area around the small cafe. The oriental cook is busy making coffee, do-nuts, pancakes, and setting out eggs and meats. Rose, I'll call her, a feisty 140 pound redhead about 30-something now owns and operates the cafe.

Her mother, getting tired of working for others, collected her special savings and appropriated her own (this) business when Rose was just 2 years old. It's claimed she knew more about the local people than they knew about themselves, and was ever ready to share new in new or exciting gossip. The people had always been fond of her, especially because she made them feel like family. No one ever heard her speak a foul word, **but**, everyone knew that you didn't mess with her either. She had a strong 'constitution' and apparently, the weight to back it up. It's been told, that once she even held up the back of a small car with her bare hands while a tire was being changed.

But that was long ago, and the facts about those circumstances have dimmed with time. Rose is her mother's daughter. All the way. Stocky and sharp-minded she carries on in her mother's shoes. She is just as respected as her mother and people love to drop by to see her. She has no children and has never married. As for men... Well, she's had a few flings over the years, but she never saw anything in any of '*them*' worth keeping... and she'll tell you so. She told me as much. However, she's had her eye on one I've already named as Mark, for several years now. They are seen often together and appear to be close, but she said she won't talk about it to anyone... including me. Further, she very much enjoys keeping the other women in suspense and "Anyway" she said, "It's none of their business!" Rose and her cook are just about finished with their preparations when their first customers come through the door. Greeting Rose, they sit at the counter and review her simple menu. Others are beginning to file in and it looks like it's business as usual.

• ▲ •

LouAnn, Greg's mother, had seen the pickup in the barnyard and figured that the boys would be hungry. The table is set and Jeff, Greg's father, is already finishing his breakfast and reading the paper when the two boys come through the screen door. "Morning, guys" greets LouAnn. Greg leans over and kisses his mom on the cheek while Tom replies with "Morning Mr. and Mrs. Holdeman." "Morning boys" Jeff says from behind the paper.

Eyeing the feast before them, they take no time in sitting down and indulging themselves. "*Boy*, am I hungry" announces Greg, taking a drink of orange juice." "Yeah!" follows Tom. "Where's Billy?" inquires Greg's mother, knowing about the 'stopover' in town. "I don't think we're going to see him anytime soon" says Tom. Greg imparts "He's in the barn sleeping, he's not feeling very well, sun poisoning I think..." Observing their slight burns, LouAnn says "You boys should know better. You know how fair skinned he is" with a sympathetic tone in her voice. "Maybe I should take some aloe-gel to him." Jeff, now standing, downs the last of his coffee, kisses LouAnn offering "Gotta' get to work, you all have a good day." As he proceeds out the door he says "Guys, use some sun screen next time."

• ▲ •

Arriving at the lake, is a small caravan consisting of a mixture of unmarked dark blue vans and cars. Going unnoticed for the time being, they park and the men gather around each other. Some are dressed in uniforms, some in 'plain clothes' and yet others are wearing what looks like white, light-weight protective coveralls. The uniformed men are holding clip boards and seem to be directing the conversations, motioning with their hands once in awhile. The lake and surrounding area is tranquil and the sun is well above the Eastern horizon.

THE SIERRAVILLE EXPERIENCE

The air is calm and the sky is blue and clear. A flutter over a nearby lake reveals that a flock of ducks is preparing to land on the glass-smooth water. Driving up the road is a local forest ranger, out to check the lake and the camping areas. He is totally unaware of the activity that lies ahead of him. Meanwhile, the men in the white coveralls have spread out and are searching the area with what looks like metal detectors. Occasionally, one of them stops and collects a sample of the sandy soil and puts it into a plastic bag. The forest ranger encountering the parked vehicles, stops his truck and climbs out to investigate.

Two of the plain clothed men approach him, intentionally blocking his path to the other vehicles. They involve themselves in conversation with the ranger. "We won't be here long" voices one of the men. "What's going on?" inquires the ranger. "Well, we hate to admit it, but an Air Force transport plane flew over this area last night and accidentally air-dropped some supply platforms that were supposed to be used in a field exercise quite a long way from here. We don't know the exact location of where they came to rest, or whether or not they broke up, but we've got to find them. There is some highly sensitive gear involved and we're here to recover it. As soon as we find it, we'll be out of here." Given the palatable explanation, the ranger bids them good looking and returns to his truck and his duties. He is entirely unaware of the reports of strange lights from last night.

• ▲ •

Back in town a woman I shall refer to as Betty has opened her home salon for business and is tending to her customers. Two women are under hair dryers, one is waiting her turn and Betty is busy doing nails for another. The atmosphere is moderately mixed with the din of equipment and multiple conversations the women are having. The radio has been playing country music from a Reno station behind the counter when a news segment comes on:

"This brief note just in from our Las Vegas wire...."

"An unidentified Nellis Air Force Base source has unofficially disclosed information to our associate field reporter indicating there has been an extraordinary increase in documented UFO sightings in many states during the last few days. An unprecedented internal act, the official at the base indicates that he wishes to remain anonymous, but cites this information as authentic. He suggests he feels that it's time the perplexed public knew the facts and therefore decided to leak the information, in lieu of national security directives and potential jeopardy to himself. He says they can't explain this phenomenon and indicated they are taking the necessary measures to follow up on as many of these sightings as they can while attempting to keep it hushed up."

"He also indicated that NASA and other agencies have become involved in these investigations as well. Various tracking stations, we were told, have reported as many as several hundred unidentified targets entering U.S. and other airspace's in the last week alone. Reconnaissance planes available in some of these areas particularly in Nevada, Ohio and Florida report no close contact although their radar's have briefly locked on to a few of these elusive targets. As the source at Nellis put it, 'Just when they think they have them, the targets disappear into thin air; taking off at speeds exceeding 40,000 miles an hour.' Our station will keep you posted on this interesting story if further information becomes available... Now for ..."

The ladies have all gone quiet as they stare toward the radio, then at one-another. "What do you suppose *that's* all about?" questions one lady. "Seems kind'a ridiculous to me" voices another. "Well, *I* think it's exciting!" exclaims a third. "You *would* Dorris, you're into all that far out space and paranormal stuff" a lady says just out from underneath a hair drier. That lady continues, "Listen girls, if there was life on other planets, don't you think we'd know about it by now? Especially since we've sent up so many satellites and probes or whatever they are? I mean, *come-on!* It's the 20th century, *surely* if these things existed we'd have evidence by now..."

"Not if '*they*' don't want to be found" says Dorris. "And anyway, who says we don't. How do we know the government isn't still hiding all kinds of this stuff from us?! Remember what happened with the Orson Wells radio broadcast in the '30s? Lots of people went nuts-o; they just couldn't handle it. Of course, it **did** depict us being invaded by the Martians, but that was just a story!"

"You know" Betty says, "She's right, some people were actually offing themselves because of what they imagined might happen to them. The entire country was in a panic. They must've looked *pretty* foolish to the government... all that fuss over an imaginary story. I think we've got to blame that situation on wrongful perception and panic being generated from not having enough accurate data to work with!"

"Suurrre.... don't you see, that's why we never get any *real* information from the government? They *know*, or at least they *think* they know, that we can't handle it!" voices Dorris. The lady getting her nails done adds "Well, I'm not so sure that's the case any longer, what with all the books and movies about extraterrestrials and such. I think *most* people are really open to the idea that other intelligent life exists out there... somewhere...", now pointing to the sky.

"PUT your hand back down, you're dripping" exclaims Betty.

THE SIERRAVILLE EXPERIENCE

• ▲ •

Greg and Tom have finished their breakfast and continue to sit at the table. Billy has awakened from the 'dead' and is meandering toward the house. *"Hey, Where are you guy's?"* he shouts. Peabrain is following him and is continually jumping up and down on the back of his legs as he trods. 'Stupid dog, no wonder he calls you pea-brain. I know worms smarter than you' he thinks to himself. "In here" comes a voice from the window. As he walks through the door LouAnn pushes a glass of cider juice into his hand, "Here drink this... It'll make you feel better." "Better than *what*?" He continues, "Now I know what moths feel like after they've hit a bug lamp!" (laughter breaks out from all, even Billy, now loosening up) "Moms got some breakfast for you if you're hungry." "Whoa... Maybe toast or something" Billy replies, "Sorry Mrs. H, I'm just not very hungry right now." "Understandable" she says. "When you're ready, we'll tend to your burns."

• ▲ •

The ranger meanwhile, satisfied with having inspected the next lake and campgrounds and finding them to his approval, has left the area and is heading to his next location. The small group of government men have about completed their immediate job and have rejoined one-another at the vehicles. "Basically, the only thing we found was some soil containing very slight traces of crystal like substances near where a car seems to have been parked over on that knoll" says one of the men in white, pointing. They compare notes for a several minutes and later a gentlemen walks to the knoll to take some pictures.

Back at the main group of men: "We've got to find that car" says one of them in uniform, "It may be our only lead." When the photographer returns, someone takes a fast setting plaster cast of the tread marks. Then they repack their instruments and gear. "O.K. we're history" someone else exclaims. Climbing back into their respective vehicles, they leave the area as they had arrived. The ranger, still driving, hears a short report about the local sightings starting on the radio and pulls over to listen to it. *"Wait a minute!"* he says out loud, and sharply turns his truck around. He quickly heads back to the lake. The caravan however, is long gone when he arrives. He drives around hoping to find them still in the area...

• ▲ •

Folks around Sierraville are now deeply engrossed in their activities and are going about their daily affairs. Many farmers are busy in their fields. Some are actively laying out the massive watering-systems-on-wheels and others are spraying for insects. The postman is making his rounds, stopping to chat every now and then and the daily entourage of tourists and passers-by are starting to show up.

Some are coming here because they've heard about the hot-springs, some because of the stories about the place being highly spiritual, according to Indian legends which permeate the local history. Most though, just drive through enjoying an outing in the 'back country' and occasionally stop for a burger or gas. It's also time for hunting season and many come through here on their way to their special 'stomping' grounds. Even now an International loaded to the gills with camping supplies has stopped to refuel at the gas station. Having also heard a UFO report, the driver kids the gas station attendant about 'watching out for flying saucers' as he pays for his gasoline. The attendant, puzzled, asks him to explain...

● ▲ ●

Billy is feeling a lot better now and the boys decide it's time to go find something to do. They walk to the truck and pile in. The engine uh-uh's and whines, then fades to a chug, clink. "Oh damn" says Greg trying to start the engine again... I left the lights on... the battery's dead!" Out they get... frustration in the air. "Boy" says Tom "You must'a been really plowed last night." "Guess so" Greg answers, shrugging his shoulders. After trying to push-start it, they look for tools to take the battery out so they can attach it to the charger Greg's dad keeps in the utility shed. Later, finding what they need and having removed the dirty old battery, they stand around and exchange small talk. "I thought you were going to make a really big scene last night, there with Mr. B" says Greg, wiping off his hands, to Tom. "Why'd ya' do it?"

Billy and Greg are now looking intently at Tom. "What are *YOU* guys lookin' at?" (silence) "It wasn't nothin'"... (looking down and kicking at the dirt with the toe of his boot) "S'my business anyway." "You almost got us all busted last night, I think we've got a right to know!" replies Greg emphatically. "I don't know why... It's real strange, I can't really explain it" insists Tom. "Oh *c'mon* Tom, you can do better than that" suggests Greg. "*LOOK*, I'm tellin' you guys, I don't know why...... *I don't.*" Greg and Billy see the empty look of puzzlement on Toms face and decide to drop it. "What did you say about a medal, or something last night?" questions Greg. "It's not a *medal*, it's a gold symbol of some kind the ol' man wears around his neck" states Tom, "and I've seen it before." "What did it look like?" probes Billy. "Like an upside-down triangle with a dot in the middle of it, that's all." Greg pipes in "You know, he was supposed to be into spirits or something a long time ago."

"That's right" says Billy, "My grandparents once said that he has the knowledge of an Indian medicine man; At least that's what they told me years ago." "That's complete rubbish" counters Tom, "He's just a waste of other peoples air, there's *nothing* special about that ol' coot."

THE SIERRAVILLE EXPERIENCE

"All he ever seems to do is hang around... Bet he's never worked a day in his life! Beside that, he sure doesn't look like any Indian to me. And I should know!" "Well I believe it's possible" says Billy. "Yeah right" Tom snidely comes back, "And I guess I'm the Lone Ranger!?"

• ▲ •

In the little country grocery people are shopping and squeezing this-n-that for freshness. Down one isle, two ladies almost run into each other as they scan the shelves paying *absolutely* no attention to where they are going. "Oh, it's you!" says one of the women. "I'm so glad I ran into you, *so to speak*" the other giggles. *"Wait'll I tell you what happened last night...* My daughter was out at the lake with her boyfriend and they had a really strange experience..."

• ▲ •

In Truckee, the Highway Patrol has had a barrage of calls about flying saucers and strange lights being seen over and around Interstate 80, in the mountains near the Donner Lake area. Their investigations reveal no tangible evidence so they can only file these reports into the seldom used "Unexplained" files. Sightings and reports of sightings have now been lightly noted in some progressive newspapers in California and Nevada. Stories of unidentified flying objects are even being carried by some of the major television stations overseas, as witnessed by their communities, unfamiliar with what is occurring in yet other areas of our globe.

- - - - - - -

People in general everywhere seem to take such reports in stride. I know very few people who do not believe in such things. For the most part, I think everyone is very interested and excited about this kind of activity. The churches on the other hand, and as usual, keep pretty darn quiet on this particular subject. This is just not a topic the Church establishment easily relates to and I believe it could *really* be a problem for their faith-specific doctrines if real evidence were ever made available to the masses at large...

- - - - - - -

Meanwhile in Sierraville, the sheriff's department is investigating a local farmers report of strange marks in his fields. Held at bay at the edge of one of the fields are several groups of locals when John, having been notified, rolls onto the scene. "What do we have?" he asks a deputy as he gets out of his cruiser. The deputy describes the details as they are presently known to John. The two then engage in conversation with the farmer and he restates his findings to the sheriff. "I was [crop] dusting this morning when I spotted some strange marks in an adjacent field. I flew over them a couple of times to get a better view. At first I thought somebody got into the field and just was being destructive to my property, but when I got a good look from overhead I knew something else was going on... That's when I decided to call you guys."

"Wha'd you see?" asks John. The farmer takes out a small piece of paper and quickly sketches something on it for the sheriff. "Wow... That looks similar to some of the marks that have been reported in Europe" points out the deputy. "They're just over there" indicates the farmer. "Lets have a look" replies John. The first pattern in the hay they reached was a set of circular impressions. They were in a line, North to South. The first was a circle about 4 feet in diameter. All of the hay was flattened to the ground, yet none of the stalks were damaged in any way. The next pattern was a *ring* about 4 feet wide with a diameter of about 30 feet. There were nine more smaller and flattened circles after the ring. All of them different sizes in diameter. The entire length of this pattern was about 127 feet as far as the three could make out. The next pattern about 200 feet West of this one, was really unique.

It appeared to be that of a humanoid form about 50 feet tall, with it's arms out from it's sides, palms up. Over one hand was a triangular shaped object, over the other was a round ball with streamers formed around it. All of the hay was again matted down in an extremely precise fashion. "What do you make of all this?" the farmer inquires. "Looks far too professional to be pranksters, especially since I don't see any footprints or tracks of any kind" responds John. "I have no idea" he continues. He then arranges a flight with the farmer for later in the day, to obtain overhead pictures for his report. Back at the group of onlookers, a man is leaning against a dark blue van. He is wearing a suit and sunglasses, and is standing alone.

Surprisingly, no-one takes much notice of him there by the other parked vehicles. On a hill overlooking the area is the rest of his entourage and the other vans and cars. Those men are taking pictures of the area and writing things into their notepads. One man is talking on a mobile telephone. This group goes totally unnoticed by the people on the ground below them.

As the three men in the field walk into the clearing by the cars they are almost surrounded by the small group of awaiting people. The unknown men watching silently from their hilltop vantage point are now taking pictures of the crowd. A young man is seen to approach the sheriff and talk to him. (more pictures) As the crowd of 15 or so people start to disperse, the men take close-ups of all the vehicles with their powerful camera equipment. The man at the van is opportunistically getting ready to leave while the people are focused on the sheriff and the farmer.

• ▲ •

Greg and the boys finally have recharged the old battery and are installing it into the Ford. Peabrain is laying in the shade on the porch, head on his paws, lazily watching the boys at work.

THE SIERRAVILLE EXPERIENCE

LouAnn starts out of the screen door with a plastic tray of cookies and glasses of milk when Peabrain decides to come back to life. *"No"* she says firmly to the shaggy animal as she makes her way down the stairs. Peabrain, feeling dejected, lays back down and watches sadly as the potential meal moves out of range. "Thought you boys might want something to snack on" she says reaching the truck. "Thanks mom" Greg responds. The three finish up, clean off their hands and sit down on the tailgate to enjoy the treat. LouAnn has gone around the house to check on the line of clothes she'd hung out to dry earlier. "You've got one of the best moms in the *whole* world" Billy says, quickly gobbling down his 2nd cookie. **"Peabrain"** Greg calls out, **"C'mon boy!"** Peabrain literally *flies* off of the porch, knowing that he has a chance at those goodies after all.

• ▲ •

In town there's talk all over about the UFO sightings and now many know about the young couples experience at the lake. It's a very small town and nothing goes unknown for very long. Reports about Charlies unexplained field art are now being relayed as the hottest news items. Conversations concerning Area 51 in the cafe are intense. Even though lunch has been over for a while, the place is packed with deeply engrossed individuals. The air is full of excitement as everyone gives their thoughts and opinions about the events taking place. One person makes a comment to Rose. She responds with, "I hope they're here to help out, we could certainly use it. We've really made a mess of this little old world. Do you realize that in just 200 short years, we've almost made it un-inhabitable!? People lived on this planet for thousands of years and then here *we* come... *MODERN* man. Because of our thirst for profit, our selfishness, we mess it up for everyone."

"WE didn't mess it up" comes a strained remark, "Big industry did." "And we let them" continues Rose. "*Everyone* has to take some responsibility. Had there been a little less greed and more care about the environment people wouldn't have to drink bad water, breathe polluted air and worry about toxins in the food, to say nothing of all the chemical and nuclear dump sites." "I don't think that's fair. The little people like you and me didn't have anything to do with making decisions that affected that" responds another. "No" says Rose, "But we haven't exactly voiced our opinions to those-that-be, have we!?" "What can *we* do?" questions yet another.

"Individually, we can raise the consciousness of the community we live in. We can boycott items that are part of the problem. If enough communities join together we can arrest and stop destructive and endangering industry. But there's a catch... and you know what it is. Most people aren't willing to give up *anything*! They think, *MY* little this or that isn't enough to hurt anything, and so it goes."

IT BEGINS

"Until ALL people *EVERYWHERE* decide that enough is enough, we're going to whittle away at the little we've got left until there's nothing, *and that's scary!*" One of the customers interjects, "We've started recycling things." "That's good, but it isn't enough" replies Rose. "We have to make a global decision *NOW*, to stop pollution and the destruction of ALL of our natural resources. Are any of you willing to reduce the driving of your cars and trucks, or write your congressmen demanding cleaner combustion engines or new energy sources? Would you really be willing to stop using energy made from nuclear or coal burning generators? Are we willing to go out today and buy solar collectors that produce hot water naturally, and solar panels to generate electricity... Probably not, it's perceived to be too involved or complex and it's easier to use what the power company delivers at an exorbitant price to our homes or businesses."

"Are people really willing to boycott ANY product made from the wood being savagely ripped out of the rain forest? Or willing to stop buying foods that have pesticides sprayed on them? Would any of you be willing to stop buying ANYTHING that pollutes water as a by-product of being manufactured? Or to stop buying fish caught in those multiple, mile long floating sea nets? Are we seriously willing to pay more for necessities to help underwrite the cost of recycling *everything* that doesn't easily biodegrade in a few weeks or months time?"

"And what about us as a people? Are any of us overly willing to share with, and help the down-trodden and homeless, except out of what we feel is occasional embarrassment or shame from other's input around us? What about the disharmony between the various sects? Will the prejudice ever end between the nations of races, between the haves and have-nots, between religious communities, between corporations? Are any of you willing to have, take, and do with less for awhile, maybe years, so your children, or their children can have more later? Are we really willing to save the planet from the seemingly inevitable total environmental destruction!?" The place is dead quiet, all ears are now listening intently to Rose. Some are even pondering what it might be like. She has made her point, and everyone knows it! One quietly adds that she should run for office...

• ▲ •

Greg, Tom and Billy have left the farm and Greg is enroute to drop the other two boys off at their respective homes. Tom lives on the outskirts of the town where his family also farms. They keep a low profile and are meticulous in all of their work and affairs. They fight hard to keep a clean image so their acceptance remains intact. Tom's family has few traditions anymore and live by the sweat of their brow.

THE SIERRAVILLE EXPERIENCE

To exist in the white-man's world has meant giving up certain ways of life and losing the understandings of the 'old' ways and methods of interfacing with nature. Billy lives between the two and his dad, being a superior mechanic, is occasionally seen at the small single-strip airfield. Billy's family is highly but not rigorously religious, yet he has developed a very open mind. His parents taught him about believing in himself and not having to be part of any clique that he might encounter, no matter what the pressure. They taught him that anything is possible and to look for reasons and meanings behind events that occur in his life. They taught him that life is good and *IT IS* what you make it. From this, he has learned to be intuitive, to have an acute desire to understand anything new he comes into contact with, solid internal strength and he is known to be dependent on no-one. He likes who he is, he just wishes he were older. I once told him I wouldn't mind being younger... he couldn't relate. The way he put it didn't help *me* any... "You're not *that* old."

On the way, the young men's imaginations run wild. "Wouldn't it be neat, if they stopped here for an extended visit?" asks Billy. "Just think what they could teach us" adds Greg. Billy continues "It's too bad our government treats us all like children. I understand that Project Bluebook was never really shut down, just renamed, and they continue to collect data. Even the CIA is reportedly involved. Why, I've heard from several sources that President Eisenhower suffered his first heart attack after learning that several craft were left at an Air Force base in Nevada for us to study while he was in office. Supposedly the pilots of those crafts told the officials there that when they fully understood the technology and principles behind how the spacecraft operated, they'd be back to open up communications with us. Apparently they didn't want us to look up to them as gods or something... Weird, huh?"

The boys get into a deep and philosophical discussion on the subject as Greg drives on. Eventually they reach Billy's home and he jumps out saying "See you guys later." Greg pulls out onto the main road and heads towards Tom's. Not much is said between the remaining two as they are both mentally contemplating the news release and its' possible implications. Finally they reach the ranch. Tom jumps down from the cab and bids Greg 'thanks' for the ride. Greg turns the truck around and starts back the way he came. Driving home, he finds himself lost in the dizzying thoughts of Sierraville possibly being contacted from an advanced race of Man. In light of his second sighting he thinks to himself, 'I've always known we weren't the only ones'.

• ▲ •

Back in town John is in the process of holding a small meeting at the station.

He feels that there is enough information available to take the reported local sightings as potential fact. Therefore, he has typed up some instructions for the other officers concerning internal guidelines for any unexplained local (saucer) activity and what they should do, if they encounter such a situation. He is in the process of sharing this information with the others, indicating to them that all effort should be taken to be reserved, remain calm and get the details as factually as possible. For the time being, he also suggests that no information be divulged to anyone outside of the department.

He states that "We don't want to cause undue emotional stress on anyone, nor do we want to turn this town into a gigantic easter egg hunt. We will release any information we have, only when it is deemed accurate and verifiable and in the peoples' best interest. Until then, any information gathered, independent of it's nature, will remain 'classified' until further notice."

• ▲ •

The young man who had the strange experience at the lake, has finished his dinner with his family and is helping remove the dishes from the table. The television is on and everyone is talking about the upcoming news report. Once the area is cleaned up, the family members converge on the living room to relax. A vehicle is heard to pass outside of their home. Unexpectedly, a knock is heard at the door and the young man's mother gets up to answer it.

Opening the door, she greets a man in his early forties nicely dressed, who asks to see her son. In the drive she notices a dark blue sedan and then motions her son to the door with an expression of 'Somebody's here for you, but I don't know who they are' look. He greets the man and is asked to step outside for a minute... he agrees and shuts the door behind himself. The unidentified man introduces himself as being with the United States Air Force, as a member of a transport recovery team. He has identified the young man's car, as the car on the knoll by his tire tread.

Going over the 'story' of the misguided aircraft and lost equipment, he wants to question the boy and proceeds to ask his permission. The young man nods his approval thinking how exciting it is to be talking to someone from the Air Force... at HIS home! Eventually, he is asked if he saw or heard anything the night he was at the lake. The boy describes the bright light and his feelings at the time, but he doesn't give the well dressed man anything to work with other than verifying what already seems very obvious to him.

• ▲ •

Mr. Beckworth and I had spent the entire day inside engrossed in conversations of all varieties. Much of the foregoing I was later able to reconstruct after interviewing many of the participants.

THE SIERRAVILLE EXPERIENCE

Mr. Beckworth had informed me a little about what was happening around town during our talks this day and suggested that I would soon be able to verify it all. He was accurate, uncannily accurate. Then he asked if I still had the viewer on me, I said "Yes." He said "I've picked up on a really distressing situation. It involves the President, his advisers and others of clandestine but extremely powerful influence. Hand me the viewer, I want to show you what is happening tonight in Washington behind closed doors." I did as he requested and was saddened by what I eventually saw. Our nation's leader had decided to do what no other had, or was willing to do... to break the silence surrounding the truth concerning extraterrestrial activity. I had found myself looking over the shoulder of one of the advisors. In his hands was a press release generated by the President himself.

It read:

Ladies and gentlemen of the Press and the viewing audience...

Soon we will complete a summit meeting concerning an ongoing global experience. A level of which has been unknown to contemporary man. Due to overwhelming evidence and my personal convictions on this topic, I have decided to come before you tonight to speak on a subject kept concealed for much too long. One which I feel could have a profound impact for the world as we know it.

That subject concerns the persistent cover-up of the existence of spacecraft which are not of our own design or technology. There have been countless reports of spacecraft of apparent extraterrestrial nature being sighted around the world for many years. I'm before you now to confirm to the best of our collective scientific knowledge that this in fact, is the case.

The vast number of reputable observers and the data gathered by our various intelligence agencies lend overwhelming credence for the high probability that many of these sightings are genuine. Although I am not prepared at this specific time to explain further, there exists much concrete evidence of actual visitation and landings by these craft.

In light of many recent events taking place all over our world, I simply can not ignore the unusual circumstances any longer. To put many at ease, let me confirm to you that there have been no reports of destruction or damage of any kind being caused or linked to these recent sightings.

Nothing and no-one has been reported as missing or taken on-board these craft. Further, it appears that no-one has been harassed or in any manner otherwise, detained or interfered with by whatever intelligence operates these vehicles. For lack of a more complete explanation, it appears that these visitors may just be monitoring us, as we would monitor a situation for a news report. It is possible however, due to the vast numbers of reported sightings, that these unknowns may be getting ready to make contact with us.

I would stress to you, the American people, that perhaps a time has come that we may soon be receiving a gift of a magnificent nature. A chance to experience science fiction turned reality. I would hope and pray that no-one would take aggressive action towards these vehicles or intelligence's, should a situation make itself available. We will soon have an organization set up for anyone having an encounter or sighting to be able to openly contact us. We need and desire your input and your assistance; That is my secondary purpose for holding this conference.

People, we have a potentially fantastic opportunity before us! Let us work together to make their welcome if that is their desire, as open and friendly as possible. Truly I say to you, I believe that we are on the verge of an awakening and an exciting new age. When, and as further information is available on the present situation, I promise I will make it known to you. All of it, you have my word.

For now, I thank you and bid you all good night.

The room is quite intense with emotions. The military minds are dead-set against letting the President follow through with his proposed release. He ignores their statements about possible strategic capabilities and of keeping silent. They try to convince him that such a release will prove detrimental to the nation's confidence in the scientific, space and military communities. He said "Isn't it already too late; Haven't we done enough damage? It may raise a few eyebrows and some will be able to say I told you so, but in the long run won't it also reestablish some faith in government policy? That even though we admit there has been a cover-up we finally had the courage to spill the beans to the public? We can take the heat, it won't last forever. We took the freedom to hide it, now we need to take the responsibility that comes with full disclosure." He listens to many more arguments against disclosure, some suggesting that he will never have a chance at a second term if he proceeds.

THE SIERRAVILLE EXPERIENCE

He later decides to convene for the evening, telling them all he'll take their arguments under advisement and get back to them. Several men I do not recognize demandingly stay alone with him in conference. What they said and insinuated, infuriated my very being. Without hesitation, they confronted the President and firmly told him that if he decides to go ahead, he may be predisposed to the experience of an unrecoverable 'accident'.

I'd heard of the 'Grey Men' of world policy and financial control, but now I saw and heard what I believe to be several of them in action. I couldn't believe it! I wish I could say that I could pick them out of a line-up if I had the opportunity, but I can't. Beside that, no-one would take action on hearsay alone, no matter how strongly it was presented. The images experienced by the viewer are clear as can be, yet after one leaves whatever energy field he or she is in, the images fade out only leaving the net worth of the experience. The memory of having it and knowing what went on, but the explicit detail falls away for some reason. Like reading a book... one knows what he or she read, but they can't specifically tell you word for word what is on any one page. I'm guessing that it's the same type of principle. Mr. B interrupts my barely reserved emotional inner-anger about what I've seen. "It's dinnertime" he said, "Let's go into town for supper."

Composing myself I said "Fine, but how... walk?" He calmly said "No, we're going to take your car." I shook my head at him and followed with "We can't, it's back in town." He said "No it isn't", and proceeded to open his door and show it to me! I checked my pockets for the keys... they were still on me. "Did John have it towed it out here last night sometime?" I asked. "No" he said, "I 'transferred' it here this morning while you slept. I knew you'd need it sooner or later."

So Ends Journal Two

JOURNAL 3

✳

"SPECIAL EFFECTS"

DAY 5:   There have been no further sightings of saucers the last several days. Some of the folks around Sierraville still gaze up nightly at the stars hoping to see something, but no-one ever does. Life is slowly returning to normal as the talk of extraterrestrials dies down. At the cafe, Mark is having a conversation with Rose while he eats lunch. There are three other people in the cafe, all eating alone and in their own private little worlds.

The radio is playing a Kenny Roger's song about 'space cowboys' and Mark suggests how appropriate that might really be. Continuing, he comments about the sharp decrease in U.F.O. activity and wonders what it was all about. "Probably just one of those 'flack' things" replies Rose. "You know, they happen every now and then, a whole bunch of sightings then nothing for a while." "Guess you're right" Mark responds. "Well, I've got to get back now" says Mark as he stands up, looking around to see if anyone is watching. Feeling satisfied that no-one is paying any attention, he leans over the counter and gives Rose a quick smack on the cheek. She smiles and bids him good-day.

• ▲ •

Lily (not her real name) a 64 year old psychic, is busy doing a 'reading' for one of the locals. She keeps a fairly low profile because there are those in town who just do not believe in that kind of 'stuff' and have on occasion made some rather cruel remarks behind her back. Being a loving and sensitive person, both emotionally and spiritually, that kind of talk makes her feel somewhat isolated and rejected; but she understands that she needn't allow those types of energies to cause imbalances within herself. She is very aware of the principle (cosmic law) of allowance, and this brings her peace.

51

THE SIERRAVILLE EXPERIENCE

She takes her gifts as a God given blessing and has helped many people over the years with their lives. Having lost her husband in an auto accident a few years ago, her only external source of income is the psychic work she practices. She works out of her home not far off the main drag. It is a small but very clean place. If it weren't for the out-of-towner's that pass through, and her repeat clients, I'm sure her life would be extremely hard. As it is however, she manages to meet all of her expenses and occasionally earns enough supplementary money so she can plant extra flowers in her immaculately kept yard.

• ▲ •

Billy, having nothing pressing to do, has decided to drive up to the lake. (I'm at the cabin using the viewer during this time, as per instructions.) It is another clear and warm day and he can't wait to find a place to just sit and think. Very often he gets away by himself to do this, as it makes him feel at one with nature. Walking around a bend in the shore he spies Mr. B laying back in the sand, fishing rod in his hands and his hat pulled over his face. He gets within twenty feet of Mr. B when "Hello Billy, How's it going?" rings out from under his hat.

He approaches Mr. B, and sits down close by. "Have a seat" continues Mr. B. "Already did" responds Billy, smiling. "So you have. What brings you out to this neck of the woods" questions Mr. B, "Can't be the girls, I think we're the only ones out here." "No... not girls" follows Billy, "Just wanted to get away by myself today." "Explain please." "Well, I... *Wait a minute*, first you tell me how you knew it was me?!" "Must of been your cologne" points out Mr. B. Billy thinking about that says "But there's no breeze today, and anyway, I'm not wearing any!" Billy, seeing dog prints in the sand around Mr. B asks, "Hey... Who's dog?" "Hold on, one question at a time..." implores Mr. B. "Okay, How'd ya' know it was me?" "I saw you." "What do you *mean* you saw me, your hat's *covering* your face!"

Mr. B still in a reclined position, long ago identified Billy as an opened minded and spiritual person. Knowing that at last he can share some advanced thought concepts with him, he does. "I saw you with my mind, Billy." "Whoa... now *YOU* explain" returns Billy. "You've heard of telepathy and clairvoyance?" "Yes." "That's similar to what I did" "Oh, I get it" says Billy, "Like Lily does!?" "Pretty much" responds Mr. B. Fascinated, Billy inquires "Can you do that anytime you want?" "Yes I can, anytime, any place." "Maybe you could teach me how to do that sometime..." "If you want too Billy, if you _really_ want too, I just might do that." Mr. B now sits up, readjusts his hat and winds in his fishing line. He looks over to Billy and asks, "Now, What was your question about the dog?"

"What kind of dog was it? asks Billy. "It was a shepherd." "Do you know who's it is?" inquires Billy. "Yes I do." "Who's?" "Mine." Billy, knowing the story of how he lost his dog, seriously ponders the sanity of Mr. B. "*C'mon...*" Billy says, with that all to obvious look of doubt in his eyes. "Billy, I want you to stand up and look around. Tell me what you see." Billy does as requested, shrugs his shoulders and offers "Just dog prints." "Look *harder*, what's different about those prints?"

(pausing now) "I don't see *anything* different, they're just there" says Billy, shrugging his shoulders again. Mr. B continues, "Can you at least tell me what direction they came from?" Billy examines the prints more thoroughly. (another pause) "They don't come from *anywhere*, they're just around *you*!" "*No-o-ow* we're getting somewhere" replies Mr. B, "Are you sure there's no other prints on the shore...?" Billy looks up and down the shore, even taking a few steps in both directions. Returning, he sits down, hands up in the air and says "I give up, what's the deal?" "What do *YOU* think the deal is?" asks Mr. B, smiling. Pondering momentarily, Billy says "It must be someone else's dog, probably got over here in a boat." "Do you see any hull or shoe prints in the sand, besides your own?" "No." "Do you see any boats, or anybody else at all, on or around the lake?" "No... but there could have been earlier." "That IS a definite possibility, however, that's *not* a correct hypothesis. If for the moment we assume that I have been the only person here all day, then how could these prints have been produced?" Billy is caught again, "I don't know."

"Do you believe me when I say that I have been the only one here today?" Billy is now terribly confused, he really wants to believe him, but ingrained logic says 'NO WAY.' "I guess so..." he mumbles. "I'm going to make you a deal" says Mr. B, "You think about this for a couple of days, then you come find me again and we'll talk." "Okay" Billy says dejectedly, "But where do I look for you?" "Don't worry about that, you'll find me." Billy gets up and starts walking to his car, his mind going over and over what has just happened.

In his concentration on the paw prints he has failed to notice a major and obvious attention grabber. However this clue would have just led to more questions. There were in fact no other shoe prints in the sand other than his own, this he was right in observing. But because of his focus on the dog tracks he saw nothing else, not even the *absence* of Mr. B's foot prints!

Billy is almost around the bend in the lake when he pauses to glance back to where Mr. B is sitting. But to his surprise Mr. B is no longer there. (He is actually now back with me at the cabin. *Don't ask*, you'll understand later.) Shrugging his shoulders again, he continues walking toward his car.

THE SIERRAVILLE EXPERIENCE

He climbs in and anxious to share what has just happened with someone, immediately decides to pay Tom a visit.

• ▲ •

Having returned, Mr. Beckworth wants me to 'go' with him to observe Lily at work. He obtains the viewer from me and I get ready to travel... In town she is actively elaborating on some of the principles of her work for a new client, since the person is relatively unfamiliar to this science. Here's where we came 'in'... "Some psychics use tarot cards, some crystal balls, many use nothing at all. It really doesn't matter *what* they use, it's a function of *how* they use it. The function of course, is to provide a singular point of focus. *That* is what's important, *not* the item(s) at hand. Contrary to popular belief, no tools are required of an adept psychic. Those items have absolutely no mysterious power of their own. If they are used, they are just used as a tool. And of course everyone has these powers but few acknowledge or try to develop them."

"Each 'sensitive' has their own method of viewing events or 'seeing' certain things that might, have or potentially will occur to or for that individual. Sometimes we see situations for other maybe unrelated or unknown individuals during the same 'reading', or even an event that is, or might occur in a different area of the world. It should be pointed out, that all 'future' events are actually 'probable realities'. That is, everything remaining status-quo, the event is likely to happen as it is seen, but it doesn't *mean* that it will.

"The 'everything' referred to, includes the thinking of the individual involved, as well as possibly other individuals or influences having (seemingly) nothing to do with that person. The foundation for future events can be formed years, or even life times ahead of the incident, and can be influenced by the thoughts of any number of intelligent life forms, at any moment, right up to the time of the actual event. But it is *your* thoughts which have the greatest influence."

"If you can accept the fact that everything that has occurred in the past is available and stored as a unique form of memory in the ether, then understand that a 'sensitive' person can 'tune' into a past event and visualize it in his or her mind. The form of the memory may leave what is referred to as a psychic impression, or more accurately, a 'vibrational imprint'.

The impressions can be felt physically and emotionally, heard and seen as they actually happened. The imprint(s) can be gathered from an individual that has had the experience, picked up from the physical surroundings, or it may be left in the 'ether'. The ether being the typically invisible plasma of energy that fills the voids between, and surrounds everything. It exists everywhere, here and throughout the entire Universe."

"Certain psychic investigators that occasionally help the FBI or local police departments are known to be able to hold a weapon, or other articles found or used in a crime and accurately describe the assailant or where a victim might be found... and exactly what happened during the crime. This is made possible by the residual energy imprint left from the emotional energies of that particular situation. The weapon as well as the immediate area has absorbed the collective 'thought energy' at the time of occurrence and is later able to be relived or retrieved by a psychic. They don't necessarily *have* to have a physical object to hold, they can just walk through the area of the incident and collect the information that is still in vibration there."

"I'm probably getting a little deep for you, aren't I?" asks Lily. "No, not at all. I'm fascinated." states the lady. "Please, go on..." Lily, sensing an honest understanding by her client continued to elaborate. "As an example, *some* of the various 'ghost' reports you may hear about are actually residual imprints of vibration... 'living' thought. Living, in the sense that thought is the purest form of energy and it can not be destroyed, although it can be altered. That energy, can last forever or vanish at the *thought* of another thought; one of the proper *intensity* and vibration to replace the prior thought."

"Residual vibration is a by-product of creative thought. Residual effects occur with many of the thoughts we have during our earthly life. Every thought we generate, *creates*. Some thoughts are created with a small amount of energy (intensity). Some with a magnificent level of energy, resulting in apparent 'miracles', as in the case of Jesus and others. However my dear, there are no miracles, *per se*. These manifestations occur only by the joint effort of multiple loving entities... with ourselves being the initiator."

"Miraculous events remain quite unexplainable for most of us. We don't generally believe that *we* can impact circumstances in life this way and are simply awed by others who have these wonderful and impressive experiences. So... from *accepted* disbelief in our *own* higher abilities, we choose to label unexplainable events as miraculous. It's *so* much more comfortable to think that only someone 'special' could possibly manifest miracles, not lowly us. You see, our thoughts are real. We can't touch them physically, but they exist. The fact that we ask a question implies thought. For without the thought, an event can not take place. Speech as an example, is a materialization of thought although it is a rawer form of manifested thought. Thought is alive. It has it's own energy, it actually *is* energy... of a *spectacular* nature."

"Thought activity actually governs the Universe. Many might find this hard to accept because it isn't tangible. Yet neither is the electricity we use but we readily accept *it's* existence, don't we?!"

THE SIERRAVILLE EXPERIENCE

"The same for emotions, everyone has them but they can't touch them. Yet every thought is *based* on some kind of emotion. Weak or strong, wispy or prevalent. There are so many areas of metaphysical science that people generally regard as occult, or without merit. Sadly because this is what we are taught; and some people perhaps unconsciously, refuse to believe that they *actually* have basis in fact. We can hinder, confine and restrict our lives by how we embrace certain ideas and concepts. This occurs mostly through lack of proper information and/or very limited thinking! You see, *how* we think is what actually defines our *own* individual reality... I'm sorry, I didn't want to get this far off track. Let's get back to the ghost example."

"As far as a specter sighting is concerned, if one is trying to determine whether or not the 'energy' is active or passive, a clue may be found in the events that take place. Scientists study specter events to see whether or not they happen the same way over and over. If they do, they can conclude that it is 'passive' residual imprint energy. Say you hear about an country hotel that has a lady ghost wandering around. She is seen at 9 P.M. in the foyer, then she is seen to walk up the stairs, down a hall and then she disappears through a door to one of the rooms."

"Maybe she is seen every night, maybe she is seen on only one special night of the year, but that's not important. What *IS* important, is the consistency of her sighting by others, and the consistency of her actions during the sighting. If the events repeat *exactly* from sighting to sighting, then you can rest assured that what you are viewing is a residual thought imprint, passive energy period. The event being an ongoing manifestation of that woman's thoughts. Her thought imprints can linger around for centuries, or for a very brief time. "

"A lot depends on the vibrational intensity of the emotion, of the thoughts that were produced by that individual at that time in their life. The apparition might be her personal thought vibrations [usually] from a deeply emotional experience she may have had. On the other hand, if there is a difference in her actions she could be stuck between planes. Planes of Life that is, and there are many of them."

"If this were the case, the sighting would be considered 'active' imprint energy since *intelligence* is associated with the event. She may have passed on so quickly that she hasn't realized that she is in spirit form. There is an intermediate vibrational boundary between our physical plane and our first destination after death. Sometimes we linger there for a while adjusting to what has happened, then proceed toward the tunnel of Light. The darkness and emptiness around us at transition, separating us from the tunnel and our Source, is often referred to as the Valley of the Shadow of Death."

SPECIAL EFFECTS

"Many times a soul enters this realm and because of his or her preoccupation with the physical and/or not realizing that they have transitioned, they may not be aware of the presence of the portal that lights the way 'home'. They become stranded or 'stuck' at this plane, but only until they notice the Light or come to understand they are no longer physical and therefore free to continue. Since they are extremely close to the physical vibrational field their essence can be witnessed, and they can and sometimes do tamper with the physical environment they left. Most often though we speed away after lingering for a brief duration (up to several days) to our Source, for our life review and reunion with other beings familiar to us, so we can proceed with our soul advancement."

"Getting back to vibrations, some people are sensitive to advanced vibrations (essentially higher in frequency) existing or occurring from other planes of life. We physical's can sometimes hear, see or feel vibrations of those particular types of energy. Am I losing you?" "No, I don't think so. Is that how we sense good or bad vibes from someone?" "Yes, but that is a much less refined part of the overall capability we have. We give our undivided attention to typically only the physical plane because that is where our focus, our quasi-reality is. This materialistic focus limits much information from various sources that otherwise we could have access to. The process you are talking about describes a fundamental use of our *physically oriented* extended sensory perception ability."

"This ability, or natural asset, lies in what is referred to as our 'Higher Self'. The cosmic or etheric form from which we came into the physical from. That element of us which exists beyond the physical dimension, yet is part of the essence of all that we are. Because thoughts are real, because they are a form of energy, they can be picked up through the ether as they make a vibrational imprint on our consciousness. Positive as well as negative (emotional) thoughts can be experienced, sensed if you will, as can their intensities and impending immediacy. Sometimes a person may just 'feel' a light emotional imprint, at other times an entire mental 'picture' can be formed in the mind. This picture (understanding) may allow you to avoid harm or enjoy knowing something pleasant is about to happen... to you, or perhaps someone else."

Lily now has the lady drink a cup of natural loose-leaf herbal tea. (the variety doesn't matter she told me later, but implied a natural tea should be used over a 'manufactured' one for our body's vibrational [harmony] sake) She explains to the lady while she's sipping the tea that the reason is two-fold. "First, *I* as a medium like to use tea leaves as my focus point and tool as that is my usual method of 'seeing' for someone."

THE SIERRAVILLE EXPERIENCE

"Secondly, the fact that a client is holding the cup and drinking from it, impresses the cup and the leaves from that individual's specific energy vibrations emanating from their aura. The aura being the extended life-force or naturally occurring etheric 'life-light' and interactive vibrational energy with which all things, living and inert, are composed. A person's aura contains their specific thoughts and reflect what kind of a person they truly are *inside*, no matter how they act on the *outside*." When she is finished drinking the tea, Lily takes the cup from her and pours out whatever liquid still remains. She uses a wooden stir-stick to move the leaves around the inside surface of the cup. (pausing, she studies the leaves) "Wonderful" she says, "You just got a raise!" "Yes I did, and it's about time! I really needed it, my car's about to fall apart." "Isn't that great!" Lily expresses. "Let's see... (pause... one of several Lily takes in order to focus) "Do you want to know a little about your guide?" "What's a guide?" the anxious lady responds.

Lily goes into another dissertation with the woman. "A guide is like a guardian angel, one who 'looks out' for us and assists us in times of extreme need. They differ from guardian angels in how they interface with us, although they are still spiritually enlightened entities or BEings. They primarily help in directing us; they are spiritual teachers and advisors. By spiritual, I am not implying religion or that you must belong to any particular religious sect, or that you need to give the appearance of being religious either. Those who strive to continually 'show' others their religious conduct and/or impeccable weekly faithfulness have completely missed the point. They are doing nothing for their soul growth. The concept of Spirituality resides in the attribute of Love."

"It is a special condition of heart and mind which is used to comprehend and interface with life. A spiritual person is non-reactive and has a firm conviction, belief and understanding, a *knowing* that all things are of God; or a Supreme Being, if that makes you more comfortable. If we truly believe that all things are of God, then we must believe that we also are of God. What God is then, is a part of all of us. Do you follow?" "Sure!" "Great."

"Understand that the 'Church' is an institution which was initially developed by *men* based on a divine ideal which unfortunately digressed; resulting in much domination and misdirection of others. I'm not saying that *that* institution is bad, the basic premise is actually very good. Today, many people *do* feel that they obtain assurances and have questions answered by attending church. A person who goes to church may experience peace and tranquility and may very much enjoy the camaraderie of his fellow parishioners. He may also feel that he is able to get closer to his God and is therefore able to experience an emotional 'high' by attending. This is good, if this is what he senses. But God is everywhere, and as I've said, all things."

"He doesn't make His presence known *only* at church. God is available to all, at anytime, anywhere *YOU* desire, for part of Him is with you always. Very few wake to the fact that they needn't be pressured by social conformity to go to church to be *with* God, because they already *are*. A church setting may in fact amplify our inner emotions and feelings, and that's great, but our God Presence is *always* with us. The Church ideals have changed somewhat over time to accommodate contemporary thinking, but the doctrines many times remain clouded and veiled in misunderstandings. Misrepresentation because of the interference of *man* and his ignorance of the actual messages, and in some cases, their true meanings."

"It's a known fact that the Bible has undergone generations of re-interpretation. Changes were made to accommodate beliefs, customs and understandings at the time, *each* time. Some material was never put into it because those pieces of information would give *too* much knowledge to the 'common' man. Knowledge that would let him understand more about who he is and his relationship with God. Certain material was deleted because it was felt that only the 'Church' should have this knowledge. Some data wasn't entered at all because the 'authorized' scribes of the Church didn't even *begin* to understand what the information implied."

"Unfortunately, all organized religions still unwittingly persist in their misguided philosophy of the separation of Man from his God, by however their 'God' is referred to... Mohammed, Yahweh, Buddha, Allah, Jesus etc. Understand also, that a benefit of having so many types of religions is that it offers a growing soul opportunities to gradually interpret different messages, which may attribute to that soul's seeking to understand even more."

"As growth occurs within a soul - from exploring, comprehension and deriving what 'truths' are meaningful for that individual - they may eventually leave one church for another, adding to their philosophy and interpretation of organized religion. As they reach toward their awakening, they will see that much important information is lacking. Particularly the vast spiritual power of the individual and how significant that is. Sometimes occurring as a result of additional life cycles, they will ultimately come to understand the profound statement: The Temple [of God] is within. The physical temple (the Church establishment) is not representative of this understanding, but it is a great place to begin comprehension of Spirit."

"I think I understand what you mean about Spirituality. This opens a whole new direction of thinking for me. Please... Go on." Lily refers back to the 'guide' definition. "A person can have one or several guides throughout his or her physical lifetime(s), and also during various levels of etheric life."

THE SIERRAVILLE EXPERIENCE

"You may have had an agreement with one of these entities, prior to your re-incarnation into this life so that *that* omnipresent 'form' keeps you on your designated path. Or perhaps your foremost guide is actually your Higher Self, or that which many refer to as our Overself. Then on the other hand, you may have been assigned a guide by an even higher level of spiritual 'ISness.' You see, there are as many levels of existence or ISness, as there are colors. Incidentally, a guide is not God, I want to be sure you understand that. God is God, and everything else is *of* God."

"Okay, so what might a guide provide for you? Let me give you a small example... Intuition, where do you think that ability comes from?" "I have no idea, I've never given it any thought." "Not too many people do. Actually it can come from at least four different sources, or a combination of them. One source is that of our Overself. That part of us (spiritually founded) which resides in the etheric, or higher vibrational plane, on a continual basis. We in the third dimension, are actually an *extension* of ourselves. We tend to think that all there is [to us] resides in this physical frame... Not true. It's very hard for people to comprehend that there are *multiple* levels to our existence other than just the physical *one* we perceive. From this higher plane our Overself communicates thought to us... most often, as intuition. As an urge to do, or not do a 'thing'."

"Number two, which can seem very illogical to the multitudes since many tend to deny any possibility of prior existence(s) and even if they don't, they may not be in touch with their higher capabilities enough to use the information, could be from a 'memory-lift' from a prior experience in another life time concerning a like or similar situation or decision. Having experienced some 'thing', we can retain an inner '*knowing*' about that situation forever within the higher dimensions of our consciousness."

"This endowment has nothing to do with physical brain cell processes; although now there exist various arguments that some or all experience is available from subsequently patterned or encoded DNA. They argue that once the DNA is modified, there occurs a chemical reaction which takes place that modifies the condition of brain cells, thus thought. When a similar experience is encountered thereafter, we have a feeling of similarity or familiarity."

"I don't doubt that this scenario could perhaps exist for some of our really *extreme* experiences or those that experiences which upset, tamper with or cause temporary modifications to our bioelectrochemical processes; but I for one, find it very difficult to believe that all of our millions of trivial and other experiences, and especially the attribute of *intuition*, could ever be associated with or to a genetic function of the physical self... I suppose I could be proved wrong someday, but I really doubt it."

"The third source could be from our ability to sense or perceive the right solution or thing to do, by the auric *energies* surrounding the 'thing' to be decided on. If we were 'sensitive' enough to vibration we could detect the right solution for any given course of action. This though, this is not something we develop overnight. It comes with an extremely expanded understanding within... of how everything around us is connected by energy interfaces, and what types of energies those are."

"Or perhaps four, from the careful and caring 'thought direction' of our cosmic guide. In many instances, this may be the case. I'm sure you've heard many others comment: 'I should've gone with my first feeling or choice'... because their second or third choice ended up being the wrong one." "Yes I have. I've even said it myself, *dozens* of times." "That my dear, is a *very* ordinary occurrence. We tend to ignore Spiritual input and guidance because we generally aren't able to interpret that they are in fact spiritually caused or generated, and because of that we choose a wrong direction by application of patterned self. That's what Jesus was trying to tell us when he talked of hearing with proper ears. We mentally argue within ourselves that the other choices available to us seem so *logically* better... yet I've never ever known logic to prevail over Spirit input and guidance."

"As we mature and experience a particular life existence, our thought processes can grow or expand, *if* we allow them to. Spiritually now, by how open minded and receptive we are to new ideas, how we conduct ourselves... which is internalized thought manifested externally, and by which types of thoughts we cling to as our basic modus-operandi. In other words, by what thoughts we embrace. As we change spiritually, and we do whether we're conscious of it or not, we may acquire a new guide or guides that best relate to the level of spiritual understanding that we possess. With successful incorporation of various spiritual comprehension's into our 'BEing' our guide(s) may leave to allow for others of enhanced knowledge to take their place as their design with us has been fulfilled."

"One of our guide's purposes then, is to assist us in our evolvement and direction toward achieving spiritual enlightenment and our employment of those understandings in all that we do, think, say, act, feel, hear. Until ultimately through this growth, we need not repeat our physical lives and we can go on to a *greater* life experience. Is this still making sense to you?" "I believe so, go on..."

"As we develop and grow, God grows; but in terms of joy for our success. The experiences we have as individual's God is party to. He, and I use that term quite *generically*, experiences all things through His creation of all that exists. One day you will understand this. Man, is a reflection of the spirit of God manifested on a lower order."

THE SIERRAVILLE EXPERIENCE

"We have been given gifts of creation and dominion over all things, because we *are* of His Essence. Only now through divine evolvement are people everywhere starting to wake up and smell the proverbial coffee. They are coming to understand that there is in fact, a well defined higher order and purpose. Many now see that the meaning for, and of their rigid lives has holes in it's 'given' interpretations. Like worn puzzles, the pieces don't really fit together any more. We are in the process of questioning the fundamentals of the Church, political organizations, suppression, reasons for military necessity, financial institutions and comptroller's agenda's, social welfare, health and insurance programs, and government leadership and direction."

"As well as developing serious interests and desires to investigate such things as psychic awareness and abilities, hands-on and spontaneous healing, extraterrestrials, black holes, infinite space, how does evolution really occur, creative intelligence, the concept of the soul, and who are we and where do we go from here?! People are now sensing that there is a greater energy, knowledge and influence which exists above all else, and they *want* it in their lives. People are beginning to shift from using standardized and empirical thinking to developing an expanded consciousness."

"They are doing so by modifying what types of knowledge or philosophy they embrace as 'truths'. The attitude of *care* is also being developed within these individuals. Look at the global shift taking place toward protecting the environment and various species of plant and animal life, it's wonderful. Many of these individuals are having perhaps uncustomary, but plausible spiritual experiences. These real experiences become substantiation that there *is* benefit in whatever effort they are putting forth. Their early-on experiences only *hint* at the possibilities awaiting them. These experiences create new realities and most are quite conscious of what is occurring. Able to be experienced as a result of *their* determination and embraced perceptions, because they chose not to be sub-consciously directed by other's thought patterns, or rely solely on what they have been taught in the past as to what is and isn't possible."

"So many are opening up and starting to be able to utilize their higher powers because of their belief. Unfortunately, established science in general still treats certain intangible events as mystical, manifestations and delusions of emotionally disturbed minds, mass hysteria and in general ignores the reality that these capabilities *are* real. *This*, my dear, is a terrible tragedy, but we will see it all change... and change in *our* lifetimes. Now let's examine the beginning of physical Man and what occurred... I speak of the times subsequent to the Adam and Eve personalities, highly advanced entities. The 'Fall of Man' is generically understood as: When what was created, [Man] turned to Self for reliance, direction and the means to all ends."

"The Fall has been one of the greatest misunderstandings that has ever perpetuated time. We tampered with our strong connection and association with God, the infinite cosmic understanding of who we are, where we came from and why... slowly ignoring our spiritual communications and guidance, and have suffered the consequences since. Self became ever so more important, to *itself*. The lower we allowed our vibrations to spiral, the denser we became in the physical. This process put many restrictions upon us. We could have corrected our thinking, but didn't, and as a result lost many capabilities. We moved more rapidly toward evolving a totally physical form by thinking that we had to, or could rely on ourselves (only) for all things. We actually began to *believe* this."

"The more that thought was perpetuated, the more entities that took up that thought and *thought* about it (global consciousness) the more *real* it became. Over time, the thought was so deeply ingrained, studied and taught, the separation became infinitely wide. One of the side-effects of such tampering was the inclusion of a physical death, a condition which hadn't been known before. So you see, when Spirit who transcended from Light become Man and decided that he was in charge of all aspects of his life, then that is when the real division of Man from God occurred." "Then how does free will fit in?" asks the young lady. "We all have free will, and we have authority over what we will experience. Remember, if you believe God is all-powerful, then surely it stands to reason that he has free will. If you accept that we are of God, then believing that God does not limit himself, you must conclude emphatically that He does not limit us. For by doing so he would be limiting aspects of *Himself* and *that* 'equation' makes absolutely **no** sense."

"As for the Fall, we chose to violate the Laws knowing full well the repercussions, thus putting our spiritual growth in retrograde. We got knocked down a big notch - To the level of vibration which we were then dwelling upon. That level of vibration brought with it associated vibrational circumstances. We have never been removed from God's hand or His desire to see us break back through the barriers of Self to return in glory. Only by the 'space' created by our actions (thoughts in particular) do we feel alone." "Then what you are saying, is that we always *have* had a direct link to God. We just *think* that we don't. That we are separated only because we choose so or were taught to be. That our thought processes exploited the weaknesses of our form through thought about Self, and that we *can* re-establish that link anytime we change our thinking and make a conscious effort to do so?"

(Lily claps her hands, in excitement), "YES, yes; That was a mouthful, but I believe you've got it! Now do you better understand how creative positive thought, sincere desire, positive emotion, solid belief and particularly: faith, affects our realities?"

THE SIERRAVILLE EXPERIENCE

"Unfortunately for most though, many will choose to believe more in themselves rather than in the bedrock of our Source... so their many strained realities seem dim and unrewarding. Do you see that without a true knowledge of our relationship with God we are merely limited to Man's thinking, and how we then *keep* ourselves from experiencing something greater? And that 'something', far and above exceeds the experience of the purely physical (dimension). "Yes" the woman replies, "I recognize how we are taught from a basis of limitations all our life."

Lily continues, "It's easy to understand why we elect to reincarnate. We choose to, to continue growth and gain further understanding so we can eventually return to the Godhead. The ultimate collectiveness of the families and entities of the highest orders of the Light of God. We DO eventually choose to come back, maybe here, or perhaps somewhere else in the Universe. Because once we escape our three dimensional forms and take up our cosmic form, that being pure thought, we can look back on all we haven't experienced or accomplished. At some point in our understanding, we truly desire to *fulfill* ourselves as God intended us to do. Directed by His will not ours. For only He knows the best and straightest path to travel to attain our individual glory."

"Some of us come back to this plane of existence having already made-the-grade, so to speak. Usually to help others, and by our own choice and with very advanced spiritual attributes and abilities. We might assume the role of becoming a doctor, or a new products engineer, a teacher or even a transient on the streets." "Kind of like angels?" the woman asks. "No... not exactly. Angels are a very special creation of God's. Their stays are typically brief and usually unexpected. They provide wonderful tasks such as helping us in certain situations, or delivering messages to us. They intercept our prayers and relay them to the Source instantly for review and action. Their main (soul) task is providing a highly specialized caretaker service to us based only on the emotion of Love. They are truly magnificent BEings."

"*We* on the other hand, may return with an insatiable desire to elevate the consciousness of society by what ever means available, before physically returning. You must know somebody, or know somebody who knows someone who seemed to be gifted in some way, for no apparent reason? Such as a girl prodigy pianist or a boy that seemed overly creative as a child, who turns out to be a research or design engineer?... Even though no-one in their family history had an aptitude for that kind of ability? Or how about the teacher who instructs on a subject so well that he or she truly stands out as a special or master educator, or the minister who can expound so infinitely well that none miss his messages, or the doctor who is so very gifted that he overwhelmingly excels at his profession?"

64

SPECIAL EFFECTS

"There are explanations for those types of behavior and knowledge, and they come from a *cosmic* level of understanding." Lily continues "I realize this has been involved, but I feel that you are having no problem with the information. Please let me know if you are." "Oh no, I'm taking in everything you've shared." (smiles) "Very well, let's get back to your guide again. It's not critical that you *believe* you have a guide, but you do... we *all* do. How do you feel about that comment?" "To tell you the truth, I've never sensed anyone around me. I *would* like to know more about my guide, but honestly, I'm not sure I understand how this guide thing really works. How do I interface with my guide?"

"Let's try to break your question down. The reason you may not have sensed anyone being around you is probably because it was never discussed, at least *not* in a format that allowed you to feel okay with the idea. Some children have what adults call 'imaginary' play friends. Most doctors and parents instantly, or soon after discovery of them, discourage this type of behavior because they feel or 'know' there is no such thing, or they fear or don't understand what they can't see, hear or touch. They will typically use the excuse that if the child persists in this behavior pattern, then it will ultimately prove to be detrimental to their psychological well-being and mental health, etc., etc."

"The behavior is perceived as a problem, instead of an *asset* or *gift*. The child may in fact be communicating with it's guide or guides, and if you think about the *possibility*, it's very exciting. Parents will step in to stop this form of behavior very rapidly, or completely ignore what the child is trying to communicate. When they insinuate that there really isn't anybody there, sooner or later the child looses that direct link. Why? Because they believed their parents or wanted to respect their input, or because it might mean punishment if they don't quit their odd behavior."

"Young children have *very* open minds. They haven't *learned* what's impossible yet according to Man's limited knowledge, and they are easily influenced. Even a new born, once their eyes can maintain some focus, will look into the air above peoples heads and watch (at) invisible *something's*. Isn't that obvious proof to us that something wonderful is occurring to them? If they could only speak at that age, what mysteries they might unravel. Children absorb all the data that is thrown at them because they are *thirsty* for knowledge. Most people do not understand that, they don't know *how* special children really are. Under the right guidance and teaching philosophy, every child could be a genius in one or more fields... I'm not exaggerating, *every child*." She continues, "As we grow up, we learn more and more about what *isn't* possible or what *isn't* real, again, this according to the 'documented' sciences."

THE SIERRAVILLE EXPERIENCE

"But you have to remember, Man and his semi-finite intellect lost his connection to the infinite source of all knowledge. By doing so, he found he was then limited to the physical world around him. He had lost touch with his unseen worlds of energy and knowledge. Over time he didn't even *remember* that he once *had* the connection to the Source, because he now believed *HE* was the source. 'It' was created when *HE* made the bricks and mixed the mortar. 'It' was possible if *HE* designed it. Gravity can not be avoided because *HE* said it couldn't be. He only openly admitted to having five senses until fairly recently. But as the sciences continue to develop they find that there is more and more that they really do not know, and can not answer... yet. So now Man finds (assumes) he is existing in what *seems* to be only a physical environment, without any understanding that he (by internalizing globally accepted thought patterns) put *himself* in this restrictive plane of existence."

"Further, he is quite unconscious that he even did so and doesn't see the result as anything *but* reality, and of the sometimes harshest kind. Now do you understand how the reality everyone accepts came into being?" "Yes... I think I do." "The child is taught from the Book of Reality According to Man. So many coming from the same school of thought agree that this is all there is, and it is the only thing that *is* real. We believe it because we are taught to believe it, in spite of the fact that it is grossly in error. Jesus expounded that we need to have the pure hearts and minds of innocent children to be able to hear, see and feel with the necessary spiritual awareness. Without this, we become blinded by our environment and gradually loose our connection to the truth."

"There is so much we could gain if we would only pay attention to some of our special children. But what papered and educated self-conscious doctor would ever openly admit to his peers or to the world, that he listens to a child who talks with unseen entities? Not too many. But pure hearts can receive some *very* special attention, some of which is only available for the RECIPIENT! You see, it is possible that as a child you once communicated with your guide and possibly even saw your guide though others didn't. *They* weren't suppose to. Your guide is *your* guide and therefore has only a single focus... YOU. They do however, work with more than one entity at a time, but any communication between you two is meant for you alone; unless of course instructed otherwise... by your guide. It's really no wonder you don't feel any presence around you... we don't normally sense such things."

"There are many special and evolved people which have regained this capability or brought it back with them, and they can be found all over the world. Some teach about the Higher Self and the Source, some write books and others give lectures and hold seminars."

"The information that they have been 'given' in many cases, has been distributed because of the direction to do so from their guide(s). *Why?* Because people are searching for something that explains God and the true meaning of life. People are now ready to learn who they are, all that they are, and why they are."

"Some guides may actually appear to you, and others may simply be 'channeled'. Do you know what that is?" "I've heard the expression, but I don't fully understand it." "Channeling is a form of cosmic communication. Information is obtained from the etheric and passed to the mind for physical interpretation or utility. *Typically*, a three dimensional entity like you or me can receive our communication as *thought* impressions or sometimes even as inner-voices, from our guide (or guides). In many cases the spiritual information is accompanied by an urging to make the channeled information available to others through the written word."

"This is because the guides may desire to have that information disseminated to as many as will take advantage of the enlightened material. By enlightened, I mean information of a spiritual nature. Information which can open the heretofore closed recesses of the third-dimensional mind about who we really are, who God is, and what we can be and experience. The information is meant to give us a deeper understanding of the (spiritual) power we all have, but fail to recognize or believe in. It is meant to put us in touch with our true essence and to *recognize* the Source of All That Is."

"Our three dimensional existence is *not* our true reality, it is only an experience we choose to have. This goes strongly against accepted dogma, scientific understandings, many philosophies and religious beliefs. It is considered an outrageous statement to say that we live *as*, and *in* an illusion. Who do you know would give you the time of day if you were to say that to them? Probably no-one. (nods) By illusion, I don't mean that we *dreamed* up who we are, or where we live or what we experience. Yet we create for ourselves, all the conditions that we do in fact experience."

"Further, they are temporary experiences and on only *one* plane of existence. A plane of existence which presently doesn't come close to defining reality or what we really are or what our potential is. Keep in mind the 'Fall'. We identified so closely with the third dimension that over time we lost track that at one time we *were* able to experience, and be more... *MUCH* more. We still can and *are*, but we have to recognize that fact *before* we can encounter more. Once we truly believe it and think it, we can start to experience it. And like anything else, it takes time and practice, patience and perseverance. You must *KNOW* that it is real, that you *ARE* greater than your physical being, that you are *NOT* limited in any way except to the extent that you *believe* you are! This is what the Masters have learned."

THE SIERRAVILLE EXPERIENCE

"Do you understand what I mean by that word?" "No, I don't... But I've heard that word before..." Jesus was a Master, Buddha was a Master, Paramahansa Yogananda was a Master, many of the 'channeled' BEings are referred to as Masters. They had realized at some point in their experienced multi-dimensional lives that they were greater than perhaps even they gave themselves credit for being, and therefore chose to experience it. They realized that because they *ARE*, indeed, they *had* no limitations."

"Do you remember the story in the Bible about Paul in the boat with the others during a storm? Jesus commanded Paul to step onto the water and he did. And he didn't sink... *Right away* that is. He lost sight of himself temporarily and was captured by the sight of Jesus on the water. Then his left brain kicked in. It said 'Wait a minute... I can't do this!' and what happened?... He sank into the water. He was conditioned to believe that this kind of feat wasn't possible by mortal man."

"I better explain 'left brain'. Science has found that the left side of our brain contains the logical portion of our thinking apparatus, or capability. Here is where we draw on learned experiences and beliefs. The information residing here is *our* individual Book of Knowledge. What we have accepted as real or not as far as our thoughts go, remain here to be used whenever we need the information. The right portion of the brain is the creative and conceptual part. What enlightened people attempt to do, is redirect their right brain thoughts to the left part of the brain, to retrain and reprogram what priorly was considered to be negative or restrictive accepted thought. As an example, perhaps you don't believe in reincarnation. You may one day get enough new information on that subject to really *consider* the possibility of prior existence's. As is the case with any yet unaccepted thought pattern, if you hold those thoughts of reincarnation with enough conviction you might begin to believe them."

"The more you think about the *possibility* of something being 'real' and begin to accept it's reality, then in time you may reprogram the left brain into believing it as real; changing the priorly restrictive thought pattern. The next time it comes up in a conversation you will have no trouble giving your opinion(s) on that particular subject, because now it isn't shadowed in doubt or disbelief... You have accepted the *possibility* entirely, replacing the old left brained belief with a new one. You may even wonder why it was so foreign before since now it might seem so easy and comfortable to relate to. This is the usual process of reprogramming left brain beliefs... accepting possibilities which may not be able to be immediately or empirically proven."

"As far as the term Master goes, it is a generic term. Somehow we humans want and mandate order in our lives and experiences, and this term alludes to the fulfillment of this need. Cosmically, there is no such thing."

68

SPECIAL EFFECTS

"For us, these are individuals which have MASTERED the thought of who they are, what they are and their purpose in life, and because they KNOW there is more, they choose to experience it. Some then, might eventually become 'ascended' Masters. A fancy word implying movement into another life realm of vibration; a higher one than before. Physical masters can transcend the environment of the third dimension to one of the many higher dimensions, by alteration of their vibrations."

"They no longer have to experience physical death or aging because they no longer believe the reality of it, contrary to what they were taught to believe at the time. They choose a new reality... one that is absolutely *real*. Real, because they accept nothing else of a *lessor* thought. Real, because it actually IS. Now there are many grades of Mastership. This is because like school, we learn in stages. We can continue to grow spiritually almost for forever. Therefore, there are many different levels of Mastership. So really, each Master is but a student... always learning from a Higher Source. Don't be concerned with the term *Master*, we are all Masters, and we are all students... ascended or not!" (giggles)

"Back to channeling. A guide may be a Master on one or many levels apart from us. They can make themselves seen to their 'student', heard and even felt. They can rematerialize from the ether into a totally three-dimensional form, as a two dimensional etheric form or Light Body, a speck or beam of light or as a shadow, or in many other ways. We might *never* see them, but if we do it's usually to make us feel more comfortable, or sometimes it's for verification or impact. They can temporarily remain here to guide or teach us and they can eat and drink as we do if they return physically to this dimension; although this is fairly uncommon. They can communicate through 'automatic' hand writing through our fingers on a computer keyboard, typewriter or a piece of paper; they can express themselves through thought to our subconscious or they can be heard to speak what seems like audibly to our ears, or directly to our consciousness."

"Many times we communicate with them in our sleeping states. We can feel their presence *if* we are receptive enough by various sensations in, on or around our body, a heaviness in our hands as we write down enlightened thoughts, an electrical charge in the air, a cold sensation or in a myriad other ways."

"I'd also like to explain the word cosmic to you. Cosmic basically refers to a greater accepted understanding, the essence of which contains all Universal knowledge. That which exists beyond time and space and *definitely* beyond our basic and simplified three dimensional terms and understandings. The infinite data bank of all experience, reality, thought, wisdom and perpetuity. The Cosmic Consciousness then, is of God, the All in All."

69

THE SIERRAVILLE EXPERIENCE

"To understand that God IS, as are we, is to understand one of the *most* important aspects of enlightened thinking. People attempt to place God in long robes on a great throne; physical association, but not correctly perceived. Many different religions have vastly different ideas of what God is, but hardly anyone realizes the simple fact that God just IS. He can be to us anything our limited and restrictive left brained concepts can imagine, but to understand the absolute and *greatly* superior thought that He simply IS, is *far* beyond most of our capabilities."

"We accept His BEing but we vastly limit His concept to *our* level of understanding, a rather poor level at that. Yet that is changing even now. BEing, is the actualization of the state of 'ISness'. We think in the simplified terms of 'being', of *our* existence... a 'human being'. A form of life, substance with an intelligence. 'BEing' on the other hand, is the higher inner-realization of all that we are; and that we continually *demonstrate* our wisdom by what we think, say or do, from a focus of *harmony* and *love*."

"We're not just an accidental three dimensional form, an entity which experiences only five senses. No, we are *much* greater than that! But most of us don't acknowledge it. We accept the air that surrounds us as a fact. We may ask: Why does it exist?... but we never question that it does because we KNOW that it does. Faith of mind and matter, *requiring no proof*. If we could only have that kind knowingness about *ourselves*, what a difference that could make to the world and to our own spiritual growth. The Masters have accomplished this realization and they understand the totality of their BEing. This is what I tried to explain before. They *ARE* and they *KNOW* it. They no longer restrict their thinking in any fashion, by having escaped the limiting three dimensional thoughts that we tend to accept as personal 'truths'."

"Boy, I'm really going on aren't I?" "Please don't stop. I feel like I have been asleep all my life. The information you've given me is extremely interesting, I'd like to know more." "All right then, in some written material you may come across the ambiguous word: truth. *This* is a truth and *that* is a truth, but somehow the inexperienced reader may be left to try to glean out what the author means by '*truth*'. I'll try to explain. There are cosmic truths and there are individual truths. Cosmic truths contain the foundations for All That Is. By now you have probably formulated what that means."

"Individual truths are unique to each individual or entity. As an example, Your 'truth' about a point of philosophy may not be someone else's 'truth', and that's *okay*. If *YOU* believe it, then it is true for YOU. There are as many truths as there are Carter's Pills. Do you understand?" "Perfectly." "Let's say you believe a black cat crossing your path will bring you bad luck. This has become a truth for you from childhood."

SPECIAL EFFECTS

"Some people may kid or condemn you for that kind of thinking, but for *you* it is a reality because of your accepted belief patterns. Perhaps when you were young you were told this old superstition. Let's also assume you internalized that thought, because it seemed believable. Then later you have an experience with a black cat. After which you also experienced something you might call 'bad'. From then on, if it is your choosing, you will remember and *BELIEVE* that black cat's bring bad luck. Of course there is no such thing as luck, I hope you realize that... Then even later on in life, should you experience a black cat suddenly crossing your path, you get all tensed up with negative emotions and fears. You *KNOW* something is going to happen, and let's say it does. Now we are talking about manifestation. Manifestation is the end result of bringing into form, a *thought*. It is creation. In the example, you believed something bad would happen and it did."

"The error of thought here was, you blamed the cat. WHY? Because that is what you were taught, or that is what you chose to believe. In reality, you brought the 'bad' event into your own life by your own will. (the lady frowns lightly) Yes, you *'willed'* that 'thing' to happen. No-one would admit that they ever 'will' bad things to happen to themselves, but they do... many times. It isn't intentional, but nonetheless it is a fact. It is an unconscious left brained act, and as I said earlier, all thoughts are real things. They can and *do* create situations and circumstances!"

"We think that *our* thoughts are just personal things. We think that they *only* stay within our minds, locked away and secret from the world... Wrong! They are available to everyone, anyone, seen or not seen, anytime. Our thoughts as well as all other thoughts, including those from the far ends of the Universe permeate the ether. They have their own set of frequencies at which they operate. Thoughts are the fastest kind of energy and are almost *instantaneous* in their travel. Depending upon the *directive* energy we give a thought, determines or impacts how or if it will manifest, or to it's full potential. That energy is always electromotively charged with either plus (+) or minus (-) [emotion based] potentials [feelings] or a combination, and the resultant potential determines to what degree a thought can be made manifest."

"So you are saying that when *we* create certain events which happen in our lives, that they originated in part from our emotions at the time of the thought, and the result can be good OR bad?" "Exactly my dear, exactly. Let me ask you a question... Did you decide that you needed a raise at work, or did you get it unexpectedly?" "Yes, it was unexpected because it wasn't time for my review. I just knew my financial situation and I knew I needed more money." "Then you DID create the thought... from your feeling of need! When did it occur?" "When did I think about it? or when did I get the money?"

THE SIERRAVILLE EXPERIENCE

"When did you think the thought that you needed more pay?" "During one tense moment." "Then understand it was at that time you generated the foundation for the manifestation of the raise. What emotions were you feeling at the time?" "I was feeling desperate and that it needed to be now." "When did you receive the raise?" "Two weeks later." "And how much did you want your raise to be?" "A hundred dollars or so more a month." "And what was your raise, how much did it increase your monthly salary?" "One hundred and four dollars!... (long pause) "Wow... did I *really* have something to do with that?" "Yes honey, you did. Bet you thought it was coincidence didn't you?" "To tell you the truth I don't remember giving it much consideration other than I thought what great timing!"

"And indeed it was. I believe you may now be able to convince yourself about the fantastic *power* of the mind and just how dynamic thoughts are! All of the conditions necessary to bring forth the end result were initially generated by you. Then your desire was acted upon by a creational energy and higher authority! The pattern was... first the thought of the extra money, because you had a *sincere* need, second the thought of how much, third the thought of when and last but vitally important, the *intensity* of the emotions *behind* the thought you had at that moment."

"Do you see how uncomplicated it can be? Once you believe you were the causal factor involved in manifesting your raise and believe it occurred because of your cause and effect action, then I would hope that you try to practice what you have learned in other areas of your life. There is *no end* to what you can accomplish, but you *have* to believe you can and be the driving force behind creating the desire to experience these wonderful things. But also understand that we can not misuse or abuse our thoughts for manifestation. They must be based on needs, *not wants*. Our personal understandings of cosmic laws, which includes such things as intent and beliefs in a structured higher authority, directly impacts the observed results."

"Through God all things are possible, isn't that what we are taught? Why then, don't we *believe* it?" "Because we have learned to depend only on *ourselves* and lost those higher understandings when we gave up our higher connection with God?" "That's right. How do you feel about that statement, as far as you as an individual are concerned?" "I realize now that I am *not* alone, and that I should focus on learning more about my relationship with God. I believe, because of your kind instruction (smile), that God really is within me; and that we *can* do things that in the past I didn't accept that we could. (pause) This has been so *enlightening*, as you put it! I see I've got a *lot* of self-examination and changing to do. I can hardly wait to get started!" "Wonderful" says Lily. (another pause to study the cup)

SPECIAL EFFECTS

"Well... your present guide appears to be a very ancient and wise Chinaman." (the lady bends over to look into the cup, but can only see loose tea leaves. She frowns somewhat, looking back at Lily) "I'm sorry, I forgot to mention that I can see three dimensional views with this process; As well as moving pictures, *like movies you know*, and can even hear messages. Your guide is now emanating a huge aura of love for you. Not in the physical sense, but in the Spiritual sense. He is showing to me what he feels for you and about you. He indicates that when the time is right, right for you that is, he will make himself known to you by a very special means. He wishes me not to disclose what that is... so I will not."

"Didn't you say earlier that our guides were only for us and they only communicated to us?" "Yes." Then how is it you're able to get *my* guide's information?" "Your guide knows what, when and how to get through to you. It isn't uncommon for them to work through whatever means are available to accomplish that. I, just happen to be the *means* at the moment. 'He' knows my level of understanding because as I already said, all of our thoughts are available to anyone, anytime. He knows that I won't misrepresent him, his messages or the intent of his messages. I become a tool for him as the tea leaves are a tool for me. Do you understand?" "Yes, that makes perfect sense."

"He is instructing me to tell you to read some special material." (Lily takes a pen and jots down the name of several authors and gives the paper to the woman) "He feels the information from these authors will help you to understand more about Spiritualism and more about who you are as a beautiful and living part of God. He sends his blessings to you and wishes you well. (pause) He has left my vision now. (pause) What have we here? The leaves are indicating to me that you are an old soul. You have lived many times before... you bring with you much spiritual knowledge. Knowledge which is just under the subconscious layers of your mind... 'Carryovers'. That's what we call them for lack of a better term. Information that we have learned from a previous existence, yet forgotten through clouded perceptions in this incarnation. It's still there though..." (pause)

"Oh... You were once a man-priest in the Mystery Schools in Egypt. You had a great understanding at that time about life on other planets (pause) and about... telekinesis, or the ability to move objects by mind power alone. Apparently, you were personally involved in the building of at least one large pyramid. It seems you also understood the philosophy of embalming... that's *quite* interesting."

"If you're curious, you might try in your meditations to focus on this information and see if you can gain more insight to other aspects of this prior life-existence. Keep me informed, okay?"

THE SIERRAVILLE EXPERIENCE

Lily gently pushes the cup aside, "Well, I think that's about wraps up our session for this afternoon... I'm beginning to feel a little depleted from my connection. It takes a fair amount of focus to remain in that energy sphere you know... How do *you* feel about what we've covered today?" "I feel really great! I can hardly wait to see you again Lily, thank you so much... for *everything*."

So Ends Journal Three

JOURNAL 4

"MAGIC... OR WHAT?!"

Although I was previously aware of a lot of what Lily had said, I was very impressed with her simplicity and how she was able to bring her visitor up to speed in a very short time. Her client's progress told me that she was *really* desiring to learn. I actually felt the *woman's* excitement in her own accomplishment. Mr. Beckworth, informing me that Billy will be seeking him out tomorrow, invites me to participate and shares what is to occur at that meeting...

• ▲ •

Meanwhile Billy has reached Tom's ranch. Tom's mother tells him that Tom is down by the wash, target practicing. He hops back into his car and heads down a gravel road that he knows ends up at the ravine. Sure enough, there's Tom setting up some more bottles and cans. *"TOM"* yells out Billy, *"C'mere, I want to tell you something."* He motions Tom with his hand. Through the grasses and up the lightly inclined bank, trudges Tom. "What are you all fired up about?" he asks. "I saw Mr. B over at the lake this afternoon. Man is there something different about *him*..." "Yeah? Like what?" The two decide to sit down and talk in the shade of a large old tree stump. "Well, I went to the lake like I said to do some thinking. I saw Mr. B when I went around a bend in the shore and started to walk over to him." "Why be bothered?" asks Tom. "I just thought I might go over and say hi, since he was there an' all." "I wouldn't do it" indicates Tom, "*I*, wouldn't waste *my* time on that old man." "Let me tell you the rest of it..." pushes Billy. "I was walking towards him while he was laying on the beach with his hat over his face. He couldn't see me coming but when I got within twenty feet of him, he said hello to me. He called me by name!"

THE SIERRAVILLE EXPERIENCE

"Yeah? What's the big deal?" inquires Tom, "So he knows who you are!?" "You didn't hear me, I said he *couldn't* see me because of his hat." Tom turns abruptly towards Billy. His frowned eyebrows indicate that he has taken some notice and is puzzled. "It was really weird." "WHAT was?" presses Tom inquisitively. "When I asked him how he knew it was me, he said he saw me." "So, maybe he's got holes in that ratty hat of his." "No! He said he saw me with his mind!" Tom stands straight up, "Get outta' here. Now I *KNOW* he's a mental case   And if you believe him, you've gotta' have rocks up there", pointing at Billy's head. "I don't think he's a quack Tom." Tom folds his arms over his chest, "Oh really?" "Yeah, really" Billy comes back. "He said he uses power like that older lady Lily does, that psychic power... ESP!? No, that's not it.... CLAIRVOYANCE, that's it, *I think*." "That crazy ol' man? You've *gotta'* be kidding? If I were you I'd stay away from him, I think he's lost it." "Then how do you explain how he knew I was there?" "It's prob'bly just a trick of some sort" replies Tom. "I don't think so" says Billy. "That's what you get for thinkin' Bill! A bunch of nonsense."

"Then I noticed a lot of dog tracks around him." "SO!?" "The strange thing is, the tracks didn't come from any where. They were only around *him*." "What are you talkin' about?" asks Tom. "I asked him about the tracks and he said they belonged to his dog." "Oh Boy! That's about *all* I can handle Billy. You guys been hittin' the same bottle?" "NO, *nobody* was drinking. *Seriously*." "Well you know his dog is dead don't you? He died years ago!" "Yeah, yeah... I know that." "Then how in the *world* can you listen to him?" "There just isn't any other explanation Tom, 'least I can't think of any. There wasn't anyone else at the lake, and he said he'd been there all day by himself!" "So you believed him?" "I guess so." "How'd he explain the dog?"

"He didn't, he said to think about how the tracks could be possible and to look him up in a couple of days." "Boy, he sure's got you going doesn't he?!" "You know what I think, Tom?" "*What*?" "I think that maybe his dog is a ghost or something." "Have you ever heard of ghosts who leave tracks?" asks Tom. Continuing, "If I were you, I'd just forget about that junk and avoid him altogether." The two will end up talking about this for a while longer then they decide to drive into Portola for a burger.

• ▲ •

Back in town the streets are closing up and people are starting to file into Beth's cafe for dinner. A last pass of one of the crop dusters can be heard not far away. "Looks like everything's pretty much back to normal, doesn't it?" inquires Rose of a customer. "Yup, sure does" he answers back. Rose finishes taking the man's order and heads back to the counter to give it to her cook. Jeff and LouAnn were at the counter just starting their meal.

MAGIC... OR WHAT?!

Jeff asks of her cook "So how long have you been working for Rose now?" With a glint of mischievousness in his eyes, he most cleverly responds, "Sins-sa befoa glasshoppa ton gleen." (laughs, all around) "*Good* answer" says Jeff. Rose lightly plants her elbow in her cook's side. John comes strolling in, "It's chow time" he calls out. Some of the folks question him about any other news concerning the kids possible UFO experience. He says that nothing else has been discovered and as far as he's concerned, the case is still a mystery, but now officially closed.

The night elapses without incident and the people around Sierraville are pretty much back to doing what ever they did before the flap about extraterrestrials. Singular vehicles from the strange government caravan have been observed motoring around town, but they never stop to talk to anyone. Nobody yet knows they exist or who they are, they're just seen in passing and no attention is paid to them. During the darkness of this night however, they will disappear back to where ever it is they came from.

• ▲ •

DAY 6: This morning Billy sets out to find Mr. B. Anxious, he wants to find out the answer to the dog question because *he* hasn't come up with anything yet. He drives to his cabin but Mr. B isn't there, so he drives to the lake. He looks and looks but doesn't see Mr. B anywhere. Having driven around the entire lake and checking out the camp grounds, he heads back to Mr. B's cabin. Here he finds Mr. B sitting on his porch lighting a small pipe like he'd been there all along. Billy stops his car in front of the place and gets out to approach Mr. B. "Morning" Billy says, "Who's that?" (Here's where I get introduced to him.)

Mr. B continues, "Well, I see you've found me." "I almost gave up" Billy responds. "Couldn't wait, huh? Come, have a seat" requests Mr. B, arm and hand pointing to the extra chair. Billy sits down and asks him where he was. "I was in meditation and transcending." "What?" "Meditating... finding peace within myself, and also contemplating your arrival." "Yeah, but WHERE were you?" "I was right here." "What do you mean *right* here?" "I was right where you see me now." Billy, not having the understanding of inter-dimensional vibration shifting, shakes his head with much confusion. "You'll understand in due time..."

"Billy?" asks Mr. B, "Have you ever heard the expression Enlightenment before?" "Sure." "What does it mean to you?" "I guess it means a positive change a person makes in himself, as far as his thinking about the possibilities of spirituality and our higher self. At least that's what I've gotten out of the books I've read." "Good. That answer's pretty close. What does the term 'higher self' mean?" "You know, things about our greater capabilities..." "Like what?"

77

THE SIERRAVILLE EXPERIENCE

I can tell that Billy is starting to get nervous, he doesn't feel he really knows that much about the subject and he doesn't want to appear ignorant. "Some of the books indicate that we are more than we think we are." "How?" Now he really feels on the spot... Stammering, "That we have powers, the kind you hear about in legends." "Like what?" "Boy Mr. B, you're really asking a lot of questions. Is he doing that to you too?" "Not really" I said. "Sure I am... I just want to hear your opinion... So, *Like what?*" "Like being able to alter certain circumstances. Like making things happen, or creating something from nothing."

"That and more comes with a person's true and total 'Awakening'... The acceptance that we are an absolute extension of God. Do *you* think those kind of things are possible?" says Mr. B looking deeply into Billy's eyes, like a snake getting ready to strike. "I don't know, I've never heard of anyone really doing it." "Sure you have." "*Who?*" "How about a gentle carpenter named Jesus?" "Oh yeah I know that, I mean a 'normal' person." I couldn't help but chuckle - quietly to *myself* of course!

"He WAS a 'normal' person as you call it. Tho' he knew long before he came to this world as the entity known as Jesus, that he was much greater than the space that his energy-form took up." "What do you mean?" asks Billy. "He knew that because he was of God, he must therefore have similar capabilities that God has. Do you follow?" "Yeah, I think so. But God is so far removed from us and Jesus was a super being." "God, Billy, is everywhere and everything is *of* Him. What would you say, if for an easy explanation, I said God IS the Foundation and Center of Cosmic Thought?" "*EASY?* I thought he was an all-powerful entity with white hair and a giant white throne; Someone you didn't mess with?!" Mr. B laughs. "What if I told you that he wasn't a man?" "I can't believe you're saying that he's a *woman*. Wasn't Jesus his son?" 'Good question on his part' I thought.

"God is *neither* male nor female, yet His essence encompasses both energies, and even more than these. There are *many* dimensions to the One we call God. Jesus called himself the Son of God for clarity sake for the people he was teaching. Back then it would have been too difficult for common man to understand the superior thought that God was not a man, least of all a Living Thought Energy. A BEing of superior essence to all others. *Men* dominated everything in those times, so they could relate to a man being in charge as it were. Since Jesus came to us as a man, a man of wonders and miracles, then it was much easier for them to comprehend God as the Father, and Jesus as His son. Understand?" "It kind'a makes sense." "Good." "Actually, we are *ALL* sons and daughters of God. Remember what Jesus shared: "I and my Father are One?" Not only of the same essence of Spirit and creativity, but of the same focus... Divine Love."

MAGIC... OR WHAT?!

"No man, woman or child is less than another and we all have the same foundation of Spirit. By that I mean we are all *OF* God, like petals are *OF* a flower. It so happens, that everything is of God." [Understanding that Jesus is one of this world's creator's, he chooses to keep the emphasis on the term 'God' for Billy's sake.]

"All creation is a manifestation of the Almighty Thought, the I AM Presence, God. This may seem a little hard to grasp at first but consider this, God is an omnipotent, omnipresent creational life energy. He, which is the term we use in a universal way to mean God, desired to bring into existence various forms of 'Life'. So the heavens were created, and the stars and planets and the suns. Not just ours, but millions of them throughout the Universe. He then created plant and animal life and he so much *loved* and *marveled* at these forms of life that he desired to *experience* them. In order to do so, He sent part of His *consciousness*, His ISness into the various realms. One, eventually being the physical or third dimension as the creation of Man. We then, truly are OF God. Made in His image or more accurately, His *essence*. That being the non-physical form we have. Our etheric form, or soul, *is* what is created in the likeness of the essence He is of."

"God, having tremendous and unlimited creative potential, exists throughout *all* dimensions, the majority of which are totally unknown to us. Our world, like many others, exists in what is called the third or physical dimension. This is the lowest and densest of the available dimensions of thought. When God released the elevated-frequency-thought of *Man*, that vibrational 'conception' left his mind to transcend *down* through the upper levels of creative non-physical energy. The 'condensing' which then occurs, binds the necessary atomic elements together to eventually manifest into the lower ones in a completed form. When you take a higher vibrational energy and bring it into a lower vibrational field, something happens. Do you know what that is?"

"Haven't the faintest" says Billy. "The energy-substance becomes increasingly more dense and less fractionalized, until eventually at the third dimension in this case, it can materialize into a solid form. The energy was *thought* and this world was created, as was everything else from thought; God's thoughts. Man was initially created to participate *in* the third dimension, but not to be an absolute extension *of* this dimension... we, fulfilled *that* criteria ourselves! Here's an analogy for how thought (a higher, creative order vibration of intellect) becomes manifest... Water, as steam, is higher in temperature than tap water. You could show since it's true, that the molecules and atoms of the water are vibrating at a higher level because they are heated up. As the steam cools and the molecules slow down it reforms into water droplets. You see?" "Yeah, it's getting clearer."

THE SIERRAVILLE EXPERIENCE

"If you take the water one more step down it will become ice, won't it?" Adding, "Down, meaning in temperature. Thus, in frequency, or vibration." I nod in agreement. "*Right*" says Billy. "Is there anything I just said that you don't understand?" "No, that's just plain physics." "Correct, but only as it relates to *our* understanding. Long, long ago *we* decided that we were responsible for everything that happened, and that was 'created' by us. We had lost our connection to the wonders and the powers of knowing God. When we did, we were left with only the physical world you and I see. At least that's all most of us *believed* there was. That's what some refer to as the Fall of Man, the original Sin. Thereby, we lost touch with the greater knowledge that we once had. Knowledge that we are indeed god-like... that we *are* that supreme vibrational energy likeness, manifested now in physical terms. I'm not saying that we *are* God, but that we are *of* God, there is a difference. God created Man, not only here, but in different forms throughout the Super-Universe and then allowed discrete evolution of that form by whatever means that form declared for itself."

"When God had the thought to create Man, the ISness of God was the fundamental essence of His creations. A purposeful form was then attached to His particular creations, to allow experiential freedoms within the environments Man would seek to share expression in. The superior feature of His creation (before it was manifested into a para-physical form) is what is referred to as our Spirit. So... what He IS, we are an extension of. A physical form quite appropriate for our environment, initially based upon a superior and original life essence, modified by us per His loving allowance. He is then able to experience not only His creations, but 'their' personalized manifestations of creativity as well. We are OF Him, yet we retain an independent consciousness; Our own *BEing*. The two are really One. *THAT*, is a very hard thing for most people to grasp."

"Our vibrations of spirit (consciousness) are always accessible by He or others of the Light, as His are available to us by various means. We are of the same energy, and communication of consciousness travels both ways in this wonderful sameness. We unfortunately, have become desensitized to His presence... He however, has never waivered. We call our individual spirit form our *Overself*. Although it many times perpetuates on a level below the purity of the All In All, it exists on a level higher than our physical plane. From that plane we can do things of an unimaginable nature. What many enlightened people explore, is contemplating doing on this plane what they *KNOW* they can do on the next. They know because they fully accept their true relationship to God. The sad thing is, is that at the time of the original creation of Man, we *COULD* do those things in our para-physical form!"

"But because we have free will, the longer we focused on the physical and the more we took to heart that if we couldn't touch it, taste it, smell it, feel it or see it, it wasn't real. We trapped ourselves in an illusion. Little by little, we began to limit our wonderful capabilities... until there was no other 'thought' but third dimensional (physical) thinking. Now people are starting to realize that part of them is missing... The connection to God. The realization that there *is* more. I sound like a broken record, but do you see?" "Yes, I think so. Then those things that legends are written about were based on truth weren't they?" "Yes they were, and people that have opened up their thinking, like the 'Lily's of the world, are beginning to get in touch with that part of themselves that we have misplaced over the eons. That's called self-awareness, which is an outgrowth of spiritual enlightenment. Our initial comprehension [when we first come to understand the real potential] of a higher union and association with our Source, is referred to as Awakening. That's where we give mental leeway to the possibilities of a grander Power and seek to understand all we can so we can begin a transformation of spirit, *ours*. All is but One, Billy. There is nothing which isn't possible, nor which we can't do."

"I'd like to demonstrate an example of this power. Everyone can do what I am about to do..." He takes Billy's right hand. "Close your hand and make a semi-tight fist." Mr. B is holding Billy's hand in his own. "Now, I want you to close your eyes and imagine what a marble looks like and feels like. Imagine one in your fist right now." Billy does as requested. Mr. B then engages his thoughts with Billy's, yet Billy is unaware of this. Suddenly Billy says "I just felt something like electricity in my hand." "Open it up" Mr. B says, releasing his hand. Billy's eyes get as large as saucers... "*MAGIC!*... How'd you *do* that?" "That wasn't magic Billy, *that*, was creation. You focused on what you wanted to manifest, and I kind'a tipped the scales for you by focusing also. With our collective thought energy we brought it into being."

"For every person involved in a common thought pattern, for whatever the reason, the applied energy equates to the square of the people involved. This fact is as simple as I can make it without really complicating things. So basically, with two of us there was an equivalent creative energy level of four persons, but creation is not founded on this alone. You see, once you believe you are more and can do the kinds of things Jesus did, which by the way he even *told* us we could, then you will begin your path to self-realization. It really isn't hard, but it does take a *lot* of rethinking and self-examination, a broadening of patterned self-limitations and what you are willing to define as your reality. We can start the process by thanking God for everything we have and experience in our lives. For through God all blessings come."

THE SIERRAVILLE EXPERIENCE

"That is such a simple statement, but how often do we think about the *realness* of the interaction of God in our life? After we master the belief in the truth that God IS; is everything, everywhere, at all times, then the *principle* of God will no longer seem intangible and vague. We will begin to sense His presence everywhere, and within us... because He IS."

"Let's talk about Deohgey for a moment." "Yeah, do, I can't figure out if you're kidding me or not." "Billy, I kid about very little and Deohgey isn't just a memory." Mr. B gets off his chair and goes into the cabin. (I'm thinking to myself 'I <u>love</u> that name! How witty: *D...O...G*' Say it fast with emphasis on the '*oh*') In a little while he comes back out and hands Billy a picture. "THIS... is Deohgey" Mr. B says. Billy looks over the picture and hands it back to Mr. B, but Mr. B doesn't take it from him.

"Would you like to meet Deohgey?" Mr. B asks as he pushes the picture back toward Billy. Giving Mr. B that 'Uh-oh' look, Billy barely nods his head yes because he doesn't really know what else to do. "Okay, I want you to hold his picture with both hands and study it for a while. Look at his face, study the colorations and the markings, then shut your eyes and imagine him in your mind. Sense what my shepherd must feel like, act like, smell like and especially, what he looks like. Make him as real as you can, see him move and run around in your mind if possible. Then envision yourself *with* him, sitting on the porch here like you are. Can you do all that?" "Boy, I don't know... but I'll try." "Good enough."

Billy is studying the picture, trying not to miss any detail. Mr. B tells him that when he is ready to close his eyes, to put the picture down next to him and hold his hands palms up on his knees. After he shuts his eyes, he wants him to take three or four 'cleansing breaths'. Breathing slowly in and holding it a moment, then exhaling slowly and pausing before slowly inhaling again. He instructs him to clear his mind by picturing a blackboard with nothing on it while he breathes. A moment later Mr. B indicates that it's time to put him in touch with his Source. "Okay, now I'd like you to envision a beautiful white beam of light coming into the top of your head from somewhere above you. It's not necessary to see *where* it comes from, or how wide it is, only that you accept it as being from our real and spiritually founded Higher Origin."

"This Light *is* from our Source and purifies and amplifies the connection to that which IS. See the light enter your crown and begin to be absorbed into your head. Can you see the light Billy?" "Yes..." "See it permeate your skin with it's awesome pure whiteness. See it drift slowly down the sides of your head. Can you do that?" "Yes... I can see it." (pause)

MAGIC... OR WHAT?!

"Okay, see it continue down your neck and shoulders, slowly going down your arms while it also continues down your chest and back, filling all areas of your body with Light. Are you with me?" "Yeah." "Good. (pause) See it flow towards your hands while it flows down your stomach. Watch it fill your fingers and flow onward down your waist and down your legs. (double pause) See it flow out of the bottom of your feet. (pause) Are you seeing it, Billy?" "Yes."

"*Great*, now envision that the entire outside of your body is glowing and enclosed in a seamless sheath or veil of this brilliant white Light. It looks alive, iridescent and effervescent. It may appear to you as egg-shaped, a sphere around you or simply a glow extending from yourself." "I *see* it." "Excellent, you are raising your vibrational energy to an advanced level... Now visualize the blackboard again, and relax your focus." Then he tells Billy to picture Deohgey in the area of the blackboard when he is ready to visualize. "It's a little hazy, but I think I can see him." "Make him more real, Billy. In your mind you must believe that he is right *there*. So close and real you could reach out and touch him!" says Mr. B with a sense of mild urgency. "I think it's working; He seems closer and clearer." "Wonderful, can you see him move?" "Yes, his tongue is out, he's panting." (pause) "Do you see yourself in the picture yet?" "Yes. I'm in this chair on your porch." "Good, very good. Reach out in your mind and pet him, can you feel him?" "*YES*, I CAN!" Unknown to Billy, Mr. B has his eyes shut and can 'see' everything that is happening.

"Do you want to make him absolutely real, Billy?" "Yes, Let's do it." "Okay then, *believe* that he is right in front of you at this *very* moment. That he *IS* real, that he is physically here with you *now*... Call his name, ask him to come to you... NOW Billy!" Billy, caught up in the experience, forgets about his inhibitions and calls out to the dog. "Deohgey, come here boy... c'mon boy..." Suddenly, Billy smells the scent of a dog and something licks his hand. He almost fell backwards out of the chair when he opened his eyes. There sitting on the porch IS Deohgey. Flesh and Blood! Billy can hardly believe his eyes let alone talk, and I'm just shaking my head in wonder!

"DEOHGEY!" he finally yelps, turning to look at Mr. B. "Is it really true? Is he really here or am I dreaming?" "You aren't dreaming Billy. That's Deohgey all right." Billy loves animals and leaps off the chair to kneel at his side. He hugs Deohgey and Deohgey returns the emotion by licking his cheek. "I don't understand it, this can't be happening!" Mr. B just sits there smiling, watching the commotion. "How did you do that Mr. B?" "*I*... didn't do it this time Billy, *you* did." "*How?*" "You had a genuine desire to have Deohgey here at this moment."

THE SIERRAVILLE EXPERIENCE

"You also had belief in the process because of the marble. You expanded your thinking and temporarily lost any unconscious disbelief in the *possibility* of manifestation. You obviously love animals, so you had a lot of love-emotion in your desire. You also believed that he *was* real. With these 'tools', you brought forth his being from the ether into the material plane. He, as is all other creation, is *of* a higher vibrational energy. That unique energy 'pattern' exists *outside* of the third dimension and it can be duplicated, revived, modified or regenerated. Remember, anything which is once created is easily re-created by proper activation of the residual energy pattern, or etheric blueprint left by the original creation process."

"*You know*, Tom said you were nothing but hot air, he doesn't believe a word you say." "I know. I've known that for a long time. Bless his heart, he is still struggling with a subconscious *knowing* of what is real, and his conscious mind which has *learned* what isn't. At least that's what *it* thinks" says Mr. B. "There's a reason he's uncomfortable with me, but he doesn't know *why*. He isn't in touch with his higher self, he's just operating on a mental/physical basis. Because of this, he experiences ongoing internal struggles with other facets of his life and he feels uneasy; He has no tangible explanation for his feelings... He can't even *describe* them to you. This will pass however in the not too distant future. You see, we are basically a triune creature. We have a *Physical* form, that which we think of as our true self, but is only a vessel; a *Mental* self, which precipitates thought by various means to control the physical form through emotion; and a *Spiritual* ISness, or Transcendental Mind, which is our *real* self. Few give consideration to anything but the mental and physical aspects of their being. We need to acknowledge the spiritual part of ourselves, the most important part. It is *this* part that knows what we really can do and BE."

"All right, I think I understand that" says Billy, shifting, "Now tell me how you knew it was me at the lake the other day." "First of all, let me say that I knew you were going to be at the lake ahead of time." "*WHAT?*" "I picked up on your thought impressions and made myself available at the lake." "You read my mind? From clear over *here*?" "No... I focused on you, like you did on Deohgey. Then I let myself feel open to your vibrations of thought... I tuned into your thoughts about coming out to the lake." "Does that mean you can read *ALL* my thoughts?" "Only the ones that aren't too private... There are just some things, thoughts, that deserve privacy and ANY enlightened entity allows you that respect. Thoughts, *all* thoughts, are forms of energy. We have an energy around us at all times we call our aura. This is part of our life-force, an element and extension of our Overself. Kirlian photography shows the existence of this energy, however it is proof in a very raw form. There are special photographic cameras today that give a *much* better view of our aura and many things are being learned from them."

"In each aura there are color patterns. These indicate to the interpreter what kind of basic person you are and to a certain degree, how spiritually inclined you may be. Our thoughts emanate from this aura, in the vibrational form of cosmic lights, and may be tuned into by others. This is where the expression 'picking up vibes' from another person actually comes from. Auras differ from person to person, moment to moment. One person's picture may show that they are very psychic, one may show that they have a great ability to manifest. They can show if we are angry or have unresolved pains in our life. In some of these pictures you can see the White Light I've referred to."

"You can also see the 'Channel' to the crown of your head, your Crown Chakra, and how established it is, or rather how spiritually aligned or open you are. This channel indicates how connected to the Source we may be, whether we are *aware* of it or not. It is a fantastic tool with which to learn about ourselves. Now, in the average person an aura can be witnessed as only one color, or you can see several shades (veils) within the aura. The aura can be only inches from the body or be so great (large) that the picture can not show it all within the width of its frame. The more advanced people have had pictures that actually show these veils of lights to appear as 'moving'... alive. *These* auras are majestic and the light patterns appear as Living Lights instead of veils or curtains of light. They are much more active, defined and stronger."

"These individuals may not recognize anything *special* about themselves, but they are closer spiritually to the Source than many others may be. This doesn't mean that they are better than anyone else, it just means that they may be more in balance with their higher self and Source then perhaps others are. Once a person obtains one of these photograph, his or her life will probably never be the same. They have *physical* proof for their physically focused minds that there *IS* something greater about themselves. Many will take new steps toward improving upon themselves and experience a new awareness; Many unfortunately, will not. But for those that do, the desire to know more of the 'truth' about themselves becomes overwhelming. The search begins!" (pause)

"Now... lets get back to Deohgey. He experienced a real existence here on this physical plane. He as I said before, as all living creatures do, has an etheric 'blueprint'. It is not as highly developed as ours, and hasn't the utility or purpose ours has but it exists nonetheless. When he passed on, his 'coding' went on to the etheric world of existence. Because I, as do you or anyone else, have dominion over all things through the use of unrestricted thought, by properly balanced and focused mind-energy, I could call his isness into this plane by my will."

THE SIERRAVILLE EXPERIENCE

"I can call him back into my reality as a vapor form, a physical form or sometimes just close enough for me to be able to sense him from the unseen. At the lake I brought him into the physical to enjoy his company. He can be here almost as long as I want. I must release him to go back after a while though, because of the strain this dimension places on his vibrational pattern. Do you understand?" "Not really, but kind of" replies Billy. "These vibrations are heavy and awkward, much like moving around in a bowl of jello... it is difficult and extremely energy consuming. He must eventually return to recharge and stabilize his vibrations. I can also will myself into another dimension... I do this by 'becoming' love, harmony and peace, with concentrated thought and to such an extent that I can dematerialize from the third dimension. I sometimes raise my vibrations and send my consciousness into the ether while my body remains here."

"In addition, I may visualize myself as pure thought energy, or even a physical form transgressing from one plane to another. That is why I said I was right here, I was... but you couldn't see me!" "So you were like a ghost?" asks Billy. "No, I wasn't a ghost. That term is really crude, but it is the only term 'modern' man has for apparitions. An apparition is generally a person who has physically died, but doesn't know it or in some cases, hasn't accepted it. They still try to be who they were and get very confused when no-one 'here' can see them or recognize them. Some are angry, some are mischievous and some are pacifists, just as they were in physical life. The real *nature* of the departed person continues into the next realm of life, yet it can be modified... but only by *that* individual. They can also be a person who was so strongly attached to the physical plane that when they expired, their physically oriented thoughts kept them from getting into the next exciting plane of existence. They haven't recognized that they are physically dead because they seem to be able to do the same things as they always did."

"They are etheric, but are caught between the third and the fourth planes of limited thought and lower vibration. There are cases, you may have heard or read about, that have had noises occurring with the sighting(s). These cases may involve individuals that 'linger' around what was once their home. When someone else moves in, things start moving or breaking, because the 'original' person wants to regain possession of their home. 'They' don't want what they consider intruders in what *they* still think is *their* home, messing with *their* stuff, so they might try to frighten them away. It usually works..." (We all get a laugh.)

"There are distinguished people, simplistically called 'apparition-midwayers' [parapsychologists usually] who desire to help these specters, or 'spirits' out by sending them to the White Light. They act as a go-between to send them spiritually, 'Home'. That Light is a cosmic door to another level."

"That's what people who have had near-death experiences see. A tunnel with a brilliant white light at the end of it. They *intuitively* know that loved ones and a great Love Presence is at the end of this tunnel. If their time isn't up on this plane, their spirit-selves are moved back into their physical selves to finish this life-cycle. It is an awesome experience and anyone who gets a glimpse of it will *never* again be afraid to die... they KNOW it is only a transition to a higher plane. Physical death, is merely the moment of rebirth back into the *essence* that we really are. The more cognizant of that we are, the easier the transition will be if or when it occurs. Physical death needn't occur at all, that's why I said if, but most of us limit our thinking and accept that it must; a tragedy at best. Yet people on the 'other' side can transcend back into this plane at anytime. Most don't because they are learning and experiencing many new and fantastic things, or are busy elsewhere in other realms of existence."

"Some of the more enlightened ones may even choose to become guides for their physical counterparts, that being you and me. Some go on to even higher levels or planes, and *all* will study their prior lives to judge whether or not to return to the physical or another level of existence. To transcend back to the third dimension from spirit takes an awful lot of concentration and energy, beyond what you and others can comprehend but it can be, and is done. Jesus did it many times, as have many others before and after him." "What do you mean *study* their lives?" asks Billy. "Let me first share another piece of information that I'm sure you'll find very interesting. When God created Man, you, me and all of the other forms of Man throughout the Cosmos, it was accomplished in a step-modified approach. Each intellectual development was based on prior experience and code. God, and later His co-creators, ultimately conceived vastly differing worlds throughout the thought-form known as the Super-Universe, and various life-forms were developed for those particular environments."

"Some of the worlds reside in different dimensions from ours, some are closer to the material, some are higher in vibrational frequency and some are beyond even that. Some can be seen physically, some can't. Many of these worlds of 'Man' are very advanced, scientifically *AND* spiritually. Many are similar to our world and some are at other stages of evolution. By evolution, I mean spiritually. Some are closer to the realization of all that they are, and some, like us, are just awakening to that realization. Therefore, some worlds are very harmonious and peaceful and others remain in various types of conflict, again, like ours."

"Okay, back to your question. As we [here] transcend, we review what we have accomplished as individuals when we leave the physical embodiment."

87

THE SIERRAVILLE EXPERIENCE

"From this next plane, now unencumbered, we have all of our lives, memories and experiences available to us to 'study'. We also instinctively KNOW that we have areas of our BEing that we will desire to change for the better. We judge how well or poorly we've done [how we handled our experiences] and then understanding that we can't progress to the next 'grade' so-to-speak, *without* improvement, we might choose to reincarnate to experience certain changes in ourselves before continuing. OR... we may decide that we didn't get an opportunity to experience something in particular that can only occur in the physical. Reincarnation becomes a personal commitment to ascertain, develop and experience Universal Truths and Spiritual perfection. It's a lot like school because we are forever learning."

"Now for an eye opener... God never judges us. *WE* judge ourselves... contrary to what we have been 'taught'. God basically judges *no* entity, ever, for to do so He would be judging Himself." "Because we are OF Him, right?!" interjects Billy. "Right. There is an exception though, but only one, and that is in the case of the knowledgeable who willfully expound the denial of God AND perpetuate the subduction of others into this belief... Hindering their soul growth or harming their evolution of spirit. This, is the greatest sin an entity can initiate. God is perfection, and everything He created is good. 'Bad', is a manifestation or an act of a 'created-entity' alone, not God. We can and eventually *will* be perfected, but because of the Fall it has and *is* taking time. The *length* of 'time' has been up to us, not God. He patiently waits and lovingly watches and is willing, through the gifts he gave us all, to help at anytime."

"But WE have to recognize and utilize our awareness and understandings *of* His Life Force Energy within us, in order to accommodate any changes for ourselves. We alone, pull ourselves up the ladder of enlightenment and spiritual realization. As we do, we grow and as we grow we are able to experience other wonders in our lives, and later, in new dimensions."

"Dimensions so great, they would boggle your mind, your three-dimensional mind that is. Life you see, is forever. A 'living' thought-form can not be (generally) destroyed, but 'it' can experience many, many things... including different types of life, in different planes of existence." Billy asks "Are there real places called heaven and hell?" "Only to the extent you believe there is, Billy. If you believe in Divine creation and Love and consideration for all living things, in sharing and taking delight and joy in all that is created by only seeing and experiencing the greatness and beauty, then you can have heaven here or in any other plane of existence. Heaven is a *state of heart and mind*. If on the other hand, you believe there *is* a hell and you 'imagine' all the terrible things that *people* say to be true, then you can also experience that. Here, or even more easily on the other planes."

88

"The magnitude of reality resides solely in our beliefs. If in this plane you always think the worst is going to happen to you and then it does, you believe the world to be a pitiful and terrible place... *You* in fact, have created those thoughts, and thereby have placed *yourself* in a hellish existence. Then after you pass on, reaching the *other* side, those thoughts might be very ingrained. You can actually continue your own torment once there as well!"

"In another example, you might have been taught that hell is a real place. You may have experienced what you'd call a hell on earth and you may have been taught to imagine the terrible concepts of fire and torture in the after life if you were 'bad'. Then reaching the next plane of existence, harboring thoughts that you believed you *were* bad, these thoughts could be so strong that you may '*create*' a condition for yourself and truly experience pain and suffering. However, it is *only* a condition YOU have created, just as you create various conditions for yourself in this plane of life."

"Fortunately there are guides on the next plane [as well as on other planes] that will help you eventually 'see' that those thoughts are an illusion. An illusion of your own making; That which YOU created for yourself, *not* God. That 'illusion' principle works *here* on earth as well." "Boy that's weird" says Billy. "You must understand that in the next plane, creation or the manifestation of thought happens *instantaneously* and with voluminous power because you are no longer *limited* by the third dimensional realities and laws. From that plane of existence, we have vast information available to us to study and learn from. What is and isn't real, what is and isn't 'good' for ourselves. From that review then, we can see how we create reality and how we can modify and evolve our BEing or remain stagnant, the choice is *always* ours."

"To put your mind at ease, at the center of the Super-Universe there is indeed a 'world' called Paradise. This place is much like you'd imagine heaven to be but ever more so, and the loving, learned and committed Souls of Light will attain residence here. But a 'state-of-heaven' can be realized outside of Paradise, anywhere you are, in any dimension of reality... I will leave Paradise for another time however, for it is a lengthy discussion."

Billy asks "Is there really a devil, if hell doesn't exist?" "There IS an entity called Satan. This entity was originally one of the more achieved and loving spirits in the Super-Universe, at least in our sector. He desired to know God and worked at this achievement profusely. At one point in his evolution however, after seeking all the avenues he believed were available to him, he began to conclude that he couldn't prove the existence of God... Eventually he began having strong feelings that the concept of God was merely an intangible abstraction and therefore unworthy of merit."

THE SIERRAVILLE EXPERIENCE

"When he couldn't absolutely prove the existence of God to himself, he wondered why he should promote to others, such a ambiguous concept... He had lost his faith. Falling from stature as a heavenly and godly being, one who interfaced with many realms and worlds, he began to produce and expound vibration on these planes that God didn't exist. His less-than-positive thought creations were 'felt' at all planes in which he participated, from the highest levels down to the physical. He eventually got many once wonderful and heavenly souls to appreciate, collaborate and work with him in extending and perpetrating this thought. Of course these kinds of thoughts brought with them reduced vibrations, and creativity *based in disharmony*."

"We entities of the physical realm open our etheric doors to these vibrations when we dwell in negative thoughts, ill feelings, selfishness and other similar negative thoughts. His influence and energies can precipitate into our very *being* by our allowing rips and tears to form within our etheric reflection. Simply put, our aura. We make ourselves available to these negative energies by having negative thoughts. We literally give he and his workers the keys to tamper with our lives and various attributes of soul."

"We attract their attention by our generating disharmony, because their affinity is *FOR* disharmony... Darkness, as opposed to Light; Negative energies, instead of positive energies. He and his workers see the changes of form and lights in our aura and then seek to take advantage of every opportunity to invade our 'space', modify our behavior and control our attitudes and minds... if not our physical forms in some cases. Like will *always* seek like! That is why one should ceaselessly focus on the Light, God, his workers and utilize attributes of love and harmony in our lives. They can't break through our protective barriers if our convictions are strong enough. Light *always* succeeds!"

"President Roosevelt once said 'We have nothing to fear, but fear itself.' Fear is a negative vibration of thought upon which these beings of darkness can play. Havoc, that is. Fear as an example, is one kind of invitation to these entities to which they enjoy adding energy. They can literally amplify negative vibrations within us like: stressed indecision, feelings of loss of control, mental and emotional disorientation, panic, internalized pain, fright, and all the other types of less-than-positive emotions if we allow them to."

"Look at relationships and marriages if you want a substantial example in the material world of what can happen when they get a hold of us! Of course we have the power to fix these situations individually, but seldom is it used. We can't see past our own noses in these cases, to comprehend the larger picture of what is going on. I'm not suggesting that the dark forces are the only reason for separations and battles."

90

"There *are* other reasons as well, but these devious forces don't make it any easier for us and their influence will lead us to make personal decisions (usually in haste) which will never be right or proper for ourselves. A disastrous result of creative energy!"

"There is also a 'world' which Satan has created to house 'his' souls. Much like Paradise, it is the extreme opposite in vibration and condition. The reference to 'hell' comes from experiences many humans have had over the eons in which they have had a brief opportunity to be in a dark, tortuous place of sub-reality. This experience was handled by Jesus or other BEings of Light to show us what kind of energies we were creating for ourselves, and what the outcome of these thoughts would be if we continued in this way. We were never in danger, shielded by the Light of Jesus or the wings of those angels, but it sure is a good way to get our attention isn't it? Those types of experiences are protected 'looks' into the 'world' of Satan. A miserable, unrewarding cavity of holocaustic energy and deformity of spirit. Definitely not a desirable destination, but it is real... The netherworld we often refer to as Purgatory. There legions of entities within this realm, just as are there legions dwelling in the realms of Light."

"Universally, the balance has always been with the Light; particularly as *that* sphere is where God prevails. Satan is not a match for God, of lessor evolved BEings yes, but not the Creator. At one crucial point in time now very close, he and his followers may all be *permanently* set aside from the rest of creation to dwell in a sealed macrocosm, therein forever. This final act however, is predicated on Satan's and his entourage's repentance and alteration of spirit. Even he and his followers still have an opportunity to make a choice for change, and this is out of God's love for all of them."
"Boy, is this heavy!" says Billy. "I had no idea about the illusion thing, or for that matter, Satan. I think I'm really beginning to see what you mean by the word spiritual."

"Spiritualism is very complex, yet it is *so* simple" says Mr. B. "It can be as hard as we make it, or as easy as breathing the air that surrounds us. It's up to us, as to what we *accept* as our reality or how we *limit* our reality, and especially by which powers we drawn upon. Whatever else we might do, we DO create our own reality by *how* we think, what we focus on and where our basis of energy is placed. If we believe that we *have* limitations, then we certainly will experience them! Remember thoughts are a very powerful and awesome energy and ALL thoughts create. What you choose to believe *IS* what you'll experience, here, now or on the next levels of existence. The work, which *some* people will call it, required to mentally expand and grow is made so much easier when we are totally open to the God Consciousness concept as it relates to our true self."

THE SIERRAVILLE EXPERIENCE

"Therein, will you find complete and total freedom... Having a better knowledge of the various influences around us certainly doesn't hurt either." "Are you a Master?" asks Billy. "*Well...*" replies Mr. B. "Am I more powerful than you? No. Am I more in touch with the reality of who I really am? Yes. Am I a Master? Only if *YOU* believe me to be. Are you a Master? Yes you are. What a Master is to another, is what *that* individual perceives him to be. All Masters are students, always learning more about the Infinite, and all students are Masters, at one level or another. Please don't think because I can do exotic or outlandish things that you are any less than I, you are not. You just haven't awakened to all that you are, and underlined believed in that realization. God gave us all things, not to just a chosen few, but to *ALL* Mankind. We are only separated by what we perceive to be 'truths' for us as individuals."

"Never compare yourself to another, ever. That is self-destructive. It makes you less, in *your* mind, than someone else. It creates separation and limitations, or really, the *illusion* of both. To say 'I can't ever be or do as good as so-and-so' sets up thought energy which will manifest in forms that *WILL* keep you from achieving. What you should do is first recognize your worthy qualities, then recognize the positive qualities you see and admire in others and attempt to incorporate them into your life."

"You should focus on only your good qualities, not the lessor ones. The lessor ones can be developed, or at least accepted in time for what they are and represent... hues of personality - not considered to be good or bad, they just are. Remember no-one is perfect nor shall we ever be, only God is perfection, yet we can all seek to attain perfectionism and thereby grow as close to being as perfect as is possible. Negative thoughts about yourself or someone else, should never be created. These are very ruinous forms of energy, and those kinds of thought-energies WILL precipitate into your mind and life even more so if you continue to have them."

"That alludes to one of the principles of the Commandment, 'Love thy neighbor, as yourself'. If you precipitate harmony and love, these thoughts go out into the ether and later come back to you in one or more forms of 'good'. When you entertain 'bad' thoughts, these too will come back to you, thus the truism 'What goes around, comes around'. This *is* a truth, a cosmic truth. The more you see 'good' in life, the more your life will be filled with 'good'. The more you take to heart and believe and think 'bad', the less bountiful and enjoyable your life will be. Is this making sense to you?"

"Yeah" replies Billy, "I see how we make our own life miserable or pleasant, but I didn't realize that we have an opportunity to alter our reality. Especially in terms concerning the simplicity of: 'how or what we think'."

MAGIC... OR WHAT?!

"I see now that what we send into the ether will always return, so it's best for our growth to learn to focus on only the positive." "I'm pleased with you Billy, *very* pleased. I want you to know that you are about to help someone close to you to 'see the light', as it were. Don't dwell on that statement, but you'll be able to recognize the event when it happens. Because you *care*, you will provide an opportunity for that person to experience something very special and help to cause a great change in that person's reality... by <u>their</u> acceptance of information you will provide. God bless you Billy. Now I'm afraid I have to get some chores done, so if you'll excuse me, I'll see you again... soon." Shaking hands, Billy says good-bye to us. He will then drive to the far side of the lake to contemplate what he has just learned. As he does his head is full of thoughts.

He thinks 'Just imagine what this world would be like if *everyone* would think only positive thoughts and cared more for others than they cared for themselves. Can we ever *really* have a world of peace? Is it really possible? Mr. B sure is a lot more than I thought he was.... Oh h... (recalling dusty scuttlebutt) I only heard what I was told from other people, interpreted what I wanted, and probably imagined the rest. I only <u>*saw*</u> the outside, I never once thought about the <u>*inside*</u>!'

- - - - - - -

Billy has just realized how flawed most of our thinking is. How unintellectual we really can be and our tendency toward sometimes believing that we are somehow better (or less) than someone else might be. He sees that this is but one of the small thought patterns that set up the negative energy and forces resulting in the separation of all nations of Man, and Men within all nations.

- - - - - - -

Inside the cabin Mr. B asked me what I thought about what just occurred while he made some tea, Chamomile... '*Great*' I thought, 'I'm really not in to the Squaw Tea flavor'. He looked at me, smiled and said "It does take some getting used to." I told him I was impressed. That it was all *super* informative, and it all made perfect sense to me. I shared that having had an extremely logical mind for most of my life, I had usually looked for substance, and had greatly desired *empirical* proof from which I could then make decisions regarding new information, particularly as it concerned spiritual questions. I've learned that *that* wasn't such a rewarding trait to have; that many times in the past it kept me from growing by not being able to properly evolve. New growth would have enabled me to attain further spiritual understandings, but I had held my own self back! "It's amazing what can take place when we open up" he said. "I'm glad you invited me to participate" I followed.

93

THE SIERRAVILLE EXPERIENCE

I then asked Mr. Beckwork about the Dark Ones having the ability to read our minds. He said "Directly? No! They exploit our weakness and capitalize on our imperfect traits by analyzing our energy patterns."

"Because they can see our auras of lights, which reflect who we are and what *energies* lie *within* our thoughts, they essentially only interpret these as to whether or not we are vulnerable to their passions. Well focused, grounded and spiritually positive individuals can never be harassed by these entities, so there is no need for fear. They won't bother with those of us who are of greater constitution and faith but they may tamper with our acquaintances and significant others, perhaps of lessor constitutions, in an attempt to create negative conditions. Conditions which may result in turmoil for those therein associated. They can try, even manifesting many workings in attempt to sway the more fragile of us, but if our convictions are true and our faith strong, especially in light of having a good spiritual comprehension, we will never vacillate and they *will* give up to frustration... and rather easily.

- - - - - - -

Mr. Beckworth then began to apprise me of tomorrow's events... That man is *never* without an adventure up his sleeve. This is almost like being part of a movie making process; knowing what is generally going to happen, then becoming involved in witnessing the specifics of the events as they actually unfold in reality. They are unforgettable experiences. *This whole encounter is!*

- - - - - - -

It's getting late in the afternoon and Billy, having found a cozy place at the water's edge, has been sitting there and pondering. He begins to really appreciate the wonders of the life around him, including the tiny life that meanders through the grasses and the weeds. It is all very inspiring to him and he now feels that he better understands the beauty of creation, of *all* creation, and for the first time. He will sit until darkness falls over the area, contemplating nature and the heavens. When the stars begin to shine, he will wonder about the other worlds that exist out *there*.

Eventually, a chilly breeze reunites his mind with his body and he knows it's time to head home. As he does, he will note a thin wisp of smoke rising from the area of Mr. B's cabin and he will continue to speculate on why this peculiar man is sharing such fantastic information and knowledge with him.

So Ends Journal Four

JOURNAL 5

✳

"TIME FOR A VISIT"

DAY 7: I had left Sierraville last night to touch base with Mary, get some extra note pads, my tape recorder and blank tapes... my fingers were falling off from taking so many notes! Mary *really* wanted to go back with me but couldn't since she had no 'comp' time coming to her at this point. She was one unhappy camper. After an early breakfast with her, I took off. Mr. B had suggested that I go over to the hot springs by myself today to meditate and just relax. As I drove I was very much looking forward to the warm and soothing waters of a mineral spa and the fresh smells of the piney forest.

• ▲ •

Today Billy arose contemplating what he will do. He also wondered what, if anything, he can share with his parents about Mr. Beckworth. At the breakfast table the three of them are indulging in blueberry pancakes and sausage. Billy looks at his mom and says "I saw Mr. B yesterday." "Oh-h?" his concerned mother replies. "What did *he* have to say?" his father interjects with a partial frown. Realizing that he was treading on thin ice from his father's look and tone of voice, he quickly responds "He just showed me some things he's doing around his cabin. He's a real nice guy." "I don't know him that well son, but I don't think he is the kind of person you think he is.

'Boy, if he only knew how right *that* was' Billy privately thinks. "Why do you say that?" he asks. "Everyone knows about BW honey" his mom follows. "Knows? Knows what?" Billy asks. "They say he is just a down and outer. You *know*, an outcast of sorts." "He drinks too much..." his father offers without looking up from his plate.

THE SIERRAVILLE EXPERIENCE

"Have you ever seen him do that?" asks Billy. "Well, no, but I understand that's all he does. I don't know how he exists... He has no job that I'm aware of and he just seems to hang around. I don't think you should associate with him, you never know what might happen." Billy realizes that his parents have believed what some people have said about Mr. B. 'If only I could convince them that they're wrong' he thinks. He decides suddenly to go-for-it... "He was also telling me about what we can be." "*What*?" replies his father. "You know, what we think and how we think... how that can change our lives. Real positive thinking kind'a stuff." "Change *our* lives?" chuckles his dad sarcastically, "Doesn't look like it's helped *him* any!"

In behalf of Mr. B Billy responds, "He just is satisfied with what he's got, he doesn't believe in having to appear as other people expect him to. He's just himself." "I don't care, I still say that you should avoid him. He's just too far removed from the rest of us... if you know what I mean" implores his father. Billy can see that there's no need to continue 'pushing' Mr. B, so he changes the subject. "I'm going to go see Tom today and maybe do some target practicing." "Well, just be careful" his mom pleads. "Oh, I will. We always watch what we're doing." "That sounds like a good time, have fun" his dad shares as he leaves the table to get ready to go to work. "Help you with the dishes mom?" "No, I've got 'em." "Okay, see you later" he says as he exits out of the kitchen. "Bye" he hears as he heads toward the front door. "Bye" he hollers back, shutting the door behind himself. 'Boy, wait 'til Tom hears what I've got to say now' he thinks as he gets into his car. Starting the engine he heads out to Tom's place.

Arriving, he sees Tom working on a tractor by the large equipment building and he walks towards him. "*Just about done*" Tom shouts to him. "*O.K.*" Billy yells back. "I've just got to reconnect the battery, and I'm all through" he tells Billy, now almost at the tractor. "What was wrong?" asks Billy. "Had to replace the starter. Those things don't seem to last long in this old thing." "Should've got a John Deere" Billy nudges. "Well, that's that!" says Tom, "All done... What are you up to today?" "I've got some fantastic things to tell you" exclaims Billy. "Let me get cleaned up and we'll go for a ride" Tom replies. "Great!" (minutes elapse...)

Tom returns and the two get into Billy's car and ride toward the hot springs. "*SO*, What's this all about?" inquires Tom. "Mr. Beckworth" replies Billy. "Oh-h, not *him* again!?" "Wait 'til you hear what he told me" implores Billy, "He's a *really* neat guy!" Tom looks out his window and mumbles, "I hope you aren't gettin' your string pulled by that ol' man." (silence) "Tom? What do you know about Spirituality?" "What?" "You know, being in touch with a higher force, believing in powers that some people might call unreal."

TIME FOR A VISIT

"All I know, is we had lots of powers years ago. But the white man restricted and confined us so, that we forgot about most of them." "Yeah, like what?" asks Billy. "We used to communicate to and with Mother Earth. We could talk to her, mentally that is. We could talk to the sky and make it rain if we needed water... stuff like that." "Do *you* believe in those things, Tom?" "My father used to tell me about many such things when I was little. He's never told me anything that wasn't true... So, yeah, I guess I do believe in them." "Can your dad do any of those things?" inquires Billy. "I don't think so, but he used to tell me about unique things a very special medicine man named Black Elk was able to do... He was Sioux, you know!"

They finally reach this small community's lodge and park the car. The two walk into the building and give the receptionist several dollars to be on this privately held property. Admission fees obtained from visitors help to keep the rather large acreage preserved, and provides the means for the ongoing upkeep, modernization and restoration of some of the property and buildings. The hot springs are on land that is known to be very spiritual and full of special vibrational energy. If one is 'sensitive' at all, they will immediately feel the positive energy shift.

The owners of this spiritually based resort and healing place live in rustic, even rough simplicity, and with a very environmentally conscious attitude toward Mother Earth. It's left in a natural setting so people can enjoy an opportunity to be with, and experience nature. This isn't a place a group would come to 'party'; besides, it isn't allowed. The area is extremely peaceful and wildlife of all varieties can be seen and heard. The folks that visit here regularly come to meditate and generally like to dwell on the higher aspects of life. The out-of-towners that stop by learn very quickly about the tranquility of this place and intuitively follow the guidelines while respecting the various activities which occur here.

Billy sees me in the large redwood bath as they head West into the forest to find a place to sit and talk. He introduces me to Tom and invites me to go along, suggesting to Tom that I had been a witness to some of what Billy had encountered. I dry off while they wait for me, and we eventually walk around the hill to the far side where a twenty foot teepee is stored for special ceremonies which occur here. "*Okay*, now tell me about Mr. B" says Tom. "He finally told me about his dog." "Yeah?" "He even let me see him" "So he's got a picture, what's the big deal?" "NO Tom, not a *picture*, the real *thing*!... *I* saw him!"

"I thought his dog was dead!?" questions Tom. "Nope... Well... I *guess* he *is*, but Mr. B can bring him back to this plane." "*What are you talking about, have you lost your mind?!*" responds Tom, looking from Billy over to me.

THE SIERRAVILLE EXPERIENCE

"Mr. B told me about what we really are, our Higher Self, the spiritual part. He told me about powers we all have that we've lost touch with." "Like what?" "Like manifesting." "So he *manifested* Deohgey..." smirks Tom. "Yes... he did." "*What?*" "Well, not exactly, he had *ME* do it!" "*C'mon* Billy, your just messin' with me, aren't you?" Billy remains quiet. I'm just grinning, which frustrates Tom even more. "*Aren't* you?" asks Tom again. Billy shakes his head 'No'. Billy fills him in on the details about the marble and how Deohgey was brought out of the ether.

Tom is spell-bound, giving Billy his complete and undivided attention. "He told me some things about God and our relationship with Him. He told me about various levels of existence's and reincarnation and about why we should never judge anyone. It was *fantastic*! He also told me about auras and what they can mean, and about what a ghost really is." Tom is wordless for the moment. "He talked about enlightenment and what thoughts are and why we should 'hold' only good thoughts. I think he's a Master!" "Master of what?" asks Tom. Billy tries to explain the term and sees the confusion in Tom's face. "Like Jesus was master of his reality. That's how he did all those miracles." "There's nobody *ever* gonna' have abilities like Jesus." "*THAT'S* the point Mr. B was trying to share. That kind of thinking is all wrong."

"I looked through the Bible and even found where Jesus *TOLD* us that we could do what he does, and even *greater* things than he did! But nobody today believes they can do those things, only someone very special. But we *can*!" Billy goes into a lot more detail with Tom. Time passes and we will hold a long conversation contemplating what it all means, to us as individuals, and to the world as a whole. Birds of all varieties have been cheeping and calling, and the scene is very relaxed. "Boy, I hate to admit it, but it sounds like you could be right about Mr. B" admits Tom, "Seems like he's really got his act together. I wonder why he lets everyone think he's just a bum? Why doesn't anybody know more about him?" "Only Mr. B knows the answer to those questions Tom" replies Billy, smiling. "We'll have to ask him sometime."

Suddenly, the snap, crack of a branch invades the quietness around us. "What was that?" asks Tom as the two jump to their feet. "I don't know" answers Billy. We look around... v-e-r-y carefully, yet see nothing. "Might have been a deer, or a bear" suggests Billy. "Better a deer than a bear!" Tom exclaims still eyeballing the area. "*There*" I point, "It's just a porcupine." The little fellow winds his way through the brush and finally disappears into the undergrowth. "Feel better now, Tom?" laughs Billy. Tom punches him in the shoulder. "*Hey*" cries Billy. "Hey, yourself" says Tom as the two sit back down.

TIME FOR A VISIT

"Do you want to try something?" Billy asks, sensing Tom's seeming acceptance of everything that's been said so far. "What's that" he asks. "Let's try to focus on Mr. B and see if we can communicate. Maybe we can leave here and go visit him!" Tom reluctantly agrees to try. Purposefully declining the invitation, I said "I'll just sit here and observe."

He and Billy sit appropriately and begin the cleansing breaths as Mr. B had taught Billy earlier. I just look on because I already know what is going to happen... The two concentrate with all their muster for several minutes, then in their heads they hear "I understand". "DID YOU HEAR THAT?" shouts Billy. Tom nods, "But where did it come from? It seemed like it was inside my head!" he states. "*It was*" says Billy, "From his consciousness to ours. He sent his thoughts to us, like we sent ours to him." "This is spooky" implies Tom. Then very near to us a mist begins to grow, but not because of any element of the weather... The mist takes on a denser appearance and soon an outline to the apparition becomes noticeable. It quickly solidifies as the form of Mr. Beckworth.

"Greetings" he says. Billy is totally amazed and Tom is absolutely dumbfounded. Tom, not really sure of what he is seeing, then reaches out for his pant leg. "Is he *real*?" turning to ask Billy. "Why not ask *ME?*" suggests Mr. B. "*It talks*" says Tom, quickly backing off. "Of course I do, what'd you expect?" "I don't know" replies Tom. "It seemed more appropriate for me to come to you, than the other way around. May I join you?" inquires Mr. B.

"Sure" responds Billy excitedly, "Sit down." "How did you do that?" asks a nervous Tom. Mr. B shares how he accomplished his feat. Tom's head is full of all kinds of questions and Mr. B knows it. But before Tom can continue Mr. Beckworth says "Prior to answering *those* questions, let me share some things with you Tom." Mr. B goes into a heartfelt discussion with Tom telling him of the reasons he feels the way he does about himself and other things. Tom nods occasionally and is trying to grasp everything Mr. B is offering. Somewhere in the midst of all of this new excitement, Tom completely turns his thinking around about Mr. B.

"How many people know about the *real* you?" asks Tom. "Only you three do... for the time being." "What does that mean?" asks Billy. "That means soon, very soon, others will begin to see and understand. But not *quite* yet. A certain set of events will pass first. Tom, I want you to know that in another life we knew each other very well." "What?" responds Tom with a perplexed face. "That's right, you and I were great friends in a time long ago. That is where your 'memory lifts' are coming from. (pause) You've heard of the Pit River Indian Nation?" "Sure, hasn't everyone?" "No-o, not *everyone*" answers Mr. B.

THE SIERRAVILLE EXPERIENCE

"You and I were very respected in the council of that tribe, we were considered great medicine men. Shaman is the term most frequently used today." "*YOU and ME*?" "Yes, Tom. We were aware of many great things. We foresaw events to come. We saw the infiltration of other humans, and the destruction of many Indian civilizations and cultures. We also saw that in the future there would come about a much needed change in Mankind."

"This change is supported by a supreme cosmic plan (an alternate but needed intervention) and Divine Love. It brings with it understandings of our true Selves and the Infinite. The understandings that allow man to live with man of all colors and nations, and even with the wildest of animals, in a very harmonious relationship. At that time, everyone is seen as anothers complement and equal, there are no wars, no violence, no illnesses, no hunger. There is peace, and only peace. Life of all types is revered and considered highly precious. Man helps man and each understands that the potential of creation is theirs. They awaken to what reality is, and who they are. You and I made a pact to be part of those changes, Tom."

"That's why I am here now. That's why *you* are here now. Living in the third dimension and in Sierraville, as was arranged." "I don't understand" says Tom, "I have no memory of any previous life, or any spiritual life either, as *Billy* puts it. I never knew you before I moved *here*!" "Tom" says Mr. B in a very gentle tone, "For the most part, none of us remember a spiritual existence. If we did, our limited third-dimensional minds would probably go frantic because we would realize that the capabilities we had 'there', we don't *seem* to have here."

"There is a Higher reason as well. If we remembered, we'd live in continual frustration, confusion and anxiety, and eventually neglect our purpose by under or over-doing... Wasting the bulk of this experience. We volunteered for life here ahead of time, and planned and coordinated with others to work together toward common and/or independent goals before returning. It is very possible that we orchestrated our entire present life path, including different roles and even deciding upon our overall soul assignment. We chose, accepted and agreed to encounter many different experiences and circumstances for further personal growth reasons. If we knew what those were, we'd avoid most of them and radically hinder our development."

"During our earthly lives we usually don't recall what our purpose(s) are to be, and we will encounter faces and friends which give us special feelings of recognition, closeness or familiar warmness. A knowingness that they are unique. These are actually part of our collaborators in our purpose, and perhaps theirs as well, even though we may not recognize it at the time. Meeting up with them, we hopefully fulfill some purpose which was priorly arranged."

100

TIME FOR A VISIT

"They may remain extremely special to us afterward, or even come into our lives as an adversary. It is all part of *our* collective planning and our growth... to see what we do and how we do it. Other individuals and circumstances come along independently of these, again to see how we handle those situations and ourselves. Some of those entities are actually angels to see how we respond to an event, taking note of what or how we think. Particularly in how we handle the small events in our lives. It's the little things that are most important, not the large ones we encounter or do! The little personally based efforts we unselfishly render for positive purposes."

"There is also a cosmic reason that our powers are kept under para-elastic wraps. The attitudes of 'modern' man are basically misaligned. Contemporary Man for the most part, lives trapped in the sad illusions of want, money, things and domination..." "Yeah, I'd agree with that" replies Tom. "Very few maintain spiritual lives because they are unaware, 'asleep'... as they have been for thousands upon thousands of years. What do you think would happen if a few leaders of some countries, or corporate chairmen, or even some bankers had unlimited powers of say, manifestation?" "There'd probably be a *real* mess on our hands; They'd try to control *everything*, and destroy what they couldn't" responds Tom. "Exactly. Man customarily seems to be so focused on *his* own little and private world of possessions and himself that nothing else, *as a general rule*, matters."

"So... the *unenlightened* Man of today can not be allowed to totally recall and use the gifts he naturally has, because of what he'd do with end up doing with them. 'He', is *so* predictable. However in the near future he will be given that opportunity again, but not until certain changes take place in the world and especially, in how 'he' thinks." "What kind of changes in the world?" inquires Tom.

"Mother Earth may see many unexpected natural catastrophes, some of a magnificent nature. All of these events will prove to accomplish *one* thing. To make Man understand that a greater power exists above all else and that the hardened concept of self for *SELF* is of no thing. It is nothing, meaningless. The whole greatly outweighs *that* Self. Man's focus must be redirected to a Higher Source, helping others and recognizing that ALL life has meaning and *no-one* is more important or greater than another. He will learn to share and to do for others, because he *WANTS* to."

"There will be a lot of help available for him at that time also. These will be guides, three dimensional and multi-dimensional, all being from the Consciousness of God. Can you comprehend the magnitude of the changes, Tom?" "Yeah, but it sounds kind'a scary." "For many it could be extremely frightening. But multitudes will evolve during the Time of Transmutation."

101

THE SIERRAVILLE EXPERIENCE

"The ones who have a solid spiritual spark will be cared for, and as I've said, there will be abundant help available." "What about those that aren't?" asks Tom. "Well, some will leave during these times as their life path was finished and/or their purpose completed on this plane. They will go on to yet higher realms. As for the truly unlearned, they *will* pass on during the changes. They will have fulfilled their, perhaps unconscious, desire to spiritually fail... Cause and effect... Not in the sense that if they fail now they cease to exist at all, but they'll continue on elsewhere to come to grips about how self-centered they lived their previous lives here. They *will* be given another chance and they will continue to grow spiritually, eventually coming to 'see the light', as it were. Some may choose to return in due time, to reincarnate back here after the Great Changes... changes in themselves and our planet."

"Until then however, they won't be allowed to smudge or tarnish the new beginning for Mankind on Earth. They will participate in other dimensions and other realities, but not here. The time for Man on Earth to be what God intended him to be, by Man's own recognition of what he truly is, will be the 'call of the day'. It is *imperative* that everyone begin to acknowledge God, and the positive ways of living if they are to have a chance at reducing the impact of the Changes and participating in the New Age events. And how *great* and *exciting* they will be for those remaining."

"Are you talking about Revelations, like in the Bible?" "Yes Tom, I am." "But that foretells the destruction of the planet and most life, who'd want to be around to see it?" "What John saw was the eventual *probability* of global disaster... a *probable* reality. If Man continues on the same path he is on, *THAT* situation *will* be witnessed, and only as a result of our foolishness. It doesn't *have* to happen like it was foretold though. People are awakening to the realization that there IS more and when a more positive, collective consciousness permeates the ether and small positive changes in how Man operates and thinks start to take place, the potential alterations can and WILL be minimized."

"But certain changes must take place in order that Mankind turns to the power of the Infinite, God, and thereby looses sight of himself in the process. I'm not saying that *everyone* is tarnished, there are a lot of beautiful, loving souls on our planet. But the *collective* negative thought consciousness of the *entirety* of Mankind continues to permeate the ether, overwhelming the good vibrations. You *know* what kind of condition our planet and the people are in. People as individuals and in groups can change that situation, and as it happens, this is going on even now. People in general are tired of the old ways and desiring something different. But significant changes must occur globally, to get *everyone's* attention. Some will alter their behavior and thinking, unfortunately, many will not..."

TIME FOR A VISIT

"The status-quo will remain in place for awhile and *many* will be 'out' for themselves when the changes start to happen with greater frequency."

"Incidentally, the world will not be allowed to be destroyed. Mankind has been given rope-length after rope-length, and all he's managed to do is hang himself. A greater consciousness has said, 'Enough-is-enough, there is only so much rope left and we refuse to let out any more.' The end of the era of Man for *himself* is almost over, it can't and won't be allowed to go on. As this age subsides and is emotionally but quickly forgotten, a beautiful, inspiring and *awesome* new age will be born. That is what you and I agreed to be part of a long time ago, we are to be teachers for others to follow and learn from. Billy will also be a part of that, *I think*" says Mr. B looking over to Billy.

Billy shouts "Oh yeah, I want part of *that* action. If you think I can help, then count me in." "So be it" replies Mr. B. "What about him?" (me) asks Billy. "He's already working on his assignment" Mr. B responds. "Teachers" exclaims Tom, "There's so much I see wrong with me now, I couldn't *possibly* be of any help to anyone else!" "Not true, Tom. The fact that you admit it and are willing to change, will eventually allow you to cleanse yourself of the old ways and thoughts. However, the choice will always be yours. God does not interfere with your free will. Now, what do you say, are you willing to *bet* on the odds potentially in place, or would you like to be part of the healing process, a light to others?" "This is all so much, so fast, I still can't get over how you appeared here!" (silence, as Tom thinks) "I think I would very much like to be a part of the Changes." "Good, then we will begin."

"So you know that I speak the truth about our pact, as I sense some doubt, I will take you back to see our agreement unfold." Mr. B moves to sit across from Tom, who is now eyeing him in questionable wonderment. "You two will also be permitted to view these scenes from antiquity, *however*, you will remain here and 'pictures' will flow into your mind. Shut your eyes and begin the breathing process and engage the White Light. Remain still and at peace; When you are done with your cleansing and relaxation breaths, visualize the blackboard again. *Forget* that we are even here!" We eagerly do as Mr. Beckworth has instructed.

"Okay Tom, take my hands. Billy has told you of the breathing process and of the White Light, do you understand these well enough to use them?" "Yes, he did a good job explaining them to me." "Fine, close your eyes and do as I instruct." Tom follows every detail to the 'T' and all of a sudden finds himself floating *above* his body with Mr. B, but their astral forms are no longer holding hands and seem upright.

THE SIERRAVILLE EXPERIENCE

Mr. B, is of course directing the entire process by his stupendous command of thought. Tom, experiencing some uneasiness thinks, "Am I dead?" Mr. B penetrates his consciousness with, "No, you are in your etheric form now... See that shimmering silver cord?" Tom thinks, "Yes." "That is your etheric connection to your physical body, like the umbilical is to an unborn child. If you had passed on that connection would have thinned out and separated, releasing you to go on to the next higher realm." Tom feels more at ease now and is very conscious of Mr. B's new thoughts. He instructs, telepathically, for Tom to 'see' what he is 'seeing'.

They go far back into time, traveling at the speed of thought to an Indian settlement not far from Mount Shasta. They are overlooking the entire area from far above the sacred mountain. They glide ever so easily downward, toward a fairly substantial settlement far below them in a meadow. Tom wonders, "Am I dreaming now?"

A thought returns to him with an impression of joviality, "We are really here, Tom. Time does not actually exist, not in the sense you believe it to. But thought is always present, all thought, even past and future. You can experience either. However, since the past includes *actual* events recorded in the ether by completed (manifested) thought, they are the ones most significant. We could if we desired, actually view the creation of the planet or the solar system. Nothing is impossible. The future for the most part, is only probable and may not happen *exactly* as 'seen'. In either case Tom, we can't alter or interfere with these events, we can only view them."

They glide even further down. Tom is admiring his own Light-Body when Mr. B points out the activities going on. They listen to the Ahjumawi conversations, understanding them perfectly. They also view various scenes of living, cultivating, hunting, cooking and especially, several important ceremonies. "See how they communicate with Mother Earth and give their blessings to her. They are returning the blessings 'She' gave them. They have a complete understanding of their relationship with 'Spirit'. They live in harmony *with* Nature (Earth Spirits) and Mother Earth (Grandmother), the Helpers (Holy Ghost), Tunkashila (Son), and Grandfather (Wakan Tanka) [God]."

Tom is overtaken with emotional the feelings he is perceiving from the Indians' consciousness. He now understands what Mr. B has been talking about all along. "*THIS*, is what we must return to. Not the old Indian livelihood, but to their spiritual *awareness* and how they live as a *part* of life, not separate *from* it." They leap ahead in time several years. The encampment has changed somewhat, but little else has. Mr. B points out a structure and they glide through and into it. Inside several medicine men are sitting around a small fire. They are inside a sweat-lodge.

Each is wearing a loin cloth and passing around a ceremonial pipe. Wet herbs are put in the fire and the heated stones are occasionally sprinkled with water to alter the ambiance within the lodge. They hear prayer-type chanting. *"That's me"* thinks Tom.

Although two of the men seated below do not look like 'them' today, each easily recognizes their prior physical forms. Tom identifies the emblem around one of the men's neck as the one Mr. B now wears. The men are in the act of transcending from the third dimension. They will leave their physical forms as Mr. B and Tom did, and go into the future. Several places into the future! Mr. B and Tom follow along with the other astral spirits. They visit the Plain's and watch the settlers creep across their lands. They see how these people live and how oppressively and differently they think. 'They took no time to even try to understand who the original inhabitants were, or what they represented.' 'Taking, always taking. Never giving back.'

They go further and witness massacres of people, buffalo and the wolf, and the ultimate formation of indecent reservations ushering in the beginning of the loss of most of the native ways. Sadness permeates the ether, a great sadness. Tom becomes emotional. An etheric tear seems to grow in Mr. B's eye as well as he also is caught up in the sorrow of the moment, for *all* of the people, and Mother Earth. Then they go even further. To the times preceding the Time of Transmutation... the early 'modern age', with a brief stay to observe.

Traveling yet further, they view the consequences of Man's conquest of others and the continued pillage of the Earth. Beyond this they go... to witness the Earth's final rebellion and the conscious awakening of Mankind. Now a beautiful scene appears before them. The Changes have taken place, peace and gentleness has finally won out. There are scenes of men caring for others and living in harmony once again. It is 'understood' that Man has finally come to his awareness and has chosen to live life as God had meant for him to live. It's beautiful everywhere; Lush, green and abundant. Life is good, *VERY* good.

Then there is a 'mass' decision to return. Almost instantaneously the Ahjumawi men are back 'into' their physical bodies and regaining their awareness of the same. They discuss the events viewed and later leave the lodge. Two however, remain inside and talk further. They discuss returning in a future life, to help in preparation of the people for the Time of Transmutation. Tom is quite aware of who the two are and realizes that his duty, by his own arrangement, is to follow through on the service he has offered. It is his desire to fulfill his past agreement with the present Mr. B. "Have you seen enough, Tom?" "Yes, Let's go back." "Think upon you and I sitting as we were. That is all you need do to return."

THE SIERRAVILLE EXPERIENCE

A pulling sensation is felt by the two of them and they swiftly find themselves within their own physical bodies. "What'd you think?" asks Mr. B. Tom, Billy (and *I*, I have to admit) are 'blown-away' with this experience. "*Great!*" "*Fantastic!*" "*Man!*"

Tom continues, "*Mr. B*, I want to apologize for how I've treated you in the past. I had *no* idea you were such a special person. I guess I took for granted that everything people have said about you was true. But nobody *really* knows, do they?" 'That took a lot of guts' I thought to myself. "I accept your apology, Tom. It's true, few people really ever perceive another individual, deep down inside that is. People hide behind so many facades, or fake and altered self images that they can't truly be known. Only the more 'aware' can 'know' another individual." "How come you haven't shared the *true* you, with anyone besides us?" asks Billy. "It wasn't time and I had not yet received permission to do so. I had to fit in and live in this dimension as a 'regular'."

"Maintaining a certain station in life as per my plan. Years ago, I had a road act that earned me a simple living and brought laughter to others. But eventually I lost sight of why I was here and what my purpose was. I got caught up in the pain of the people and the slow destruction of Mother Earth. I began to see and embrace only the negative side, forgetting that Man himself had caused it, and that he could change the circumstances if he wanted to. That's when I started drinking; probably more than I should have."

"When Deohgey died, my world fell out from underneath me. I had at that time, trapped myself back in the illusion of the third-dimensional mind. Eventually I left the big cities and was drawn to Sierraville by an unseen urging. Here I regained my focus and purpose, and retrained myself in spiritual philosophy. I became reconnected to the Source, but it took a lot of work, even for *me*. I've been around so long now people just see me as part of the town, basically taking no notice of me... which is fine."

"I *needed* it that way, a face everyone knew, but ignored. Until now. The Planet is on the verge of rebirth, and recently I have been given permission to help re-align Man's thinking. This is my starting point, my first classroom. I become a teacher and by the way, *we* have an excellent *Principal*." We understand completely, who and what Mr. B is referring to.

"I don't understand why you need permission" asks Tom. "After my realignment with the Source, I began to share communications with a greater intelligence. They, and there are many, are referred to as the 'Great White Brotherhood'. Not white as in skin color, but because they are ethereal. White, because they are of the magnificent White Light of Divine Thought, they are *of* God's right hand so to speak. They are truly accomplished and enlightened entities."

"What all do 'they' do?" questions Billy. "That is far too in-depth for you to comprehend yet. Let me just say that they are supreme attendants and overseers of Life, all Life. That will suffice for now. They operate from the unseen, sometimes through other Enlightened Ones. They are available to all. They can be called into service here only by a person desiring to grow and to learn. Maybe I should explain that a little more. You have free will, you will always have that. Enlightened Ones can not interfere with you in any way. They can *only* respond to a true expression of desire, and with approval *from* an individual. You can call their consciousness to you at any time or just as easily stop the communication."

"Are there good and bad enlightened entities?" asks Tom. "Remember, *bad* is not part of the equation. *Man* creates negative, by loosing sight of the positive. On the next level there are indeed entities which haven't grown as they should. Some of these haven't come back to continue their growth, for one reason or another. They might not even be aware that they need to change, *yet*. On the other hand, they are not permitted beyond that level of existence either. These unenlightened entities can also be called upon and some of these may actually be of the severe forces of the netherworld called the 'dark' ones or 'shadow' forces. When an individual opens their mind up for communication, many different entities can partake of that experience. That's why it's imperative to prepare to communicate by surrounding ourselves in White Light. This Light is *pure* and of God."

"External negative energies can not readily co-exist in or near this Light. It is like oil and water, there is a separateness that is maintained by the differences in vibration or frequency. When we visualize this Light around us, we purge the immediate area and prevent unwanted guests. If one accidentally gets through from improper preparation on our part, we simply tell it to leave. You see, *all* entities must respect your thoughts or commands, but only to the extent that you **believe** what you are thinking. By that I mean, they know what your convictions really are."

"How do we know the difference?" asks Tom. "The truly spiritual entities will always be of service to you and give you a feeling of peace. They desire to do anything possible to help, but only at *our* request. The others however might give you great clues. Such as feel restrained, although there is nothing around you. You might begin to feel uneasy, aggressive or sense negative emotions, such as anxiety, nervousness or fear. Don't give them *any* negative emotion to work with. Make sure you have purged yourself of all disharmony prior to the act of communication, and stay focused on only a spiritually positive entity. I will say that initiates should stay away from the ouiji board and like devices. These items are excellent conductors of energy because the users are very focused and *expect* results."

THE SIERRAVILLE EXPERIENCE

"Communication in this manner is not recommended because the user's awareness is on receiving *anything*, instead of receiving *truth*. The best method of communication is simply thought based."

"In any case, if your communication is fairly good and you ask who they are, the others could play games with you by the way they answer. Which incidentally, they will never answer straight-forward to a question of God, the White Light or any other associated concepts. They may even offer information, predicated on *your* personal convictions, which may be counter to the truth yet seem believable. These are all clues to discovering that they are not the ones we should be communicating with. As a schooled and prepared individual, tell them, *firmly instruct them*, to leave. They *must* obey, that is Natural Law."

"If they do come through, it is a sure sign that we are not prepared enough, or perhaps strong enough in our convictions. Remember, they look for and are attracted to imbalance and disharmony within us, or those around us. We must be at peace. Then, ask for an entity of the White Light or of God. Project and focus on an entity which can help you from where you are in your spiritual growth cycle. An entity which is best suited to help you the most will become available. Sometimes you may have multiple entities sharing time with you. Often information comes through which is applicable to the masses. That's how many illuminating books come into being."

"These people transcribe the information, by what ever means they collect the data, and release the document for publication. These physical people recognize that they did not author the material, rather, they assembled into a form which becomes bound and is presented to the public. That is what they must do as they recognize the importance of the information for all Mankind. *That* boys, is but one method the Enlightened Ones use to divest spiritual knowledge and awareness to the masses." He now looks directly at me for some reason.

"Are you enlightened?" asks Billy. (Mr. B laughs) "I believe I am, but I am not finished with my lessons. We are never quite finished. There is always more to learn and do. Both of you are also enlightened, you *do* realize that don't you?" Billy and Tom look at each other, then at Mr. B. They nod. "You don't *believe* it though, *do you*?" pushes Mr. B. Billy questions "You just seem to understand so much and are able to do so much, what can we do?"

"Careful... there's that destructive separation 'thing' again. I've been at it a long time, and I've accepted my true identity, position and capabilities. I have no limitation on my thinking. You boys will learn that you must disassociate your 'patterned' self, *from* your true self. Your third dimensional selves, that is what must be re-examined."

TIME FOR A VISIT

"The more you entertain the possibilities and reality of the Greater you, while realizing and giving thanks that it all comes from God, then you will eventually come to *believe* in the greatness of what you are... and what you are *OF*." "It feels so impossible..." says Tom.

"Practice *DOES* make perfect. Belief in the Infinite and having faith is not an easy task for some. Believing in yourself can be just as hard, or harder. *Living* for yourself is very easy however, but is not of any benefit to you spiritually. We must try to live for the benefit of others. Do your best to see, share, seek and think only good and positive things. This kind of philosophy is very foreign to many people. Their limited and sorrowful realities are all they know, and *truly* all they are interested in. They may appear outwardly comfortable, yet deep inside they may complain loudly and be filled with turmoil, frustration and intolerance."

"They ask: 'Why can't *I* have a better life?' 'Why do these things always happen to *ME?*' They'll always find reasons to push their problems on someone else, and blame their experiences on others. It is rare to find an individual who accepts what has happened as *choice*, or *cause and effect*. When they're offered alternatives, they say 'Change is too hard, or it can be put off'. Neither is true, and time *is* of the essence. Dare to experience all you can be. Developing peace and harmony within yourself is not as great a task as one might imagine... desire and proper intent are all you need. The rest will come as a natural outgrowth of your positive attitude and efforts."

"Now... it's getting late, and I must return. I trust we will see each other soon?" "*You bet*" comes a unison reply. Mr. B stands and says "Until then." Then in a twinkling, he is gone.

Tom and Billy remain seated and motionless. The quietness of the forest is everywhere. Tranquility pervades the very ground we are sitting on. "What do you think *now*?" asks Billy in a very quiet voice. "I don't know what to say" responds Tom, shaking his head mildly. "He is the most fascinating person, I've ever met. I can't wait to learn more."

"Billy, I'm truly ashamed of myself, and I'm angry." "*At what?*" "At being taught so many untruths, and at having let others unconsciously mold who I am. I guess we get so trained in listening to others and responding to them, that we ignore our own inner voice. Mr. B is definitely one of God's chosen!" Billy jumps in, "That may be true, but it starts with *us* Tom." "Yeah... I guess you're right."

Tom asks me what Mr. Beckworth meant by the term 'memory lifts'. I shared my understanding, that it referred to experiences of one or more past existence's, the memories from which reside within our overself. These memories can be faint, strong or remain subconscious until needed.

THE SIERRAVILLE EXPERIENCE

We will sit for a while longer, sharing general dialogue about this fresh 'Philosophy' and talking about the past events we were allowed to see. Tom will then share his experience of astral projection in every detail he can remember...

So Ends Journal Five

JOURNAL 6

"MIRACLES ABOUND"

Mr. Beckworth and I spend this evening together for dinner and some casual exchange of ideas, then I will head back home a few hours later. He said would like me to be available again in seven days. I will take this time to organize, and clean up my notes, download more data from my tapes and take care of other business at hand, in preparation for returning. In my absence Billy, Tom and Mr. B will have gotten together a number of times for continuation of their training.

• ▲ •

DAY 14: Once again I leave a frustrated partner behind and head out to Mr. Beckworth's. I'm lucky she is the kind of person who is still willing to speak to me. She commented that I'm having all the 'fun' while she works, coming home to an empty house (with the exception of our pets). Research and learning (I could have logically argued as a man) is not necessarily considered fun... *but*, I didn't dare. (I will acknowledge however, there *is* a great deal of excitement that has gone along with all this!) I tried to gently explain that he had said that he desires to have only me accompany him at the present time, and that in the near future she will get a chance to meet him. That seemed to help smooth some ruffles...

As I arrive at Mr. Beckworth's, Tom and Billy are going out to see Greg. It's been awhile since they have seen each other. He is finishing up his chores when the two arrive. "Thought you guy's forgot about me!" he says. "No, we've just been busy... *REAL* busy." Tom and Billy quickly give each other that 'knowing' look. "Doing what, if I can ask?" inquires Greg.

THE SIERRAVILLE EXPERIENCE

"Oh, Hi boys" says LouAnn as she comes out the screen door. They offer their hello's back to her. *"Greg, help me pick some vegetables for supper, will you?"* she calls out, heading around to the garden on the far side of the house. *"Okay mom, be right there."* Peabrain will tag along. "Looks like we might be in for some stormy weather" says Billy to Tom. "Looks that way" he replies. They are sharing some small talk when the other two come back around the house. LouAnn goes inside and Greg rejoins them. Peabrain tries to get right in the middle of the group. "Sit down fellow" instructs Greg. The boys are deciding where to go fishing tomorrow, when suddenly a jack rabbit scurries along the front fence and into the road. Peabrain *leaps* off the ground like a lightning bolt, and charges after it.

Turning his head slightly Greg shouts "Come *back* here you dumb dog!" None of them are prepared for what is about to happen. On the roadway heading into town against the sun is a pickup, approaching fast. Peabrain, with his full attention on the dodging rabbit is unaware of any impending danger. The driver can barely see the road, let alone the four legged objects running all over it. A hard metallic THUD, immediately followed by assorted banging sounds are heard and frantic yelps of pain riddle the boys senses. They instinctively turn... *"Oh my god*, he's been hit..!" screams Greg. They run out and down the road toward the shrieks of his badly hurt pet. Greg's heart is pounding heavily. The driver abruptly stops and runs back to see what he hit.

Vital fluids are on and around Peabrain. He has quieted down and doesn't seem to be moving at all. Small whimpers are all that is heard from the dog. Greg kneels at Peabrain's face. Peabrain's eyes look so terribly sad. Then, they close half way and he becomes silent, struggling to breath. Greg tenderly scoops his hands under his beloved pet and picks him up. "You'll be okay" he says with a tear, "Hold on... I gotcha'." "I'm sorry, I'm *so sorry*" the man offers. Without looking up, Greg responds quietly "It's okay mister. It wasn't your fault. He just wasn't paying attention."

"I didn't see him, ... I..." the man continues. "It's all right." (pause) "We can take care of him, please, you go on" Greg urges. The three walk toward the house while the visibly upset man goes back to his truck and drives *very* slowly off. Peabrain suddenly gives out a small jerk and goes totally limp. He has let out his last breath and now lies motionless in Greg's loving arms. LouAnn has come out into the yard and now sees the boys walking slowly toward her. "Oh-h Greg" she cries, running over to him. Greg looks up and can barely speak, "He... He's... *gone*, mom."

No-one can now keep from tearing, the tragedy is just overwhelming. Billy and Tom are feeling quite inadequate and helpless as they walk just slightly behind Greg and his mother. No-one speaks.

112

MIRACLES ABOUND

The vital fluids have smeared Greg's clothes and arms, yet all he is aware of is the loss of his dear friend. A buddy he's had for many years. None of the boys has ever been this close to death and it is very emotionally hard on them all. Greg senses the warmth beginning to leave the body of his friend. Billy is busy mentally apologizing to Peabrain for once calling him 'stupid' and is feeling very upset at himself.

The four reach the front yard in total unnerving silence. "I guess we better bury him" Greg's mom says softly, touching his arm. "Guess so" he sadly replies still looking down at Peabrain. (momentary silence) "WAIT A MINUTE!" Tom says loudly. "Wrap him up and put him in the truck! Let's get over to Mr. B's." Greg looks at Billy with puzzlement, "What can *he* do, he's already gone?"

"*Greg*! Come on, *do it*!" Greg is in a mild state of shock. His mind is all over the place and this command he almost unthinkingly follows, as if he were a simple robot. "*What are you boys doing*?" pushes LouAnn in amazement. "We're going to get him fixed up!" Tom says as he jumps into the truck. "Give me your keys Greg, I'll drive. You get back there with Billy and Peabrain." "*BOYS!*" yells LouAnn as they speed out of the drive. She watches until she can see them no more. Tears in her eyes, she thinks 'They've taken leave of their senses, it's all over.' She walks back to the house very much feeling Greg's pain and loss.

In the bed of the truck, Greg and Billy look down on Peabrain in reticence. The curves and bumps in the road aren't even sensed by them. Tom is going as fast as he can, while still keeping all four tires on the road. After twenty or so minutes, he reaches the turnoff to Mr. B's. He slows down somewhat because of the condition of the road, thinking 'He's *got* to be there... He's just *got* to be there...' He pulls sharply into the small drive at the cabin and runs to the door, and starts banging wildly. "MR. B!... MR..." The door quickly opens and Mr. B comes out, hands raised, "I *know*" he says, "I sensed the situation as you came into the drive. Bring Peabrain in here and put him on the table" he continues as he turns to clear it off.

Mr. B has laid out a table cloth when the boys come inside with the lifeless body. "Lay him down" he instructs Greg, pointing to the table top. Mr. B gently uncovers Peabrain and moves his hands slowly over and above his shattered body. "His back has been broken... (pause) The spinal cord has been severed... (pause) His left rear leg is compoundly broken... in two places... (pause) He has internal injuries as well." The boys remain around the table, but say nothing as they stare down on Peabrain. Greg didn't really want to know all this, folds his hands to his face and begins to quietly sob. "*Boys!* We have some *very* serious work to do here. You must try to leave your emotions of sadness behind, we need a different energy for a while."

113

THE SIERRAVILLE EXPERIENCE

"Take hold of one another's hands; You also." (Referring to me) Greg wipes his eyes on his sleeve, while the rest of us closely encircle the table. Mr. B says "Give me a moment please......"

"Now... I want you all to shut your eyes. See in your mind, if you can, the high spirited animal you know as Peabrain. See him as before, alive and healthy. *Especially* you Greg." Even with tears silently running down his cheeks, he is able to do this and momentarily forgets about the still body in front of him. "Imagine that he IS in *that* condition now! Here with us and perfectly healthy. Let your heart center feel the intensity of pure love. Greg, sense how happy he and you are to see each other. Send him blessings for a total healing. See him enshrouded with a magnificent, almost iridescent pink light. Lovingly command him to return to this world. Tell him you love him and desire his return to full health and physical life, NOW. (pause) Feel that emotion! (longer pause) *More!...* Stronger... ***Stronger boys!...*** ***Feel it in your hearts!***" he urges.

Seemingly, minutes pass by, though they are only a handful of very long seconds. Mr. Beckworth continued "All right now... Give thanks to God for his blessing, and release from your minds to manifest, your desire to have Peabrain healed. Send it into the heavens, see the thought leave your minds and float toward a beautiful White receiving Light. See your thought absorbed by this magnificent light and *KNOW* it is being answered. Know he is returning! You *must* believe it!" (long moments pass)

"He, **IS!**.. You may open your eyes." As we do, a wonderful clear-green light is moving around and through the still frame of Peabrain. The boys and I can't speak, as we are in awe. Before our very eyes the blood soaked and matted hair becomes clean and lays as it should. The body then twitches. Little twitches at first, then Peabrain takes a full breath of air into his lungs. The clear-green light has shifted to bright red and begins to fade out. Peabrain's eyes open and he leaps to his feet and barks...

Greg grabs his beloved pet with new tears beginning to run from his eyes and cries aloud, "He's *alive!...* He's *alive!* Peabrain begins to lick Greg face vicariously. The Billy and Tom are choking up with emotion. Mr. B softly smiles. Greg turns to Mr. B, now with tears of joy streaming down his face and exclaims, "How did you *do* that?! He was gone!?" "The power of *Love* did this gentlemen." The five of us will soon move out onto the porch and talk for several involved hours. Eventually the weary boys head back to Greg's. As they do clouds roll in and darkness grows over the valley. Rain is imminent. In the distance bright flashes of lightning can be seen and the breezes bring the sweet smell of ozone sprinkled 'liquid-sunshine'... Rain, to the rest of us. Reaching Greg's home, they can see Jeff and LouAnn at the kitchen table through the open window.

Hearing an approaching engine, the two come onto the porch as the truck pulls in. LouAnn and Jeff find themselves in shock. Their mouths hang open and their eyes are as large as hen's eggs. (A picture couldn't have done justice at this moment) "W-w-h-h-a. . ." LouAnn starts to say as Peabrain races up to them, tail wagging madly. "Check him out!" calls out Greg, with a huge beaming smile on his face. LouAnn bends down and becomes quite emotional, she can't comprehend what has happened. "Let's go inside and we'll tell you about it" says the gleeful Greg. They do..., and they do. Quite a while later Billy and Tom leave to go home. The introductory class of Enlightenment-101 has now begun in earnest.

During the night a fairly warm rain pelts the area with its life sustaining water. Greg is on the porch with Peabrain, loving him and blessing Mr. B. In his excitement he remembers that he forgot to say thank-you to him. He remains confused, thrilled and amazed. The two will spend the night together on the large porch swing. Over the next several days the tale of Peabrain's accident, death and restoration to health become news around the outskirts of the community. People there are talking all about the events. Since there were multiple witnesses, the rumors have an air of realism and authenticity.

The young men have been queried and questioned by some of the neighbors they've come into contact with. LouAnn received several phone calls and drop-by visitors... all there to check out the amazing story. She is known to be a credible person and is believed, as are the boys. Some of the listeners realize to their embarrassment, that Mr. B is perhaps far more than anyone gave him credit for being. Some of these want to search him out to talk to him, but for personal reasons.

Knowing that he would be deluged by the goodwilled and parsimonious, sightseers and story chasers, Mr. B has purposely and quietly 'left' the area for a while... A few people actually find and drop by his remote little cabin, but they only find me. I can't tell them that he is here - they just can't see him, so I innovate. A couple of them wait for hours and a few return the next day, but to no avail. Others in town occasionally check the cafe and bar for him. Disappointed, they always return home empty-handed. The weather has been wet on and off during this time so many otherwise inquiring others have basically stayed indoors. Greg has brought Peabrain out several times to say thank-you, but in lieu of finding the elusive entity Mr. B, he has me pass on his messages.

DAY 17: This cloudy day Greg rides out to see Tom. He asked Tom why Mr. B had left. "I don't think he's *really* gone, Greg" he responded, "I'm pretty sure he must have other business to attend too... He'll be back." The two continue to chat for a while.

THE SIERRAVILLE EXPERIENCE

The story of Peabrain, Mr. B, his miraculous 'works' and now his disappearance, have caused quite a stir in some sections of the community. Many are wondering what has happened to Mr. Beckworth and soon become concerned for his well-being, especially John. He dropped by and talked to me, and eventually invited me to dinner at his home after I told him that Mr. B was away. I accepted his invitation.

As this particular day drew to a close, dark and heavy rain clouds are seen looming on the horizon again. It will definitely be another wet night. As the meal was ending John asked if I'd like to spend the night, this I also accepted. A *real* bed for a change, how could I possibly refuse? Sitting by his fireplace with a wonderfully warm fire crackling inside, we got to know each other a little better. As we talked I said I always wanted to see what goes on in the daily life of an officer-on-wheels. He laughed and said that if I had nothing better to do, I could ride with him tomorrow. "Count on it!" I replied.

DAY 18: Early in the morning, just before the sun has had a chance to light the horizon, echoing sirens penetrate the distant stillness. There is a thick morning ground fog everywhere. South on highway 89 toward Truckee, there has been a pile-up. John has been notified and we soon jump into his cruiser. One of John's men is already there, with another on his way. The fire crews and California Highway Patrol are just getting to the scene. Ambulances are also enroute at this time. Small eerie fires are burning in several places. Metal and glass is everywhere. I was asked to stay in or next to the car. "There can't be anybody alive!" I heard one of the first C.H.P. troopers gasp to another.

The vehicles were jammed into one another so tightly, getting close enough to find possible survivors is in question. Desperately the men search for the victims as others begin to extinguish the ongoing blazes. The first rays of light are now beginning to permeate the darkness. "This'll help" one of the men thinks out loud... But no-one is found in the mass of wreckage. To everyone's astonishment, the cars and trucks are all *empty*.

"How can this be?" questions one officer to another. "Don't know" says his partner, "I don't understand it. The compartments of most of these vehicles are so crushed and compacted no-one could have gotten out; I doubt anyone could have survived either. It just *doesn't* make any sense." The other officer nods in agreement.

Suddenly a fireman shouts, "*HERE! OVER HERE*!" The fog is starting to lift and many people rush over to the fireman. There on the ground, laying in a row down the side of the East embankment, are the missing people!

116

I just had to go see. Men and women... all appearing motionless. If conditions were different, one might think they were only resting as we approached. Many have substantial tears and partially burned areas to their clothing. As another fire fighter quietly asks, "Are they dead?" several begin to stir. Hearing soft voices and moans, they charge forward to assist them while yelling out for medical attention. John is still closely checking out the vehicles. Between two badly smashed cars he spies something on the ground. Bending over to pick up the damp object, he almost drops it in shock. *'It's Mr. B's hat! Is he here? Was he hurt?'* he thinks to himself dashing over to the area of the recently found people. He checks out the faces of the people who now are mostly upright and regaining their composure. Amazingly, none of them are injured or even appear to be bruised! But Mr. B is *not* among them.

"Is there anyone else around here, besides *these* folks?" urgently asks John pointing to the accident victims. "Not that we've found so far" replies a paramedic. John and I frantically search the immediate area. Dawn is now upon us and the fog has almost dissipated. *Nothing.* No sign of *anyone* else. Eventually tow trucks are in place and the vehicles are moved away. The highway is reopened and traffic starts moving through. The burnt remainders of flares are everywhere. John and I sit in his cruiser with Mr. Bs' hat while John contemplates. Eventually he picks up the mic and says, "Central, this is Car 5, I'm 10-8, Rendezvous in 30." He turns his car around and drives toward Sierraville.

As he approaches Henness Pass, he slows and picks up the mic again. "Central?" **"Go ahead..."** "This is Car 5, check my last transmission. I'm going 10-7 at Mr. Beckworth's, I'll be 10-6 at that location until further notice." **"Copy that Car 5. Out."** Soon John pulls off highway 89 and heads to Mr. B's. Upon arriving he spots Mr. B bringing in a load of kindling. Stopping the cruiser, John quickly gets out and walks into the cabin after him. "Where've *you* been?" he asks, very relieved. "Oh, around" says Mr. B in a mischievous way "What kind of an answer is that?" John pushes. "I left the area for a while. You know, what with all those folks nose'n around an' all."

"I want to know more about the dog thing too, *but first*"... he hands Mr. B his hat. "Loose something?" "Reckon I did. Thank you for returning it, John." Mr. B lays it on his rocker. John just stares at Mr. B. "Sit down John, I've got a lot to share with you. Would you like a cup of coffee?" "Yes. I *really* need one, thank you." "Me too", I add. Mr. B pours us a cup and sits down to talk. "You assisted those people this morning, didn't you?" John asks without hesitation. "I *helped*" replies Mr. B, sipping the hot brew. "You had help?" "Yup, sure did." "Who? How!?" urges John.

THE SIERRAVILLE EXPERIENCE

BW locks eyes with him. "First, let me explain some things about myself and then the incident with Greg..."

Mr. B goes into much detail about himself and the unusual episode. Then after he is done with that information he explains the present situation and his 'help' as it relates to the early morning pile-up. The three of us go through several little pots of coffee eventually eating a small, but pleasant breakfast Mr. B graciously prepared. "What's happening here, Mr. B?" "John, the world is in the beginning stages of labor pangs." "What?" "The present earth cycle is concluding and a fantastic one is emerging." Mr. B continues trying to explain the upcoming changes and the reasons for them to John. He will leave around 2 o'clock in the afternoon. Driving away from the cabin he clears with Central. Being what he considers is a logical man, he is experiencing major mental confusion. The things Mr. B has explained to him are just *too* fantastic. But through all of the mitigating circumstances, he *has* to believe them.

He has no other choice or explanation. Further, he has no idea what exactly to put into his report about the survivors of the pile-up. At the station he shares what he has learned, at least *some* of the details, about Mr. B and the episode with the accident. As usual though and before two days have passed, many outsiders know about the incident. A lot about the incident. John had forgotten to tell the other men to keep the information to themselves... So naturally*, they didn't.*

DAY 21: Before anyone has an opportunity to seek out Mr. B again, he arrives in town of his own volition. As he has done so often before and totally unnoticed, he projected his physical self to the outskirts of the town. He walks the rest of the way to Beth's to have breakfast. He left me behind with his viewer and told me to focus on him. "Looks like we got us a *celebrity!*" says Rose with a big smile as Mr. B walks in. Before the hour is up Mr. Beckworth will be involved with her patrons at their requests and urging. Rose finds herself continually attempting to keep the level of chatter down as Mr. B talks with the eager people. He answers many questions. It seems he barely has time to catch his breath, before another one is launched at him. Patiently he continues, telling everyone that he will answer their questions as best he can. "Please, there's no need for talking over each other. I will try to answer everyone's questions, one question at a time." Inside of ten minutes a small panicked boy runs into the cafe and pushes into the small crowd.

"I *think* she's broke her leg" he screams, pointing across the street. It appears that a little girl has fallen off her bike onto a rock. "She slipped in the water" the boy loudly continues, still pointing to the girl. "Hurry!"

MIRACLES ABOUND

Mr. B moves outside to help and the entire cafe empties out after him. She cries "O-oh-h, it … it hurts really bad." He kneels by her side and puts his hand on her forehead. Almost immediately she seems to relax. "She's cracked her upper leg" says Mr. B. The onlookers can see the now discolored and swelling leg. He shuts his eyes while moving his hand over the damaged bone. Moments pass, and her leg appears to be returning to normal again. He soon asks the little girl to stand up. "Will it hurt again?" she worriedly asks. "No honey, it's all better now" he replies. She cautiously stands up and exclaims, "It *doesn't* hurt anymore!" and jumps into Mr. B's arms. He stands up with the little one still clutching and hugging him, with a completely healed leg.

A women steps out of the small crowd with tears in her eyes, trembling slightly and asks, "Are… Are you *Jesus*?" The others sense the impact and importance of her question, for they too are pondering who this man *really* is. The place is absolutely quiet. "No my dear, I am not who you believe me to be. I am an ordinary man no different from any of you. A man who loves everyone and everything under God." "How can it be that you do what you do?" comes a question from the crowd.

He puts the little girl back down and begins to share and explain some of the basic principles of spiritual energy. He talks about our Creator and the power of Love. The people are drawn tight to his every word. He attempts to instill a belief in themselves, that they too can initiate miracles. Someone asks, "Would you teach us how to do these things, Mr. B?" With a soft voice and gentle look he replies, "You already know how, you just don't recognize it in yourselves. Good people, contemplate on what has been said. Rejoice in God in everything you do and thank you for your attention." He slowly turns to walk away. Nobody moves. All appear as statues. Then Steve, an assistant minister who had been passing by, quickly steps out calling "*Mr. Beckworth, please*… would you be so kind as to offer a sermon this Sunday?" Turning back, Mr. B kindly responds "Sir, I would be honored to do so."

• ▲ •

DAY 22 finds Billy at the lake fishing. Many other anglers are here enjoying the sport as well. Hearing some rustling behind him, Billy turns to see who is there. "Mr. B! How are you?" "Just fine lad, how are you? Any luck?" "Not yet, but I've had some good bites" says Billy. Mr. B sits down and prepares his line. "How's Tom?" he asks. "Oh, he's really excited about all of this." "Good" says Mr. B. Billy turns to him and sheepishly asks, "Tell me again about why you needed permission to help others…" "Well Billy, everything works as it is suppose too, if we would only listen with our heart… instead of our confusing emotions."

THE SIERRAVILLE EXPERIENCE

"Everything in it's time... according to a Divine plan. When I made a decision to be physically here during these times, it did not give me any authority to interfere with those I would encounter on my path. Yet because of where Man is presently headed, our Cosmic Overseers, the Brotherhood of God, declared that the consciousness of Man must be given one last opportunity to be raised. Thus, only recently did certain of us receive permission to share."

"The multitudes seem cast adrift and unable to return to the Way by themselves. Acknowledging this difficult situation, the Brotherhood acting in accordance with God's Will, is allowing help in various forms to be available, if Man decides to use it. Some will, many will not. Yet for everyone who makes a conscious effort to change his or her old ways and beliefs, they jointly continue to raise the global vibrations of thought toward a more positive level. We are being given a chance to reform and to enjoy the many benefits offered us... now, *right* NOW. So *few* will understand this."

"My heart aches with the pain of what those people are loosing, and they don't even *realize* it. It saddens me greatly. (pause) At the time of the Blessing, information in many varieties was and is being given to those who desire it. Those of us who are more in touch with the *true* nature of ourselves, who decided long ago to offer our services in this effort, have been granted the approval to fulfill our desires. We had to wait until approval was given to act. That, is Cosmic Law."

"You see, even now vibrational changes are taking place around us and within us. Another Blessing. They increase daily and I will discuss these in more detail this Sunday. Until a certain vibrational field or level was available, *we* couldn't do much in the way of show-and-tell, as it were. The vibrations needed to be at a certain intensity so when we did start to explain, people could begin to experience God's gifts themselves, loosing some of their consciously restrictive thinking in the process. The increased vibrations do make it easier."

"They allow manifestation and some of the other gifts to be more accessible, in *lieu* of the past denial of our God Presence. If the global consciousness were high enough (enough people focused in positive energies) the vibrational changes *might* not be necessary, but Man in general needs help at this point. Thus, the vibrational changes. Man in partnership with his God consciousness, God, and His Corps of Light and the vibrational changes create a cosmic petri dish. I, and others like me are hopeful catalysts in this important opportunity. We are here to teach those who will listen, to understand the significance of all that is occurring. What it means, how we can promote a better life philosophy, why things are to be done this way or that... All in the name of Love."

"With the vibrational changes, those who desire change can begin to get in touch more easily, but they aren't necessary to achieve Oneness with God. When we can obtain a more defined understanding of Life, as intended by God, we can better understand what is meant by the term reality. People first must see that their reality is created by their thought patterns. What they think IS what they will or *can* experience, always. They must release all restrictive thought process like superiority, stubbornness, less-than and guilt. Yesterday was only an experience, they must not cling to it. They *must* find and know inner peace and joy, releasing any other emotional, or logical-mind activity which doesn't conform to the creative positive inner-energy of love."

"Remembering we are individuals, loosing self image and seeing no separation from God is a good first step. During the coming years we will see many great things happen to and for those individuals who make an effort. Those who do not or will not, will see their lives tumble into potentially terrible disarray. Again, some will awaken during the last moments and some will not." (long pause) He looks distantly out over the lake... "Let's do some fishing shall we?" With that, Mr. B casts his hook into the lake. Within minutes he pulls out a large catfish.

"How'd you *do* that Mr. B?" "It's all in the wrist" he answers with a give-away grin. "*No-o-o*... Really, how?" Billy urges. "I asked for a fish to allow me to take it from its' home for food, and I gave thanks to it and God for the blessing of receiving it. You can't be greedy, but if you have an earnest need and you have a higher understanding of natural laws you can be blessed with abundance."

"You see, the TRUE principles of abundance work only on a spiritual level. The thought that goes into the desire must be a positive one and one of sincere need. Wants are *not* needs and there *is* a difference. Wants usually and unconsciously fall into the Self, or 'Me-Me, I-I' category. Thoughts of possessions, greed or hoarding do not produce the necessary and *mandatory* positively focused personal vibrations required to create abundance. Since we can have anything we need whenever we *need* it, there is no justification for greed or hoarding. These are negative and counter-productive thoughts." "I want to try that" exclaims Billy. After some coaching, Billy casts his line into the lake. He has desired a trout large enough to feed his family tonight for supper. Several minutes pass by. Billy looks over to Mr. B and shrugs his shoulders. Not even a nibble...

"Why is it you believe that only I can do this?" asks Mr. B. "If you separate your (perceived) abilities from mine or compare yourself with another, *that* thought process will automatically create limitations within your mind that will only allow you to experience those limitations, instead of your desires. They are not real, only *illusions* of limitations."

THE SIERRAVILLE EXPERIENCE

"There are no limitations... unless YOU decide that there are! You must *know*, you must *believe* that you have no limitations, for truly you do not! Desires can be fulfilled at the moment of the thought, or they can manifest later; or with doubt, not at all. So much depends on your inner-peace, creative thought-energy output, the intensity of the emotion(s) generated and the *knowing* that you put into the desire Billy." Suddenly, Billy's line goes taut.

"I think I've got one!" he says excitedly. After reeling in the line, he finds he has caught a healthy 5 pound Rainbow. "*Look at that beauty*!" Billy exclaims. Mr. B just grins. Billy then mentally gives thanks to the fish and to God. "*Nooow* you're catching on!" quips the widely smiling Mr. B. He follows, "Say, could you get hold of Tom and Billy and see if you three could join me tomorrow at my cabin? "Sure" Billy replies.

• ▲ •

DAY 23: Today about two o'clock, the three young men congregate at the cabin. I assume the role of just an observer again. Mr. Beckworth begins by teaching them more about focus and then about other unique phenomenon. He also suggests that this meeting will have a few exciting and unexpected studies. They sit on his porch in deep conversation. Mr. Beckworth is in the process of teaching them something about manifestation and simple creation. "I will now demonstrate manifestation for you." He cups his hands and within them appears a flame of fire from nowhere. It is about 7 inches tall and burning brightly. The boys (and I) stare. "Doesn't that *burn*?" queries Tom. "If it did could I hold it within my hands?" he counters.

Billy reaches out to touch the flame. "Yeow! *it's* hot to me!" he says withdrawing his fingers. "Why?" asks Mr. B. The boys look at one another, stumbling for an answer. "Greg responds, "It's hot because it's fire." "No." Billy says "It's not hot to you, because *you* created it". "No, try again. You're pretty close though." "I've got it" says Tom, "It's hot because we *think* it's hot!" "YES!" replies Mr. B "Fire, as all other things in this physical world, can be interpreted as you *desire*. If you THINK one way or another about a certain 'thing' and hold those thoughts to be TRUE, then you have just created *YOUR* reality about it."

"Now, I want each of you to believe that this flame will not burn you. Imagine that it is mild to the touch. See yourself as impervious to the physical effects of the flame. I realize that you have been taught that fire is nothing to play with and that you use it only for heat or light, but now I want you to change how you interpret this 'reality', Okay? (nods) Before I eventually extinguish the flame you must all exercise your minds. You must believe that you can touch the flame and not get hurt."

MIRACLES ABOUND

"This is a test, albeit simple, but you *can* overcome. Engage the Source, draw on your power of thought. You are *all* greater than this flame."

"Go within yourselves, raise your vibrations and visualize that the heat of the flame is only an illusion. That it can not and WILL not harm you. It, is of the physical world, but you are greater than the physical world and capable of exceeding it's known laws! When you believe *that* to be true, reach into the flame." Mr. B waits patiently for them to respond. In a few minutes Tom agrees to try. Slowly, he edges his hands toward the flame. He is in deep concentration. As his fingers go within the flame, his face brightens up immensely. "Hey! It's true! It doesn't burn." He pushes his hand directly into the fire and turns it slightly back and forth. "I want to try" exclaims Billy. Tom withdraws his hand and Billy approaches the flame just as slowly. "He's right! WOW, I can't believe I'm doing this!"

"You mustn't *say* that" responds Mr. B. The fact is you *do*, or you couldn't have this experience. If you should dwell on that 'other' thought you may find yourself with burnt fingers. Do not allow the flame to have power *over* you. This small experiment shows how we have dominion over all things. If you could apply this kind of thought to the rest of what you do and think, imagine how rewarding your life could be!" Greg says "It's *my* turn, now." He approaches the flame with the same caution that the other two used.

Immediately pulling his hand back, Greg shouts "Yikes! That sucker's hot!" "Greg" says Mr. B, "You haven't overcome the learned illusion yet... You still hold onto established thoughts. I know it's hard, but you must BELIEVE." Greg attempts it several more times, but to no avail. "Don't look so sad, it's simply a matter of mind. You can practice over a small candle flame Greg. Sooner or later if you so *desire* the experience you will overcome your old thought pattern." Mr. B wishes the flame out, and so it is. "You have learned a valuable lesson today, *ALL* of you. Let's experience something different..."

He continues, "Now it is your turn (the three of them)... See that barren spot of soil over there?" (the boys nod) "I want you three to manifest a small rose bush there." "*What*?!" the boys say in unison. "You heard me, you know how... Give it a try." "How?" asks Greg. Mr. B, disappointed, slowly shakes his head from side to side.

Tom steps in "Think of how you know a rose bush to be. You know, the leaves, the thorns, the red petals." "Right" follows Mr. B with enthusiasm. "Get together and decide on exactly what you think the bush should look like, then jointly create it by going to the Source! *THAT*, which is within you and binds you to the creative power of God!"

THE SIERRAVILLE EXPERIENCE

The three chat between themselves for a bit, then decide to try it. "Don't think 'try'... think DO!" Mr. B expresses. Slowly as they focus together, the appointed area starts to mist. Appearing almost ghost like, a plant starts to take shape. "*More boys*, give it more life! It must be as *real* to you, as if it exists *already*!" urges Mr. B. Suddenly, there in front of them is a rose bush. It looks very scrawny, but there it is! Then, it leans and falls down... "You boys forgot the roots!" exclaims Mr. B laughing outrageously. Then regaining most of his composure he motions "Let's go over and examine it more closely shall we?"

The four approach the plant. Billy reaches down and pricks his finger on a thorn. "Well *those* babies are real!" he says. There are only three roses on the bush and they look slightly strange, but there they are. "The colors are interesting" Mr. B says as he bends down to smell the flowers. "No scent, but not to worry. Do you now see how very important it is to visualize *EVERYTHING* about your desire? The manifestation product, or end result can *only* be as developed as your conception and projection. The three of you had a slightly different regard as to the shade red. Thus the flowers have unusual and splotchy coloration's."

"The thought of fragrance was apparently weak and of course, there are no roots! But you have succeeded in manifesting! Be *glad*! Take joy in this experience. *Learn* from it. Practice makes perfect! You can manifest by yourselves; you do not *need* another present to do so. However, in certain cases it does help to have assistance because the more of you thinking on a desire generates ever more energy to 'do' a thing. It may also impact the speed of the manifestation process. At any rate, you should be pleased with yourselves. I certainly am. Now, for a *very* special encounter."

"I wish for you to experience life through the eyes of an animal. (looking at me) You too, if you'd like to join us..." The boys all look at each other like Mr. B is crazy while I walk over. "*I heard that!*" Mr. B says chuckling. Pointing upward, "Do you see that hawk flying high overhead?" "Yes" the boys respond. "Because of their sensitivity and relationship with nature, the ancients could tune into a skybird's consciousness and actually see what the bird saw. Today I would like you to allow your mind to sense that birds consciousness and become one with it." The boys are again looking at each other in confusion.

"It's not *that* unusual" exclaims Mr. B. "Get into a meditative position and clear your minds out. Send your thoughts into the sky to make contact with that hawks... Focus. When you are there, you will know it. You will sense the freedom of flight, the quietness of the air around you, the superb vision. The view and sensation will be astonishing! Of course, it is your extended minds which will travel."

124

"I will help guide you all although you will not see yourselves, or me. You might have a 'feeling' of someone else there, but you will be *more* cognizant of being '*with*' the hawk. Let's try it. Sit in a circle and prepare to clear your minds..." We all do as instructed and in a few moments we are indeed one with the hawk. Physically though, we are on the ground still sitting in a circle. Our Higher Selves, our higher mind consciousness', have connected with the birds'. We will experience about a half an hour in remote consciousness perception.

- - - - - - -

Remote consciousness perception differs from overself melding (a *very* real circumstance, one that I have personally experienced and can attest to) in that the former connects the interpretive aspect of a conscious mind of an individual with the conscious mind of an other individual, or intelligent creature, without the other being involved or having knowledge of what is taking place. The latter connects the spirit-self or overself of an individual directly to and *with* the overself of an individual; or for a better definition, the higher (etheric) consciousness' of the individuals briefly come together as one.

This state occurs entirely on a spiritual level, well beyond simply the conscious mind, but does allow conscious interpretation of the experience. Remote consciousness perception carries with it sensation, but not emotion - that is, emotions are not sensed from the one being perceived; where overself melding allows thought *and* emotion to be readily felt and intimately understood, as well as allowing for personal resolution (will) interpretation and/or two way communication to take place, if desired, but no physical sensations are realized.

- - - - - - -

We are energetically jubilant about the experience and will discuss it for quite sometime afterwards. Then Mr. B will delve into more aspects of our natural abilities before ending for the day with a request.

He asked the boys to each locate three other individuals, not of immediate family, to join the group. As an extension of your excitement and changes, your natural family will have a direct opportunity to learn from you in the coming times. He shared that this base [collective number of individuals in the group] could now be expanded.

"With you three, there will ultimately be nine more. With those, twenty-seven... an exponential growth and involvement. This is how we are to evolve our group as an assemblage of Light."

• ▲ •

Mr. Beckworth later informed me that he had years ago perceived the young men's talents and capabilities and that was why he introduced the exercises he did...

THE SIERRAVILLE EXPERIENCE

To show them that they were more developed than they had thought. He suggested that because of what they accomplished today, they will never again be apprehensive about exploring other types of experiences or advanced thoughts.

He said these activities were a part of their current growing process and that they were ready to expand; and further, that he would never have attempted such things if he had felt that they weren't ready.

So Ends Journal Six

JOURNAL 7

*

"CONTEMPLATE ON THIS"

DAY 43: The newly added participants have excitedly gotten involved with Mr. Beckworth and the boys in after hour and weekend studies at various locations around the community, including Mr. B's simple home. A unique change can be sensed in these new students because they have been given insights to a better life possibility and feel they have exciting things to look forward to. There is a spark of enthusiasm and energy and it can be readily felt. There are those few around town however, who have an idea of what is going on and think this whole thing is ridiculous... I won't do them any favors by putting into print what they had to say. I can only hope they eventually come around to giving the concepts a chance for themselves when presented an opportunity to do so.

• ▲ •

Lily has opened her business for the day. She has only one appointment and is preparing to see that person... For many months she's seen the unclear image of a close by spiritually empowered entity in the tea leaves she's read for other people. Lily has never shared this finding with anyone. She also knew this entity was a male, but only now does she understand who it is. She had always sensed something special about the peculiar Mr. B, positively oriented of course, but was never really sure what 'it' was. With everything that has happened to date, her feelings have been firmly corroborated as far as she is concerned. As she puts a pot of water on to boil the doorbell rings. Answering it, she finds her client. "Please, come in and have a seat. I'll be *right* with you" she says. The lady sits down and Lily soon joins her. The lady has many questions, some of them about Mr. Beckworth, some of them on other topics.

THE SIERRAVILLE EXPERIENCE

The two will talk for about half an hour before they get to the tea leaf reading. Lily goes out for the water and rejoins her client. They share some small talk as the lady drinks the tea. Lily will take the cup when she is done to interpret her visions.

"I've told you some about the changes that are coming, haven't I?" "Yes." "Then you remember that the strange weather patterns and associated natural disasters we now see are just the beginning?" "Yes, I know. They're part of the cleansing process." "You remember *why* they are occurring I assume?" "Yes. The over-control of men by others and of 'Self' importance. You've shared what Man has done to himself, others and the world. You've also told me about the Separation and that we will return to the God Principle of living after certain changes take place." "Fine. *Good*. I'll add to our last conversation then. As you are aware, there is a large increase in the spiritual movement today. People are seeking the truth about the nature of all things, and about themselves. They are slowly learning to find materials and people which can impart wisdom and knowledge to them about what I referred to as the New Age of Man."

"Yes... Go on." "It is through a raised consciousness and energy of today's man, that various changes are being brought about. However, there is insignificant energy *at this time* to avoid the upcoming challenges of global alteration. More, *many more*, must wake up to the fact that all destructive mental and physical patterns of life must be abolished. Old thoughts and thinking must be cleansed and purged. People must desire a different life and **declare** it so. They must get back in touch with God and the concepts of caring and love, time is fast running out. I feel the interval of 1997 and 1999 will be a period of substantial, perhaps tremendous change; obvious to those who understand what is actually happening."

"I also feel there will be visible assistance from other worlds just prior to, and during the latter events which may take place. There is little time remaining for those who desire transformation to do so. Perhaps only a few years... give or take. We can no longer put off until tomorrow. It could be too late, even for those with last second decisions to turn down a different path. If we can not get more souls to participate and desire a change for themselves *and the world*, we could see tribulation caused by the mass negative reflected-energy of Man unlike has ever been recorded. This includes a potential foreign war with global implications... Note I said *potential*, not definite. We still have an opportunity to alter the upcoming future events, let's pray we take advantage of the time."

"With, or hopefully without war, when the changes have begun in earnest, the inventions of destruction will be the first to be minimized. Soon gone, will be the *need* for armies and the small bands of assorted hatreds."

"The political governments will topple and new ones for the *benefit* of Man will come into being. In the beginning, people will barter their items and talents in exchange for other necessities. People will tend to forget about *themselves* and become conscious of helping *others*. They will also become conscious of a greater power... *GOD*. Small communes will form at first. Some groups of people are preparing even now for this activity. People will consciously lean towards co-existing with Nature once again."

"At that time, the Native Americans will offer their knowledge and services to all that ask, for they truly understand our relationship with Nature." "Are we going to all become *Indians*?" asks the apparently worried lady. "No my dear, we will not. However we will learn how to co-exist and live in harmony with others and Nature and most importantly, *with* the God Principle! The Native Americans have much knowledge and many of them will be our teachers." "I don't *want* to live like the Indians. I don't want to live without things either." says the lady. "My dear, you have overlooked something, we will have the power of manifestation at our disposal! After the changes take place there will exist a greater vibrational energy. This inner-energy will allow us all to overcome and continue. As remaining Man continues re-establishment with God, he *will* have the power of creation at his finger tips. We will also be given direction and assistance from many other sources. Incidentally, prior to the final changes there will be many 'safe-areas' established for us by the Light-Workers." (Spirit Guides, etc.)

"And yes, life could be greatly uprooted and disturbed for a while, maybe a couple of years, but those that remain will be of a higher spiritual nature. We won't have to live like the Indians dear, but we *will* adopt many of their philosophies because they're good ones. We won't necessarily have to live *without* 'things' either. There will be great creativity, and what we need we can manifest *if* we believe we can. Some will be able to do that right away. Some will not be able to for some time. There will be a whole new world and it will be very exciting. *Please*, don't be frightened about these upcoming changes. The changes must take place in order that Man recognizes God and ceases to dominate other men and nations of men."

"But the whole thing sounds a little scary. It sounds like you're alluding to possible world devastation" says the lady. "No... Although chaos could exist for a while, the era will become known as a world *cleansing*; there is a difference, as the world will *not* be destroyed, only altered" Lily responds. "It will be different than the one we recognize today but it will be a far better place to live, don't you *see*?" "I guess, but I'm not ready for all of that" replies the lady. "That's why people like myself and Mr. Beckworth are here. We are providers of information to help those of us who desire change, before everything really starts to cut loose."

THE SIERRAVILLE EXPERIENCE

"The information we get and give, is given us to help others prepare *themselves*. Of course, everyone has a choice to participate. If enough of us strive for change, the alterations can be minimized! Unfortunately, many will not take advantage of what is being offered. It'll be quite a sad situation for them, when the great changes are fully among us. Even now the *more intense* are on the horizon."

"How do I prepare then?" questions the lady. "Take every advantage to learn. Study the books that are out from many sources. Go to seminars as they are available. Write for information. Talk to God, He is always there to reach out to. This is the most important thing you can do. Strengthen your awareness of, and connection with God. Go within and seek to eliminate those things of and from yourself with which you are not pleased. Cleanse your spirit... First forgive yourself for things that you may or may not have done. People tend to drag so many emotional anchors of unresolved pain and guilt with them. These only hinder our growth."

"As far as obtaining forgiveness, if you feel you are lacking it, you must first sincerely give it to others in order to receive it. Do this by forgiving those you feel have trespassed upon you or hurt you. Whether or not you feel you eventually do receive it from them, you must first forgive all others. This action cleanses and repairs the vibrations of self and aura, and it is necessary for good health. Release any anger or negative emotions, such as guilt you hold on to for another, or *yourself*."

"Discharge these negative feelings to the ether, blessing them that they be released for a higher purpose and good." "How?" "One method is to use the words I just said. Another way could be by imagining in your mind that you are sitting on a high hill or a mountain top. Then imagine yourself writing down any and *all* negative feelings or thoughts you are consciously aware of, one by one on separate pieces of paper. Then mentally collect each of these thoughts you want to have healed into a bundle. Bless each one as you add them to the stack and forgive yourself and any others involved in those emotionally negative thoughts. You can also do this physically, but the important thing is that you must be honest and you _must_ eventually release them... and WANT to release them! If you can't be honest about the desire to forgive and let go, then this process will not achieve it's intended potential."

"Mentally stand up, taking the bundle in your hand, and throw it high up into the wind. Watch the wind take the papers far far out of sight... thus out of mind and consciousness. You may have to do this several times for the truly imbedded thoughts, pains or feelings, but you can eliminate all negative emotions from your consciousness by this procedure, or one like it. You will feel very good about yourself as the old (mental) baggage or emotional anchors are cast aside."

"Life should take on a new meaning and satisfaction for you if you can do this. You should feel as if a great weight has been lifted off of your shoulders when you are finished." "I have a problem with letting go of my anger for my ex-husband. It's really a big thing to me and I really hate him for divorcing me." "That's honest." "How do I get rid of these emotions? They're so deeply set." "You still love him don't you?" asks Lily. "Yes I guess I do, that's probably why I'm so angry with him." "First of all, let me explain something. Sometimes two people are just not meant to be together, for whatever reasons. Occasionally we are only meant to be together a short time; this, to learn something. These reasons are usually for our own good, but we fail to recognize that fact. Instead when a relationship ends, we say 'It's fault' for this or that... we cast blame, erroneously I might add."

"I'm sorry, but that kind of thinking is very wrong, even if it *is* easier. After all, it was our choice to form that union in the first place, wasn't it!? Further, we may have decided upon these particular unions prior to taking physical 'residence' here and perhaps they were in fact, suppose to take place. Attempt to find the lessons hiding between the pains and emotions. What did you learn from the experience? That is what you should seek out and focus on. Keep the pleasant memories, remember the good times, but come to understand what was achieved or learned from having participated in the relationship."

"You see your experience may be part of your *plan* for soul growth. Much of which is suppose to take place as priorly decided upon... In it's own way and time." "*Well*, if I made such plans why don't I remember them then?" "That's fairly simple, we give up our etheric memory so we don't impede our own progress. Our soul retains this knowledge, but our conscious minds do not. If we knew everything ahead of us in this life, chances are overwhelming that we'd purposefully avoid many situations. If we did that we wouldn't fulfill our destiny nor complete our assignment(s)."

"So we leave this information behind until we are developed enough to have a conscious memory of it. Sometimes it's hard to make a decision to return though. As a Being of Light, it takes a lot of personal courage to decide to traverse the realms down to the physical, especially if we never knew the physical before. But if you could remember the moment before you left, you'd be awed! The angels and other entities of Light cheer us on as we leave the etheric plane, with heavenly music, singing and generating much excitement. Many there are saddened about not being part of our plan, being able to participate in this kind of function, or because they aren't able to do this for themselves for one reason or another, but they all urge us on and champion us in our decisions to do so. The heavens literally glow with their enthusiasm and support."

THE SIERRAVILLE EXPERIENCE

"Bet you thought you were working all alone, didn't you?" "Yes, I did." "Well you're not, I hope that gives you some degree of comfort. We are never really alone... Let's get back to your emotions. Spirit tells me that you must also release the hate from your consciousness, it is keeping you 'grounded' in negative energy. Even if you only think about your divorce once in awhile, it's destructive to your growth because you still hold on to the negative emotions. Bless him for being him, and bless yourself for being who you are. You can not go back to 'undo', you can not change the past, you can only change today and tomorrow, by changing yourself. Convince yourself that you are both good people, even if you can't be together. Allow any potential thoughts of resentment or anger to fade from your consciousness. You must, in order to have peace within yourself. It's okay to still love him, but hold onto *that* thought only, and perhaps the loving times you had together, but none of the rest. Do you understand?" "Yes, but it's so hard."

"Try it and next time we meet tell me how you are feeling then, Okay?" "All right, I'll try it, but I can't promise you anything." "That's good enough for me, but remember, it's *for* you." says Lily. "Okay, next you must pay attention to *all* thoughts that you have. Catch yourself anytime you have or entertain a negative thought, because everything we experience has good in it." "What?" "Let me give you one reason, and one example. First, the reason not to fetter about negative experiences. Like I have just mentioned, they may be placed on your path by your own choosing; *Choosing* to experience them for one reason or another. They've occurred as part of your plan for growth." "Okay, I guess I can appreciate that."

"Now let's take a simple example of an obvious good in a perceived 'bad' situation... One day you leave work to catch the bus. Only this day you find that you've missed it. You'd probably get very upset wouldn't you?" "I guess so..." "Perhaps down the road though, there was a bad accident with the bus. Maybe even with injuries. Perhaps had you caught the bus you would have been in that accident and possibly hurt." (the lady nods her head with obvious understanding) "But you *WEREN'T*... because of unseen causes which resulted in you being late, or the bus being early."

"Nothing *apparently* negative happens without some form of *good* being involved. We may have to search hard for it being unfamiliar with this thought process, but it IS there; and never get angry... *never*. Anger is extremely destructive to our energy field. As we get closer to the apex our thoughts will gain more and more intensity and energy. What we think will come back to us sooner, and with a greater impact than you can now imagine. If we think negatively, we will experience negative sooner. If we think positively, we will experience positive sooner. Ideally, what we want to do, is retrain our minds to focus only on the positives. This may not be very easy for some of us to do, because many of us are taught reactivism."

CONTEMPLATE ON THIS

"If we negatively 'slip' while we are trying to change *how* we think, we should immediately apologize. Bless the negative thought and release it (this affects the energy *behind* the thought) for a better good, least it return to us. And it WILL return, mark my words."

"Also, when you can help someone out where normally you wouldn't spend the time, do it! Share yourself with others, pass on the message of the changes. Many might mock you or not find time for you, but all of your efforts will be blessed. Share any knowledge on Spiritualism you can. We are ALL teachers in one way or another. Create positive atmospheres around you wherever you are or go, and with whomever you come into contact with. Sooner or later people close to you will see the changes in you and then may desire similar situations for themselves. You will be able to help those individuals from your own experiences and the knowledge you've gained from others. Mentally bless everyone you see or come across. This takes a lot of awareness and focus, but you can do it. Ask for guidance from above. Then listen [in your heart and mind] for direction. What you might think is intuition may be guidance from your Overself or possibly Jesus, or some other spiritual BEing. Follow these urges. Pray to God for spiritual assistance."

"Believe in a Higher plan and believe in yourself... this is a *big* one. Most people have a *really* hard time doing this. So many of us have pain, suffering and/or poor self-esteems... Many *unconsciously* seek out others in conflict, desiring to help *them*, instead of first healing themselves. It is so easy to identify with someone in need when their needs (obvious to us, or just sensed vibration) are similar to our own. We tend to feel that if we can't fix 'us', then we'll fix (help/assist) someone else if we're presented with an opportunity. But if we can't help ourselves, how in the world can we truly help someone else? We need to look into ourselves and make a decision whether or not to become whole. This is a very difficult thing to do. Why? Because it means we must *face* and deal with our pain instead of ignoring it or pretending we can handle it. The pains can't go away until we *release* them!"

"A healing can only begin with us. It will begin by releasing old thoughts. When we say *enough!* and really desire to be free, then that's the moment our healing starts. It can continue with outside help, but to be effective it must be forged ahead by ourselves. We *CAN* heal ourselves if we want to and believe it's possible. Sure, some others of us boast about being capable of doing this, that or the other thing, but about being able to heal ourselves or initiate 'miracles'?... or manifesting? - forget it. We simply can't accept that *we* play an important part in the actualizing of these types of experiences. But we all can. We *always* could. We just forgot how from our perceived separation from God. Believe in the Almighty or what ever you choose to call Him, and believe in yourself because we are OF Him."

THE SIERRAVILLE EXPERIENCE

"Desire to have the greater understanding of spiritual wisdom in your life more than anything, and I mean *ANYTHING*. It is written, and it is true; All things are of God, and all things are possible through Him. Once you plant the seed in your consciousness about desiring to know more, you may find that you can't get enough material on the subjects of Spiritualism or Enlightenment. It will become the most awesome, exciting and rewarding experience of your three dimensional life. But remember, God and our reverence and awareness of Him is at the top of our 'to-do' list. Enlightenment is the first step towards achieving a spiritual understanding of, and a closer relationship with Him. Find time every day, perhaps several times a day to meditate. Meditation differs from prayer in that we LISTEN for guidance, instead of ASKING for supplication."

"Prayer is focused mental 'output-energy' (from *inside* of our physical selves), while meditation is preparatory for mind 'input-energy' (from *outside* of our physical selves). Our quiet times of listening allow guidance and direction to flow to and through us. Spend time sending mental blessings to people you know. Send blessings to negative situations that happen throughout the world. Send blessings for healing and protection to our Earth for her waters, lands, vegetation and air, her creatures large and small."

"Send a blessing to the masses of the earth for spiritual awakening, that the changes be gentler and minimized through our collective heightened and increasingly positive thoughts and deeds. Give thanks for all that you have, even if you don't have what you now *think* you should. Be grateful for what you *do* have. There is always someone who hasn't got even near what you have. Some people experience lack to make them appreciate things in life more. If there were no sadness how could we really appreciate joy? Of course with advanced growth, the need for lessor experiences can be done away with when we 'see' how we do control our reality!"

"Some of us may experience hard lives to help make us stronger. Some experience disastrous situations that they may know how it feels to be in that or those predicaments. All these people as they become (spiritually) 'aware', are the ones who can best relate to others having similar experiences and help them to understand that they truly exist(ed) for our benefit and growth... One can not help or teach to the fullest degree, unless having priorly learned from an actual experience. We truly make our own reality by what we think and how we interpret life experiences. The bottom line however, is that now we are all being given a chance, *an opportunity*, to examine ourselves and to decide what we really want life to be like. We can act on this information, or ignore it... the choice is ours."

• ▲ •

DAY 45: It's Sunday morning and the roosters around the small valley can be heard to crow. Not a cloud is to be found in the magnificently painted blue sky. It is a beautiful beginning for this very special day. Many people who were at Beth's are up and getting ready for the nine o'clock service. Pastor Steve is at the church making preparations for this day. He feels it will be a service no-one will forget and he especially, is looking forward to it. The Community Church might see more parishioners today than any normal Sunday in prior history. Unfortunately, there will be many having no desire to attend.

Tom and Billy have even persuaded their parents to attend! I felt Tom's parents would, but I wasn't sure about Billy's. I was glad for both of them. Steve anxiously awaits the arrival of Mr. Beckworth and has already opened the church doors. Although it is now only eight o'clock, people are beginning to show up. Soon, more are arriving and making haste to get inside the church to get a good seat. Steve greets each person at the door and at nine, he moves toward the podium.

The conversations are thick and the excitement is mounting. The time is nine-o'five but there is no sign of Mr. B. The small crowd continues to wait in anticipation. Nine-ten, and *still* no sign of him. The people are beginning to wonder what's going on and the din increases sharply. Steve instructs the organist to play 'Morning Has Broken' and the noise level subsides somewhat.

Then Mr. Beckworth is noticed standing in the back of the room. The pews go immediately silent as does the organ. Mr. B calmly smiles and greets the masses. "Good morning dear ones" he says, as he walks toward the podium. "Did I startle you?" asks Mr. B, "I didn't intend to." Soft laughter and a few chuckles flow from within the crowd. He follows with "Please pardon my sudden appearance, but I wished to have your undivided attention. I thought this a good way to accomplish that." After receiving a unanimous and positive response, he stretches out his arms and asks for a prayer.

"Father, we are among you today, to share in the message of the coming of the Golden Age of Man. An age when all men can live in peace and in your Way. The dawning Age brings us further understanding of that which you are, that we might experience heaven on earth and come to know you in our hearts."

"Bless these gentle people now, with the desire to learn and the spiritual fortitude to overcome any challenges that they may experience in the coming times. Let each man, woman and child open their hearts and minds to the glory of the God Presence and recognize their rightful place at your side."

THE SIERRAVILLE EXPERIENCE

"Allow each person to experience the joy of knowing that they are of you, that Divine wonders may overwhelmingly manifest into their lives as demonstrations of their faith and proper utilization of Universal Laws. (pause) In the name of Almighty God, I bless you all now. Amen."

Looking out over the pews, he follows "I suppose you have a lot of questions still, and certainly you may be aware of the events of the recent past. I wish to say that you *all* have the same ability to do these things. *None* of you is any different from another, save in appearance and possibly life experience. Your consciousness, the part of you that is the only real thing about you, is of God. None of you is less than another. None has less or more capability than another. You all share in that Power. In the coming times you will prove it to yourselves, over and over."

"What you allow for *is* what you'll receive with persistent faith and opening of your hearts and minds. You are all created equally and in the image of the Father. Not the physical image you perceive to be who you are, but the spiritual part of you, your (soul) consciousness. That is what is made in the image of the Father. That image is the same for all of humanity, no matter the race, sex, or color. The *essence* of God is that which is born into the thing we call our soul. Our physical bodies are only shells that *temporarily* house our soul for work and life experience on this plane."

"No soul ever enters this plane lacking or with less capability than any other. Humanity has created this 'less-than' illusion. Man alone decides to fall prey to outside 'input', ego, arrogance, and pride; pity, self-image and poverty, creating his negative conditions by his own free will. Man always has the choice to be all that he can be or *unfortunately*, less than he could be. And he must answer to himself in the end. God judges not what we do in this, past, or future lives. *We do*. We are responsible for, and the greatest judge of what we have or more importantly, *haven't* done with our life. And we can change, be reborn as it were, in the twinkling of an eye."

"But dear people, you have to *desire* it. It has to burn so brightly and hot within you, that you seek nothing else. You can not do this on a part-time basis. You can not exert yourself for a while, then revert, and so on. There must be a *continuing* effort on your part to grow and change. As for the material world around you, it is non-lasting, it is only temporary. Also understand that the physical 'things' we may hold dear to us are of no spiritual value. They will not bring us closer to enlightenment or God. They only serve to comfort the three dimensional existence we participate and believe so whole-heartedly in. Further, the desire to have 'things' far *outside* of our basic needs, typically indicates focus on Self. Sadly, we are directly or subconsciously taught to focus on materialism throughout our entire upbringing."

136

CONTEMPLATE ON THIS

"I am not suggesting that to have things is wrong, but if the intent is to show-off or feel 'better' than another, or your focus dwells steadfastly on material achievement, then the energy around you will be less than positive. We shouldn't have to *HAVE* things to make us feel worth... For whatever the reason(s). This behavior implies lack of a fundamental need being met... Love... But that is another discussion altogether. Know that with God anything, *everything*, you *need* is available to you at *your* spiritually proper request... *If* it is part of your overall plan for growth. When you realize this you will understand and accept that it is okay if you don't receive; But if you do, you'll also come to realize that you aren't without Higher assistance. When you accept that you *can* manifest what you desire, and focus on actually doing it, you will see that you are indeed a magnificent being after all."

"Also, once you really understand what your capabilities are and what our Father's gifts can provide for you and others, you can then use this information to be consciously liberated from rule by others, life and health conditions, peer pressures, etc. You will be able to truly help others. You will enjoy life to a much fuller degree because you will comprehend the more significant meaning to it, and each experience you come across, as well as coming to understand your purpose. It all begins with the power of love. That is the inner-energy and source required above all other things for wholeness, and oneness with the Universe. In order to give love away, the greatest gift an entity can offer another, your cup must first be filled, if not overflowing. You must love and nurture yourself, completely, in order to share that kind of love."

"I wish to explain what I meant by the word 'challenge'. We typically have come to believe that declaration to mean some arduous, perhaps threatening or burdening task, requiring persistence and possibly uncomfortable application of time and self. I would like you to think of this word in terms of *opportunity* instead. Challenge carries with it a dubious air, while the word opportunity insinuates a potentially positive gain as a result of our participation in an approaching situation. Our most profound and exasperating *personal* life-observation is: how we tend to feel bounced around and/or affected by *our* particular 'life' experiences. We focus much too intensely on 'Why me?'... drawing in even more unfavorable experience."

"To many of us, this physical life is one greatly overshadowing challenge. Challenge, now used in the *most* dramatic context. This emotion occurs because we haven't had access to the necessary tools to work with so as to see life's real meaning(s). As an example, how many of you here believe that among many other tribulations, defeat, disappointment, unfairness and injustice, are actually natural and normal occurrences we must experience in our lives? Situations from which we can not escape?"

THE SIERRAVILLE EXPERIENCE

(multiple hands go up) "We tend to believe in and worse yet, *ACCEPT* or *EXPECT* them AS *real* ongoing aspects of our earthly life. I'd like you all to understand, that if you listen with a completely open heart and mind, you may learn that this doesn't have to be the case for any of us, ever."

"We *can* have happiness, harmony and abundance in our lives. We need never encounter pain or detrimental life experiences again. The source of this power is within, and it is an *unlimited* source. You need only to believe it and activate it, to *experience* it. Your attitude must be that if it can work for others, then it can surely work for you as I am living proof of the fact that it does indeed work. Gentle people, I truly am *no* different than any of you except only by my faith, how I use my mind, and what I accept as *truths*. By your *own* thought processes, you can create in your life whatever you desire. Be it personal peace or contentment, joy, finances, health... whatever. The deaf can be made to hear, the lame can be made to walk and the blind instilled with sight. The sick and the hurt can be healed by proper exertion of will and love. And yes, even you dear ones can walk on water if the need should arise."

"Therefore, as you apply yourselves and accumulate knowledge and wisdom, you will be able not only to interpret better what is going on around you, but you will have the clearer understandings at your disposal to find the good in any experience, and further, be able to see beyond just the seemingly physical nature of any given event... and possibly even alter various situations at hand. We must all work together, not necessarily physically but consciously and spiritually. We need each other more than any of you realize. *To be needed*... is that not an *absolutely* wonderful sensation? How warm it makes us feel to know that someone else is willing to trust, or rely on us! How great the recipient feels that someone else cares enough about them that they are willing to give of their time and effort. This is true harmony of love-soul vibration between entities. Both are appreciative of the other, both gain and each grows from whatever experience is shared."

"Remember, Love is *the* most creative emotion... and *the* most powerful spiritual instrument! In time, if you should take up and practice some of the principles I have, and will relate, you will find your life will begin to flow more gently and smoothly. You'll find that things that used to bother you, will never bother you again. When you choose to see *past* negativeness and understand better what is really occurring, nothing can ever cause undue emotional or mental impairment again. Should you catch yourself thinking in a less than positive way while you are re-teaching your subconscious, stop, and immediately apologize for having generated such a thought, bless that particular thought then consciously release it from your energy sphere (yourself) for it's *higher* and *better* good."

CONTEMPLATE ON THIS

"That less-than-desirable energy will be reconditioned by the ether, rendered harmless, inactive and to the degree 'it' can be reused for other purposes, it will remain free and balanced... but only by this process. This practice will maintain a strong auretic harmony and balance within ourselves. You see our individual energy sphere or aura is likened unto a balloon. As we dwell and think positively, it expands and becomes more positively energized. If we think or act negatively, no matter how inconsequential we "*think*" it is, it allows 'holes' or tears in our auretic field to form. These reduce our spiritual energies and can cause sickness or bad health due to the imbalance, as well as creating and/or *attracting* negative energy or circumstances into our lives. Anytime we recognize that we have erred in deed or thought, then bless and release that causal thought from our mind, we heal our aura. Extending ourselves to others out of kindness also helps heal our aura. Also, we shouldn't spend time concentrating on the various things in our life that upset or bother us. We'll accomplish nothing, wasting precious spiritual growth time and potentially creative energy. Don't keep yourself from spiritually developing and growing into what you desire to be, and from experiencing all your God given gifts."

"If we have burdened ourselves with emotionally negative anchors, we must work diligently at cleansing ourselves. Release feelings of guilt. Release jealousy. Release pent up frustrations, anger or hatred. Release the thoughts of lack of self-confidence. Forgive others for anything you feel they may have 'done' to you. Most importantly, we must forgive *ourselves* for anything we 'think' we have done, or failed to do. Become liberal with tolerance and freer with the concept of allowance. Open your hearts and remove the barriers and walls of protection. Yesterday has passed, today is a new day. Utilize it to the *fullest*."

"Consciously be aware enough to look for any reason or opportunity to expand or grow. Think in terms of being (as of now) 'reborn'... seeing with new eyes, hearing with new ears, interacting with a newly structured energy about you. Exhibit patience and allowance in all that you think, say or do. Identify with your inner God Presence. *Learn to LOVE yourself*. Remove (*un*-create) any notions of insuperiority, inferiority, and less-than. These unbecoming attributes of self-image are defeating, cancerous and restrictive. You are not worthy of such concepts... *do not* compare yourself with anyone, *ever*. **We**, are of the **essence** of GOD. Embrace that truism, cling tenaciously to it. Realize what that means and let no other influences alter that image! This is not a selfish concept, as some might view it to be. It allows enhanced Love vibrational energy to be an integral part of us... a very *necessary* ingredient. We can not express or pass on Love energies (in the purest sense) if we ourselves are lacking from within, or denying ourselves of this Love."

THE SIERRAVILLE EXPERIENCE

"And remember, the path to self-realization is as *unique* as the individual walking it... it's distance and ease of traversement is directly up to us. Embracing and utilizing those higher concepts of thought and not allowing fear or apprehension about our success or failure, is that which will aid in our success and further our spiritual growth. Believe in yourself and that any desire you have will manifest... It has to if all Cosmic Laws are in balance and applied appropriately. Now, I'd like to share two powerful affirmations with you. When you understand and truly *embrace* these affirmations, then you have begun the reforming process of your thinking and belief in your capabilities. The first affirmation goes like this:"

"*I give thanks, I have and utilize my divine power of creative higher thought, for right and proper purposes, to positively affect and alter the nature of my reality, and in partnership with God, create in my life all that I need or require.*"

"Remember all thoughts create... keep them focused in positive energies, which includes those created for any given desire for yourself or another. A selfish desire refers to the lower mental thinking process which is devoid of spiritual understanding. The term *desire* should be thought created under the influence, and in concert with Universal Law. *We* create our own reality, consciously or subconsciously. We always will. No other influence can change that. Our belief or disbelief, faith or lack of it, cosmic understanding or lack of it impacts the quality of our life and our comprehension and manifestation abilities. Either way, what we think is what we'll experience... now and always! Come to appreciate the statement: 'Be careful what you ask for... *you* just might get it.' I refer to this statement in regards to the creation of negative thought within us. Particularly when we say or think something we *really* do not mean, or wish to happen, but utter out of frustration or anger. We cause many wonderful things to disappear or fade from our lives by negative thought activity based in haste."

"Thought is a magnificent and powerful force which directs our reality. Examining thought at a basic level, we find two options which are available. Without a more discerning understanding, we tend to create our individual reality with planar or linear thought. A straight line concept... Thought that is predicated only on empirical experience or teachings, such as: If we do 'this', 'that' will be the outcome. This is a truism, but we limit results to just the physical! We generate expectations, make decisions and plans, and exercise our will in a very limited way because we are taught to. As an example, we have learned that we can't make bread without utilizing the sum of the ingredients. *Expanded thought*, allows for circumventing various 'rules' of the third dimension."

CONTEMPLATE ON THIS

"It is absolutely possible to create bread without first having even the instruments to mix and cook it with. By manifesting it. We only have to know what bread should be like, in order to project for it. The same goes for all other aspects of our lives... health, prosperity, love, kindness, healing... To receive there has to be a real need, proper intent and focus... *but*, we must also have faith!"

"The second affirmation goes as follows:"

"I embrace only those thoughts and emotions, which are for my highest and best good; and truly desire to fulfill myself as a Divine BEing. My heart and mind are now open to all Higher Thoughts of Divine Enlightenment, Wisdom, and Knowledge which will allow me to Spiritually experience all that I can, and expand fully, that which I am."

"This affirmation enhances (by your desire) the opening of those inner power centers, or channels (sometimes referred to as chakras) for external (non-third dimensional) guidance and direction. These declarations can be used to prepare you for meditation or the study of enlightened material. Use these affirmations often."

"Earlier I mentioned something about upcoming challenges. These personal opportunities are related to various transformations of our planet. Events of Universal significance. I shall refer to these events simply as Changes. The Changes are active even as I speak, and will continue to increase in intensity and quantity. Many in the future will come to understand or perhaps think in their limited way that the end of the world is approaching as many exit from this plane for various reasons. This is not far from the truth. It is actually the *old* world of 'Me-for-Self' that is being done away with. It has begun with increased climatic and geologic activity, among other things. A healing for our planet is thus involved, and will be one of the significant results. As in all cycles, the earth also has her own. Some of you remember that I once said that everything vibrates... Everything, seen and unseen vibrates with it's own energy and intelligence. *Everything* is alive, even our own Earth."

"This could be a difficult concept to understand at first, especially since we may have been taught otherwise. Nonetheless, it is true. Man has poisoned, defiled and taken from the Great Planet for much too long. Mother Earth is now reacting (reflecting back Man's overall negative vibrations) to the wounds... disregard, lack of replenishment, care and love. Because of Man's basic and characteristic self-seekingness of glory, control and reward, multiple changes around the globe will come to pass in order to cause Man to re-examine his self-righteous and self-centered thinking."

THE SIERRAVILLE EXPERIENCE

"Mother Earth *will* have Cosmic help in revamping the face of the world. The Book of Revelation as envisioned and transcribed by the apostle John, describes the *probable reality* of the End-Times. Although what he was privileged to see was mostly beyond his understanding in terms of thought, physical items or conditions, and the language restrictions of that period, the *premise* is still accurate. Man, by the greater count of the populace of the world, has denied his God Presence and sought only to seek self-satisfaction through the lower energies of the mental and physical means. He has been so long removed from his spiritual aspect, that his consciousness is primarily unaware of it's greater existence! The spiritual aspect of Man of course, IS the most important quality of his BEing."

"As a cosmic creature, we originally entered here as an advanced triune being, and we knew it. That being our *Physical Self*, in this seemingly physical world; our *Mental Self*, or that which we use to manipulate ourselves within our physical existence, governed by many emotional blinders; and our *Spiritual Self*, which is our *real* and true identity. We as Mankind are *still* triune beings, only we've forgotten that we are. We *think* that we are highly developed creatures and control our realities through emotionally mental and physical energy. We tend to neglect the spiritual aspect... which *far* exceeds the capability of the other two."

"We only have the other two facets of ourselves purely to assist us in *this* plane of life, but this is not the plane of life we were *ultimately* intended to share expression in. *That* plane is multi-dimensional and beyond most of our capability to imagine, let alone comprehend. But we can not undergo that greater experience until we re-establish the 'lost' link to our inner and outer sources."

"We must loose the idea that WE operate alone, are solely in control, and of self gratification. We must learn allowance and that all life is equal under God, and shares in the same rights. We must reconnect with the God Principle of living and our Source, from which all blessings come. In order to get the world's attention there must be circumstances which occur to cause Man to stop and ponder... To recognize a Greater Illumination and to recognize the unenlightened paths we have chosen to take over the millennium."

"When Man recognizes that he can not prevent some of these Changes and the great scientific communities and the Churches and religions of the world fail to provide adequate answers, Man will seek something else; many unfortunately, by default. You already know what that is... Yes, *The* Source... *GOD*. We will move toward reuniting with His Thought Presence and share in comprehension of His Life Plan and Philosophy of Love."

CONTEMPLATE ON THIS

"Man for the most part will see the error of his ways and desire to learn and do more for his spiritual growth. Unfortunately, through the Changes many of us will operate under the guise of status-quo. I feel for those that 'see' not. For these will depart and be reborn into other existence's to continue on their individual paths of growth. They will be enjoined from sharing in the Golden Age with those that remain. The term 'End-Times' refers to the end of Man's indiscriminate rule over others, and *everything* else. This world however, will not be destroyed as many may fear. The world will be reborn; our earth shall take on a new glow. Precious Ones, we *are* living in the End-Times. The Changes started out slow and almost imperceiveable. Most are seemingly commonplace events. These are the birthing pangs of the New Age of Man. As a mother delivers with both apprehension and excitement, Man will be reborn in a like manner."

"Oppressive governments coming to light and being questioned, politicians being 'found-out' and increasingly odd weather patterns, are all signs of the active Changes. However these are *mild* compared to what we have in store... *IF* we do not chose to *alter* our thought patterns and structure of living. We are being given a period of time to make personal changes NOW. This is our last grace period. We've had thousands upon thousands of years to make this personal and global decision for ourselves, unfortunately we have chosen not to. Now a higher mandate has been cast. Time has almost run out to make a personal decision. If Man were to continue as he has, and is, the world *might* eventually cease to exist. Our Cosmic caretakers will not allow that to take place."

"We (generically) are as some children. Being shown over and over a better path, yet we still do as we please, thinking of no-one else but ourselves. We must now decide for ourselves whether or not we want to experience the New Age. We can't be wishy-washy in our decision. We have to make a *concerted* effort to desire change from *within* ourselves. Once we do, we must stick to that thought process like bark clings to a tree! If we 'sneak' in questionable acts, deeds or thoughts along the way and do nothing to absolve it or them, we place ourselves on an endangered species list. We can blame nothing, or no-one for the ultimate result of our carefree attitude... We are the *only* ones responsible! Therefore, we must answer for our actions, or *lack* of them. Cause and Effect. This is not a negative thing. Please do not interpret these statements as threats."

"It is only Universal Law at work. That's why we are being presented with this information now. We are being given the opportunity to partake in the Golden Age of Man while encountering the least amount of dysfunction, and gaining the knowledge to make the desired personal changes before it's too late. Truly a Divine Blessing for all that heed the message!"

143

THE SIERRAVILLE EXPERIENCE

"As for the Changes... They could be vast and many. By mass thought modifications and reuniting with our Source, we can avoid many hardships... Perhaps even reducing the cataclysmic events, *but it is too late to prevent any* modifications from occurring. Changes *are* already amongst us! Remember my statements about vibrations? There are many many types of vibrational energy. One type is upon us even now. It is an influx of spiritual resonance of the most powerful kind."

"During the Fall we were cut off, isolated from this super-consciousness energy which had been with us previously. Once this energy was removed, we slid into desolation, lack, rule by others, pain and anguish, disease, poverty, trial and tribulation. There was no longer a connection to this wonderful cosmic source of higher power and creative energy. Life for Man went into retrograde, existing only by the remnant creative energy within. The small residual fragments of a higher energy-awareness and understanding which remained, were those remembrances inside but a few righteous entities scattered all over the face of the earth. Darkness had fallen over the entity known as Man. Now all was left to us, as this is what we globally (**majority mass consciousness**) had desired, and SO IT HAD TO BE!" [Do you understand the process here?]

"The multiple creative vibrations of God and the associated causal energies were minimized. This loss was a rude awakening, yet this condition was created by cause and effect and the desires generated by Mankind. It could have easily been un-created (and at anytime) but the longer we remained focused on *self*, the will-energy to do so became weak and impotent. We got caught up in, and had to then experience the energies we had cast loose from our collective creative thoughts."

"The mental energy of the masses as a *whole*, (increasing from that time to the present) vibrates in a low-order harmonic, due to the constant and overwhelming negative thought patterns set up or released by the thinking of Mankind. We can't hear this 'sound' or energy vibration, but it is there. To try and shed some light on the present and incoming vibrational energy, I'll use an example of a piano keyboard."

"The far left key produces a very low note when pressed... we know it as low-C. The highest note to the right, is high-B. On the keyboard there are 88 different keys each giving off separate and distinct sounds, or vibrations. The keys can be played one at a time, in chords or a multitude of other ways. The harmonic vibrational energy now being delivered to us (which was primarily reactivated in 1987) can be likened to depressing low-C. Because this cosmic energy is much higher in frequency, many times beyond the frequency of visible light, it is not audible to our ears. It does exist however."

144

"With time, a higher and higher 'note' [temporally etheric chord] is constantly surrounding our Universe, our planet, and us. The cosmic notes are at first 'played' [delivered] slowly and singularly. One, then the next, and so on. As more time goes by, more notes are delivered in less time. With each change the resonance becomes higher and higher. Until the rate of change in the 'playing' or spiritual energy picks up speed and progresses ever more quickly to the *end* of it's scale, or high-B in this example [December 23rd, in the year 2012 by Mayan projection]. So, the vibrational energy field starts out as a low and slow vibration, which increases in pitch, amplitude and strength and crescendos more and more rapidly until it reaches a certain point of harmonized intensity... vibrational perfection and balance for an intended affect. The result being a movement into a new dimension of Life. Each new level of resonance we get is referred to as a 'step-change' toward this new plane."

"The creative energy influx isn't being allowed to increase faster than we, *or* the earth and our local universe can *adjust* to it. If had been 'released' full blast, it would absorb the affected cosmos, the earth and all life-forms in an instantaneous cosmic flash. It would be like pouring a small amount of cold water into a pan of boiling oil... instant reaction, and of tremendous effect on the water... it disappears entirely! We are offered this gradual increase in divine spiritual energy to help assist us on our spiritual path to self-awareness, **IF** we choose to utilize it. *This*, another blessing. That being *our* choice to choose! But whether or not we do, the energy still will continue to enshroud us... because it is time!"

"As we desire our personal awakening and consciously work on ourselves, we can utilize this energy to manifest food, shelter, perform healing and do fantastic miracles. Of course *for a short while*, this energy can be used for much less positive results as well, and we will see the effects of some of this misplaced energy. However, there will come a time after the Apex that negative thought energy will cease to exist because of the New Age Vibrational Energy which will be in place. Because the norm will be constructive and positive thought energy, instead of the scattered negative energy which we sadly accept and live with today. As we enter into the zenith of the Changes, we will have other help besides the increase in spiritual vibrational energy. Cosmic guides (many are already here) will freely operate among us, to assist us through the Changes. Intelligence's from other planes and other dimensional worlds will also be here to assist prior to transformation. Just as I and others are here now to light the way, they will follow to offer their additional assistance when the time is right. So you see, we will not be left to fend for ourselves. Many of you will already be well on your way to self-fulfillment and spiritual expression, hence, you may require little or no assistance."

145

THE SIERRAVILLE EXPERIENCE

"Now, let me discuss the Changes as they appear *at __THIS__ moment*, a *potentially serious* not-so-future reality if we don't get our collective act together! Remember, through concerted and collective effort we *can* modify the impact of the Changes. Have any of you noticed that fires, flooding, winds, and tropical storms are beginning to increase in duration, magnitude and severity?" (nods) "This is just the tip of the proverbial iceberg. Changes in political climates all over the world are also occurring. Tyrannical and other governments will topple, insurance companies, stock markets and banks will eventually go defunct and money will cease to have any value. Things and property also would have little worth. Many power plants will stop running. Most computer data bases will be lost; *Significant*, because this is the *second most influential item* which controls Man. Manufacturing and industries of all natures will cease to operate, even now electro-mechanical items everywhere are being functionally affected and witnessed so, but little heed is given these observances and so called minor inconveniences."

"Commerce will become idle due to massive electro-mechanical failures and lack of energy sources. Many major roadways would become unusable and many bridges will be lost. Large buildings in many locations may be completely leveled. Transportation of many kinds will be unavailable or be rendered inoperative. Most water purification plants will cease to function, and in many areas the water and plumbing systems will become stopped up or damaged. Fresh water will become scarce and more precious than gold. Frightening diseases would certainly spring forth from the fouled water. Epidemics and disease could easily grow to outrageous proportions. Medical help and supplies could fall far short of demand during this time. Food production will radically decrease and famine would prevail. Rodent infestations and insect plagues could occur widely due to the normally operative treatments and controls being stopped. Without a way to support ourselves, many could die from starvation and pestilence. Unemployment and loss of accepted ways of living will be the seen."

"Many people may consider self destruction, many might expire from shock and many others from the lack of basic needs and care being met. Many could perish at the hands of others; not out of hate but from desperately trying to look after themselves or their families. Some might loose the desire to continue so they will just give up. Many, ignoring the energy alterations *within* themselves will fall trap to their prior desires and focuses. Multiple thousands will probably die from the natural events that will take place. There may be massive earthquakes and accompanying volcano activity which will severely pollute our air and environments, even shutting out the sun for a while, reducing the temperature significantly. The intensities of some of the quakes could be beyond what we have ever seen or known! Where there are mountains, they may disappear."

146

"The oceans could boil, rise and fall, as parts of the land masses we know vanish while unknown others rise to the surface. Typhoons, uncontrollable infernos, tidal waves, bizarre storms and unpredictable strong winds, hurricanes and tornadoes of colossal energies will be experienced. Many others would perish in this unstable weather activity. The earth's exterior may temporarily bulge from what appears at this moment to be a great planetoid, meteor or perhaps a comet passing close by. Whatever this object is, it is on it's way even now."

"The earth will then shift on it's axis slightly, perhaps 15 to 20 degrees to re-align with new vibrational fields in the cosmos. If this occurs I believe that a dangerous period of irradiation from the temporary loss of our protective atmospheric shield will be observed. Odd glows in the night sky may accompany this event. The polar caps would melt due to the tilt and great flooding would take place, bringing more land shifts and structural impairment until they begin to reform. With the axis change the planet will be reoriented with a different set of constellations. Areas of the globe that are barren and dry might see moist climates, and vise versa. No continent will go unscathed, and few may be recognizable from it's former self."

"People will turn to the Churches of their various faiths in panic to ask for answers as these events unfold, but none will come forth from these institutions. Many will begin to look elsewhere for miracles and answers. No matter to what degree the Changes do occur, when it is finished the 'deadening' areas of pollution and poison, nuclear and waste dump-sites, even the majority of the military arsenals, weapons of obliteration and machines of war will have been basically cleaned off the face of the earth. No man shall rule another, ever again. We *will* have a new earth and a new sky, or heaven, above us. Peace and the desire to *maintain* it will permeate all that remains of the old self destructive thoughts of the prior civilization of Man. As the Golden Age begins, the physical losses of all natures of those that remain will be understood and accepted as necessary and with comprehension, forgotten."

"The beautiful and powerful energy and spiritual understandings that will exist then will overcome any possibility of residual grief. Some may even be able to directly communicate with departed ones who also will carry no sadness, as they through an enlightened wisdom, new purpose or perhaps completed life plan, will already understand all that may have happened and why. The end result of the cleansing vibrational influx will be the greatly altered state of nature."

"The physical dimension as we know it, will no longer exist even though it might appear at *first* glance to be the same. We will observe and experience a radical change in the multiplicity of energies emanating from all things."

THE SIERRAVILLE EXPERIENCE

"We will have communicative abilities beyond science fiction fantasy and interface with life-form intelligence's formally given no consideration. We will share and co-exist with many cosmic neighbors. Life will be abundant and 'miracles' will be commonplace... To the point of no longer being considered miracles, but rather the full utilization of the gifts we were given by the Creator in the first place. We will be able to communicate with plant and animal life. We will heal by thought alone. Sweat of the laborer will eventually cease to be required... more appropriately, overworked laborers will be a thing of the past. New and FREE sources of power generation will be developed so no person is under anyone's thumb for energy dependence or usage. Technology will increase dramatically, but *only* for the *benefit* of Man; not at his *expense*!"

"Every man will be his brother's keeper and Love shall dominate over all things. We will know God as we knew him in the Beginning. We will never again digress to the point of caring only for ourselves. The 'whole' will be understood to be vastly more important than the Self. We will experience fantastic new dimensions of reality and life. Harmony will exist everywhere. Man will learn to be all he can be because he will desire nothing less, EVER again! The Time of Changes and Transmutation of Man is to be a time of rejoicing, not of sorrow or fear. Yet only those of rightful heart, mind and soul will escape the things I have just foretold should they come to pass. Perhaps millions will be focused with wrongful desires or have misplaced hearts, these will temporarily experience the pain and suffering of rebirth... into new realms. And as I've said, many souls will have completed their life plans and these events are their planned exits to higher planes."

"Remember, very few of the radical complications I've mentioned *has* to occur. The magnitude of cleansing is up to us by what we are willing to change from within ourselves, and then how we apply those changes toward others. This is the single most important factor which will affect the cleansing vibrations now upon us. Knowing that the Changes are taking place for our *benefit* should also provide comfort and understanding to all that will listen. There are already those of you who are on your way, and those of you who will help guide others. Lily is one among you blessed with interpretive knowledge and wisdom directed from the beyond. She is a desiring servant and teacher to you, by right, as many of you will *also* become servants and teachers to and for others."

"Billy, Greg and Tom share intimately in the understandings of the 'Philosophy'. I wish you to consider Tom as my apprentice, and all three as your 'physical' adjutants." Tom looks at him in astonishment. "For one day I must leave to show the Way to others, and Tom is destined to fill my shoes as was agreed to lifetimes ago."

"Look not to him as better than you, he is your equal. Seek him out as a teacher and counselor, for this is what his soul assignment is. Each of you will continue to grow, and at your own rates. Do not judge another as to his or her level of advancement and do not compare yourself with another. Each has their own path to walk."

"Assist and share in what knowledge and experiences you encounter henceforth. Become of One Thought... Love. By doing so, you add positive vibrations to the community, the environment, the nation and ultimately the world plane, which substantially helps to reduce the existing negative vibrations. This will become a blessing as time gets closer to the apex of the Changes. Know that who you are and whatever your personal thoughts, truths or choices about spiritualism may be, you will always be cherished by our Father."

"Dear people, accept that you are *deeply* loved by Him. Understand that you are always provided assistance and direction from the Brotherhood of God. But each individual entity must *ask* for it, and in their *own* expressive way before they can *receive*. I sincerely desire that you all experience all that you can be. For once you begin to create miracles in your life, you will *never* be the same. You will have begun your awesome metamorphosis into the beautiful partnership with the Eternal Almighty as his agents of Love. I wish to offer a prayer now..." The people bow their heads...

"Father, in the name of Love, bless these, your Sons and Daughters now, with knowledge, confidence, acute insight, understanding and wisdom so that they might come to the realization of all that they truly are, and continue their spiritual growth that they might create miracles in their lives and exclaim them in your Name, to the world. Amen."

The congregation returns a collective, "Amen."

"I love you dear ones, each and every one of you. I have been authorized to assist in whatever manner I can. Call on me as you will. It is my desire to be of service to you. You can ask nothing of me that I will not do for your betterment. Go now, dream, pray, believe, desire, know, and create. Fulfill yourselves with the Divine destiny which awaits you. Live in peace, rejoice in life, give thanks for what you have and what you experience. Share yourselves with others. Stop to smell the roses and find awe in the precious creation therein. God is everywhere; everything is of God as you also are of the All In All. Seek harmony, cleanse yourself of old habits and thinking. Prepare to experience a new Life, and to it's fullest degree. God bless you all and thank you for allowing me to share with you today." Mr. B steps down and walks slowly with Steve through the doors of the church.

THE SIERRAVILLE EXPERIENCE

The people are fairly silent for the most part, pondering the messages provided by Mr. Beckworth. A few are silently weeping, coming to the realization of all that has been said. Many are regretting how they thought and talked about Mr. B in the past, seeing how wrongly they judged that particular book by it's *cover*.

Gradually they begin to filter outside to personally greet he and Steve. The messages have been received loud and clear as is obvious by their reactions and verbal expressions. Now it is time to put into practice what they have heard and they seem to recognize it. Better yet, there is a profound sense about them, that they truly desire it.

So Ends Journal Seven

JOURNAL 8

"MANY SIGNS"

During the next several weeks I have been at home. Mr. Beckworth spent much of his time holding more group sessions with his expanded class, now numbering ten students. The seven new ones are sincerely eager for all he has to offer. They also feel extremely privileged to have a person like Mr. B instructing them. There are a couple from the original twelve however that have quietly 'dropped' from sight. These ultimately found his material too foreign to deal with. It affected them somewhat acutely. The bottom line is that the information he continued to offer went against their comfortable mind-sets (teachings) and thus they have chosen to withdraw from it.

At today's session Mr. B explains that these persons' decisions are perfectly all right, when questioned about their reactions. He acknowledges that "Not everyone approached will desire to participate at this time. Some will have strong feelings against this information, some will not. Every soul's path is true unto itself. Every soul experiences his or her own reality, by believing in what they consider to be *their* truths about reality. As far as choices go, a personal choice can't ever be considered as 'right' or 'wrong'. Remember that there is no such thing as a good or bad choice. *All* of life here now, and beyond this plane is a continuing and expanding life experience. It is up to us to determine the benefits and lessons of each of our life-decisions, and then hopefully we work with only the resultant positive energies, to accelerate our spiritual growth cycle. By doing so, we not only advance our heart-based thinking infrastructure and positively alter the circumstances and conditions within our lives, but add to the collective (global) spiritual energy, offsetting the present world condition of imbalance."

THE SIERRAVILLE EXPERIENCE

"Sometimes we'd rather not have certain experiences, but we only draw to us what vibrational energy we send out (what we think). So some of us have longer paths to take than perhaps others do. This is absolutely as it should be. It is OUR choice, you see? We *all* will return to the Godhead eventually, and some will return sooner than others. We each wake up at different intervals according to *our* individual timing and level of spiritual growth. When we recognize that there is a Greater Power and that we are more than we have been taught we are, then the process is greatly speeded along. Many of us however, will hold onto old doctrines of life-interpretation, oxidized thinking patterns and even older and inflexible, if not imaginary dogmas. If this is what we desire, then so be it!"

"Recall the word 'truth'. Each of us will experience various truths in our lives. Even on the same idea or thought, each will have their own expression and definition of what it means to *them*. That is fine, that is how it is meant to be. Every entity has his or her own understandings. Another person's personal path is no real business of ours. It's when *we* align ourselves with the Source that we find out if <u>we</u> are on the right path. As I shared earlier, please, never judge another entity. When we do so, we judge ourselves, *and God*. God does not judge, so why would we think that we have a right to? Allow each entity, to experience and think and do what they might."

"They learn at every step of the way. Love them for being able to *have* their experiences. For by each life experience, everyone of us comes closer to knowing who they are, whether or not we take the time to think about it. Allowing, is one of the 'working' principles of the God Consciousness, and of reflecting God. He allows each of us to BE. We in turn, must pass that grace on. He never interferes with our life because he deeply loves us. *That* love is more vivid, fulfilling and powerful than anything we can imagine. With that love comes free will, or the personal allowance of the expression of self ISness. As God **IS**, *so are we*. We need to wake up to that powerful truth and take it to heart."

"God has, is and emanates unconditional love. When you can see God in all things, you will be experiencing that love. Try to extend unconditional love for yourself and others. When we do, we project only good vibrations and add to the positive energy of the rest. Go within to find and sense that love. When you do and freely give or think it, you will become as a christ *awakening*. The term 'christ' does not *directly* refer to the one called Jesus, but rather to that particular state of BEing which more closely resembles and exemplifies the true Love nature-characteristic of God. Once you truly understand then you may be able to enjoy a better appreciation for the supreme commandment 'Be You Perfect, Even As I Am Perfect'."

152

"This is a wonderful personal challenge to attain Divinity and Christos Personality, but Mankind seems everso compelled by self. Man has forgotten the most elementary and simplistic rules of living and interpreting life. They aren't hard to understand or utilize, but more often than not we choose some other easier way to live. Doing so, only means that we will continue to go to 'school' until we realize that there is more, and the *more* already resides within ourselves... we need only reach inward for it. Truly, I say that to leave self behind and to seek the inner knowledge and wisdom of God, is to lay the foundation for discovering what Life is all about. Your life, and all other life."

"You only, can pave the road to self-realization of all that you are... Sons and Daughters of God manifested in physical terms to experience the true meaning, pleasure and understanding of God's creation. Is this not a desirable goal? We *will* eventually wake up. Some sooner than others, but why wait? What possible benefit is there in delaying all that we can BE? What benefit is there to live for ourself, possibly at the expense of others, to only return and go through the process, in whatever realm, again?"

"Go within your heart and take a deep look at your beliefs. Do not hide under false pretenses or facades. Make no excuses, for absolutely none are truly retainable if growth is to occur. How many of your thoughts reflect who you *really* are? How many do not? What significance(s) do you find therein? Discard any thought or emotion which does not reflect peace, love or joy. In other words, a positive vibration; for the rest are meaningless except to keep you prisoner in the illusionary world of self-imposed limitations. Do you desire internal change, or does it look like too much work? How much effort are you willing to give? It's time we wake up. We are as a grain of sand under a mountain. The grain of sand is part of a much grander purpose, and that mountain would be greatly diminished if even one grain of sand was lost. Every grain of sand [person] is important. We tend to only understand ourselves in physical terms; but that is a less than substantial reality."

"We are an important part of a grander, more majestic consciousness. The seemingly difficult physical plane is only one of life's minor experiences, it is the *spiritual* aspect of one's life that counts. There is so much *more* to us, and it is expressed and lived spiritually. BE, Allow and Love. As always, it remains our choice. Dear ones, it is so very, very simple..."

• ▲ •

Many of his students are evolving at an astounding rate. Wonderful things are beginning to happen to them and the level of personal excitement continues to grow. One of the people who faded from the rest has come back.

THE SIERRAVILLE EXPERIENCE

He couldn't ignore the inner urge he had, and decided that he too wanted to participate! Unfortunately the other actually took another job and literally moved away. The raised vibrations, activities and lessons were too much for him. He won't be able to escape though, the increasing vibrational changes are everywhere.

• ▲ •

Today Mr. B is spending time with Tom and I alone. He shares with Tom the existence of the silver canister under his bed, eventually bringing it out. Inside the canister amid the cone and other items, are several scrolls and some charts of far off star systems with several spheres identified as being occupied by close friends of Mankind. Mr. B has instructed Tom about who these people are and how they will help in the coming times. Among the items is a significant set of what looks like metal cards. Medium blue-gray in color. Not much different in size than a deck of playing cards, Tom curiously asks "What are those?" pointing.

"Those Tom, were a gift to me in my last incarnation. I was shown where to locate them again after I began my healing here." "Can I see one?" Tom asks... Mr. Beckworth delicately takes one of the cards and hands it to Tom. "What are they?" he asks. "Basically, these are tablets of knowledge." "They don't weigh much do they; What do these symbols mean?" Mr. B replies "They were created by personalities from another plane of existence. I'm not allowed to specifically interpret the symbols for you, but I know how to get the information they contain." "How?" inquires the intrigued Tom.

Mr. B takes one of the tablets and is about to insert it into a special device, looking similar to an old fashioned personal slide viewer when he offers "Neither can I share how this transcriber actually operates, but please accept that it interprets the common language of those handling the tablets. It interfaces with that part of the mind which is involved with communication, and uses those vibrational patterns to initiate the verbalization of the record of information stored within the tablet." "*Wo-o-w*" says Tom, can we hear it?" "Sure." Mr. B then slides in the tablet and a male voice begins to radiate within our heads, accompanied by a screen of light not far from the surface of the objects facade...

A beautiful but motionless figure cloaked in Light appears on the 'screen': "I AM Alpha Five. Hereby, WE bestow the Book of Planes." 'He' explains:

"In that known as the celestial life plane, as well as that known as your physical life plane, there are seven basic differentiation's of creative matter. From what would be termed: densest to finest, these are generally classified in elementary terms recognized as: solid, liquid, gaseous, atomic, pre-atomic, etheric and super-etheric."

"The typified laws surrounding each differentiation will seem to have similar properties when examined independently from each life plane. To elaborate, when on one specific plane, matter in its particular form appears to be similar in nature to it's counterpart in the other planes. The principal difference is the frequency of vibrations of any given form of matter from plane to plane. Each progressive level vibrates at a higher rate than do the lower levels. Just as the astral plane vibrates as a whole at a higher rate than does the physical plane as a whole."

"On the physical plane, a solid appears as an inflexible item of matter. It is not however, solid; in truest reality there is no such thing... only the illusion of solidness. All things of creation are based on complex particles termed: vibrational structures. Various forms of matter have these structures tightly compacted so as to give the appearance of solidity. There is a universe of space even between these structures. Some structures of creation have intelligence, some do not; some are more densely molded, some less populated. All however, vibrate with Light. Many of these unique forms have been given the gift of everlasting Life by the Creator. The initiating creative thought, and resulting and various components and frequencies which are bound together to form a 'thing' determine at what plane that 'thing' is to share expression. Some of these creations share expression in or on many planes simultaneously. Terra-Man, being one of these creations, will develop many creative items of his own in times to come with his science. Yet his creations will be absolutely restricted to the physical plane; being formed solely from ingredients of that plane. Creations of Soul can never be created by Man, yet in the future Terra-Man will attempt to bring to life creations of his own, by manipulation of known elements. These will be of little significance, simply automatons. True and everlasting Personality and Life comes only from the Source."

"As for the other planes, they have many wonders... Life continues on these next planes with a *relative* likeness to the one you know to be termed: physical. Terra-Man will eventually learn to effect change within his self on each succeeding plane he transcends, to seek and obtain a higher and purer essence. When Man transcends the physical, the power of mind is immense yet usefully restricted by the level of spiritual understanding and wisdom that he has as an individual personality. If he enters this next plane with lower aspects of what is termed: human [characteristic] tendencies, such as having an affinity toward power or dwelling in material possessiveness, he would then be considered stranded in the more solid form of etheric life. He will be able to observe other levels around him, yet not be able to share expression in, or experience them. As he realizes his error[s] of thought and focuses on the higher principles of Light, he will alter his life essence to such an extent that he can eventually transcend to other levels within that plane."

THE SIERRAVILLE EXPERIENCE

"With each level, an individual personality will find more and more evolved personalities, with consistently higher and higher principles and understandings. Therefore, the profoundness of life continues to increase as focus on Self is done away with, and a desire to grow spiritually is embraced. With each step, comes more power of mind and a deeper understanding of how, why and when this power is to be utilized. [Just] as a personality can continue to grow, a personality can also digress. [Just] because one may give rise to advancements, it does not insure that personality will stay on that next level or plane of existence... An entity's growth and advancement is due only to that entities level of desire and sincerity, based on spiritually balanced concepts of Love..."

Mr. B reaches over and removes the tablet; the 'inner-words' and 'video' cease... "Therein is a key to why some people traverse a shorter path in returning to the Godhead, the Center of Love and creation. Those that strive forward in the name of Love find that they desire to learn more, be more, do more and care more, and they will be successful in their endeavors. Others may experience life a multitude of times in one plane because they haven't learned that there *is* more, that they *are* more, and that they need to make a concerted effort to grow from within."

"All the supreme spiritual teachers in the cosmos, all the best spiritual books in the world, all the greatest thoughts of an individual are *meaningless* if the individual concerned makes no internal effort to embrace and *use* the information to effect change from within. This is one reason why each individual walks a different path to their awakening and enlightenment. Each has his or her own rate and level of understanding. Some individuals joyously wake-up sooner than others and will delight in the benefits of a higher life expression sooner. My heart goes out to those that can not or will not 'see' or 'hear', for whatever their reason. Yet in their review, they will come to understand."

"They will return to repeat their life expressions over and over until they realize that they want to change, and that they *must* change to take advantage of the next wonderful levels of life. I can hear their pains, I feel their sorrows, I sense their burdens and I ask myself *why* do they continue as they do? The Principles are so easy to embrace and demonstrate... Why is it they dwell in the consistency of the lower experiences of living?" Tom replies "Because they really don't know any better." "That's right Tom... All we can do is pray that more begin to listen, seek and act while there is still time to do so. Time is so valuable and so short, and all could share in the Golden Age of Man if they only realized that and gave themselves a *chance* to experience it, or at least an opportunity to evaluate the concepts of Spirituality."

156

"They would do well to cast off old feelings of disharmony, inadequacy, perceived mental barriers, psychological and emotional anchors and the like, and honestly open their hearts to the knowledge that many are providing in these last days. Instead of *accepting* life's problems and challenges and *reacting* to them, they could just as easily learn to *act* in accordance with the Father's Principles to alter their realities, and experience abundance, freedom from life's trials, and the joy of life."

After Tom leaves Mr. Beckworth tells me "Tomorrow is an important day, my last here as physical mentor to our Light brigade. I have many other rendezvous ahead of me and must attend to them. In consideration of this event, you may invite and be accompanied by your partner." He then graciously sends me back home so I can bring Mary with me to share in what he has to share.

• ▲ •

DAY 65: It's Saturday morning and Mr. B is in the process of beginning special council with his group and their families in the hills near Sierraville when we arrive. "As you are aware, the world as we know it is going through various stages of cosmic realignment and spiritual metamorphosis. This is a local universe event, not limited to just planet earth and her inhabitants. Through an act of Divine Love, we are being given an opportunity to go within ourselves to seek, find and embrace an understanding of how and why we belong to this, the Grandest of Plans."

"One sign of these Changes is the vibrational-field shifts, or 'step-changes'. These are incremental energy changes which are being externally applied to several sectors of the local universe. They will continue to increase during these last days bringing in more and more spiritual energy of a supreme and magnificent nature. These vibrational increases allow each of us to utilize our power of thought for the benefit of ourselves and Mankind if we do so in the right and proper way, and for the right and proper reasons. No entity, not even I, knows exactly how much time remains before this planet is completely transfigured into a higher and greater dimension of enlightened Light and Love. Yet many all over the world have been receiving images of this imminent event."

"The time we have left allows us an opportunity to reduce the impact of the pending physical changes, by what we hold onto as truths for ourselves, others, and life. For many of us, the vibrational step-changes may already be sensed and seem to affect us in strange ways. As an example, for those entities that knowingly or unconsciously generate or harbor ill feelings for themselves or others, these individuals will find that they sense *and* experience more of these types of feelings, *more often*, and with *greater* intensity."

THE SIERRAVILLE EXPERIENCE

"Seemingly negative circumstances that occur in their lives will enflame those feelings and they will oftentimes feel ill, emotionally or mentally drained or exasperated; even to the point of reacting to some people or situations with extreme impatience, intolerance or perhaps anger or violence. The point is, we shouldn't feel that we have to *react* to anything, let alone in a negative manner. There is no benefit in doing so, and these types of responses will preclude us from our desired goals. What we should do, is *act* in kindness, understanding, compassion and at the *very least*, we should bless any given situation for the right and proper solution."

"The people that experience these types of negative trauma may even recognize these things are happening to them, but not ***understand*** why or where the feelings come from. Like attracts like, and if we hold onto negative thought patterns and emotions, we will draw more and other similar vibrations to us because of the increasing vibrational step-changes. These shifts of vibration to higher levels allow *amplification* of all of our abilities, senses *and* emotions. Both 'positive' and 'negative' emotions are amplified, so it is imperative that we recognize when we are being affected by outside disharmony or alternatively, if *we* are creating it. Because of this amplification, it is very important to cleanse ourselves of all personal negative thoughts and emotions beginning right now. The vibrational changes will also allow us to *sense* guidance from above as well as another's projection of thought with much greater ease."

"If we permit ourselves to internalize negative kinds of energies, emotions or feelings, we might *react* to them and in a not so positive manner. If we sense ourselves being affected by negative influences, we must immediately release these negative vibrations from our being. We must do this on a conscious level. If you sense yourself 'feeling' any other person's negative energy and you feel you are 'holding' it or feel it is affecting your vibrational energy in a negative way, bless *it* and let *it* go. Surround yourself with White Light. There might even be times you find yourself reacting to a person, a group of people or a situation in a manner that does not typically reflect how you would otherwise respond. *This*, is the time you should sense the obvious difference in yourself and know that you must remove these negative vibrations *from* yourself."

"The vibrational changes will allow for *greater* telepathy, extra-sensory perception, precognition and many other related capabilities to be further developed and experienced within ourselves. Some *temporary* side-affects may be noticed as the step-changes continue. These can be recognized as occasional moments of lack of motivation, light-headedness, seemingly uncaused tiredness, heavy or prolonged sleeping patterns, even episodes of slight nausea."

"We might notice a strange loss of energy, find ourselves unable to sleep restfully, or that we awake with the sluggish sensation that we haven't physically reconnected (from extended astral travel). We may even experience mild forms of memory loss, fail to complete sentences, forget what we were thinking, or perhaps find our day to be confusing and or oddly incomplete(d). We might also feel out-of-sorts, out-of-sync, or out-of touch for some unknown reason. The duration of any of these side-affects can be momentary, last for a few minutes or hours, or last for perhaps several days; and is *directly* relative to the *duration* of the step-changes of the vibrational energy increases, which are occurring in what may seem like a random fashion. They can at times, affect our emotional status as well. One of the emotional conditions in particular, and most noticed by those enlightened persons putting forth energy and effort, may be the occasional sensation of expiring."

"Most often felt in times of rest or meditation, it is an impending and confusing feeling; feeling real and not, at the same moment. What is actually being sensed is not a near-at-hand physical death, but the decided shedding of various traits of the 'old' self... the lessor vibrations of the no longer needed or useful thought patterns and emotions of the old self. Subconsciously recognized attributes of self which have no further purpose, significance or meaning due to our increasing spiritual growth."

"No longer necessary parts of our makeup, they are being done away with over time, and with development. This is *not* a conscious act, it is due to the further evolvement of Spirit within us. That evolvement carries with it a higher vibratory state of BEing. Thusly, the lower vibrational concepts fall away as they are now out of balance and polarity with our overall Personality. It is an automatic function of Spirit! A natural and wonderful transformation of Self. Our old thinking and less-than-positive traits literally succumb to the more spiritual energies and vibrations of those energies within us. They will eventually cease to exist within our essence and be little more than memories, learned lessons."

"If you sense this expiring, *be excited*, for it is a *very* special sign to, and for you of your faith, persistence and growth. Another affect of the incoming vibrations is the potential of experiencing multiple nightly 'visions', even remembering some or all of them. Others may experience moments of specially increased psychic ability or awareness. Some of us might be more sensitive or aware than others. Certainly, the informed will be even more aware and have an understanding of what is actually happening. So I suggest that you *be* aware of *how* and *what* you are feeling at any given moment. If you encounter any of these experiences, then understand they are (most likely) occurring because of the changes in the vibrational energy. Do not be concerned that they may be detrimental to you, they are not."

THE SIERRAVILLE EXPERIENCE

"They simply allow us a physical source of 'feed-back' that the vibrational changes are indeed taking place. We are being gently acclimated to these new vibrations. For those individuals that are and continue to create negative thoughts and deeds, the others of us might witness a greater occurrence (for a while) of negativeness in our towns and cities. It is possible that the vibrational shifts will affect those with an unspiritual consciousness to the point they may commit atrocities against themselves or others. They will be assumed to have gone 'mad'... these we must pray for. These conditions will distress and disturb us, but it will be our responsibility to send those situations thoughts of love, peace and harmony; As well as sending global thoughts of the same to all Mankind and pray for their spiritual awakening. Whether or not we *think* we see our desired results, we DO impact the situation(s). And by doing so, we as a conglomerate of small groups of enlightened beings *can* modify the impact of the coming Changes."

"I don't speak of only *us*, in the sense of Sierraville, but of all the scattered and varied groups of enlightened like-minds, knowledgeable and spiritually advanced thinking people *everywhere*. We can project, pray or send blessings by ourselves or in groups. What we need to understand, is that *we* as *individuals* must do it on a continual and tireless basis in order to cause a significant effect on the pending Changes. As we do this, it also increases the harmony and energy within our own vibrational (auric) fields."

"I wish to inform you that I am not working alone. There are *thousands* of teachers participating at this moment all over the world to help disseminate spiritual wisdom and knowledge to those that will listen, and truly desire change within themselves. Some of those students are proceeding at what appears on the surface to be slow rates, according to the level of understanding and *desire* that those people have, some are able to proceed fairly rapidly for the same reasons. All who have been truly awakened continue at incredible levels of progress. They can 'feel' something positive and great is close at hand."

"There are many teachers working with maybe only one or just a few students. At the present most are unknown and desire it that way. It would be very hard to teach, and learn, if a teacher was immersed in constant notoriety. That is why I had asked you all to keep what you are learning and experiencing to yourselves until an appropriate time. Tom will advise you of that time. You must have a *foundation* before you share with others. There is another reason as well... What abilities or experiences you disclose to another may ultimately be impacted by that other persons thoughts. They can actually diminish your abilities by their focusing on you or your comments with negative thought. If you do choose to disclose, please insure that your listeners are of the right understanding and attitude."

"You don't want to unknowingly diminish your own capabilities by having your creative thought vibrations impinged upon by others of less comprehension and belief. Those of us which are in-tune with the understandings of the 'Philosophy' will continue to gain more knowledge and eventually share the messages with all we can. As we grow and learn we in fact have a duty to share what we know, as it is in the best interest of the entirety of Mankind and the planet. Some people will not listen or want to be bothered with what you have to offer at this time. Do not fret if that occurs, that's okay. But don't be afraid to offer experiential input, support or guidance when appropriate to do so. Fear of being accepted is a common emotion to those of an unrealized confidence. There is no need to feel fear when you work with the principles of God. Remember, each entity has and must travel their *own* path, in their *own* time and in their *own* way. You may experience frustration or sadness because of how they might 'shut' the doors to their minds or try to discredit you."

"Do not allow these types of feelings to be held or internalized. You are at least allowing them the opportunity to examine advanced knowledge. Realize the joy and satisfaction of your giving, and of what you are giving... do not entertain the concept of grief if they wave you off. Whether or not they choose to embrace what you offer is entirely up to them and them alone. You can not and must not 'force' anything on anyone, for any reason, no matter how 'good' it seems, how well placed your concerns are, or how it might improve their lives. *They* must make their own decisions, *Always*."

"Perhaps later, at another time, they might see something in you by how well your life flows, what you experience or things that are going on around them that causes them to question and want to know more, like Bob here. Remember, *doing* is also teaching. When you live your life by embracing and utilizing the Cosmic Laws in the right and proper ways, then others can learn from your example. If they come back to you, share with them all you know. If they do not, perhaps that is what is best (for them), as each individual's path takes a slightly different course. Allow them the *right* to be themselves and learn from their experiences. This is how it must be."

"As for preparation for the Changes... We must acknowledge the *possibility* of the lack of personal needs being met during the rebirth period of our world. You have heard me comment on the potentially upsetting tribulations which were originally foretold in the Bible. You have also heard me submit that *we can affect and alter* the types, intensities, and duration's of the pending Changes up until the Apex. Some of us will not have evolved enough to manifest what we need, during the Changes."

THE SIERRAVILLE EXPERIENCE

"Some of us will have, and it will be our charge to help those who come to us, for we will be provided an abundance of all that is necessary by our direct link with the Source and our command of faith."

"For those of you that have questions as to your own capabilities, there are several things you can do, and should be aware of. First, try to put away food stuffs for at least two years. Investigate purchasing bulk, dry or freeze-dried foods or something similar. If you can, or have the means to drill a well for water, do so. Purchase fast growing vegetable seeds of all varieties, so you can grow your own gardens. Consider joint venture warehousing with others. Eventually you may expand in such numbers that the messages do spread into the cities."

"Those living in the jungles of concrete and blacktop have a more severe problem facing them. You need to share even more with those. For those dwelling in the cities where there is no place to grow food stuffs, they should convert some or all their yards, build greenhouses, planters or consider purchasing or moving to a plot of land where they can. Granted, some will not heed these words for various reasons including the fact that their livelihoods are (*or seem*) to be restricted to the congestion of the city."

"But if there is no fresh water, no electrical power and nothing on the shelves at the supermarket, what will they do? Sadly, many of us tend to live our lives in the fast lane... fast computers, fast food, fast shopping, fast cars, fast everything; and selfishly, *everything* on demand. My friends, *listen carefully* - that privilege will not continue for much longer. Share that they should not take these things for granted, they really may not *be* available tomorrow. Learn to grow a vegetable garden, bottle and purify water, so you can show others. How many of you know how to prepare and bake bread... from raw wheat? It would behoove you to learn how. Buy garden seeds... bean sprouts are excellent growers and very nutritious."

"*Plan for the worst* even though through the heightened efforts of Man, it may not come *as dramatically as is now seen*. Take note of the motto of the Scouts... *Be prepared*."

"Share that it wouldn't hurt to have camping supplies such as a tent or tarps, cooking kits and a large storage of water and water purification products and tablets. They should also contemplate assembling a good first aid kit, tools of assorted varieties and perhaps canned butane or gas, safely stored of course. We must also be willing or equipped to barter our talents or some of our items of sustenance. Such as food or clothing for wood supplies or nails, or trading one kind of labor for another. We might actually need our neighbor's assistance at one time or another, and we might need to be available *for* our neighbors at various times, and possibly throughout the latter period of transformation."

162

"What we will eventually get back to, is being our 'brothers' helper. Caring for others as we do for ourselves or our families. We will get back in touch with feelings and emotions which encompass the joy and satisfaction of knowing we are or were, of service to somebody else. How wonderful it will feel to really share ourselves with those that need our help, guidance and strength. What will you be able to do for someone needy, or what might another be able to do for you? What skills might you teach others, or perhaps learn? We should desire to *want* to help and not do it out of selfishness, or the thought that it might benefit us in some way. That comes back to 'self', and 'self' is what is least important and being done away with."

"If you *feel* that *nothing* is impossible and you have learned and embraced the Laws, then you will *know* that you will have anything you need, for yourself or others, and you need never be concerned about self. With proper application of this kind of knowledge, you simply won't even consider worrying about yourself. You will *know* that your 'supply' comes from an undimishable Source. Share this message as well, and trust that there will be *nothing* a person can't ask, that won't be answered or so done, in the name of Love. Of course, more unlimited power is available to us as we conquer the understandings of the Laws and continue to apply them in the right and proper ways. As time goes on more and more of the remaining entities will grow and advance, and soon times of apparent hardship and lack will be gone forever as the vibrations are completed."

"As each of you seeks to teach others, the level of wisdom and creative powers of the whole will rise beyond present day comprehension. All will come to understand the infinite term 'Spirit' and what is truly means. Peace, Love and Harmony will one day soon, be ever prevalent. Men will work and live side by side with men of all nations, and each will see and respect them for who they really are. Children of God and disciples of the All In All. Lights of *the* Cosmic Light. You can't now perceive how great and wonderful that life will be. Unlike anything you have ever encountered. Imagine a world totally devoid of hate, anger, animosity, frustration, stress, competition, control, and rebellion. Imagine a world with over-abundant love, friendship, courtesy, compassion, caring and being united in all causes for the further development of Mankind."

"No lack for anything, no disharmony or imbalances, no feelings of inferiority, no prejudices, no person perceived as, or being better or less than any other. No feelings of the need to be dependent on anyone. No mandatory eight-to-five jobs, no seniority, no supervisor/subordinate situations. Each person will become self-confident, self-reliant and self-sustaining, yet we will all work together as family."

THE SIERRAVILLE EXPERIENCE

"No nation controlling or manipulating any other. No requirement for money, as none will exist; *This*, the **greatest most influential item** of control, has served only to cause disillusionment and separation for all peoples of all nations. It has been, and is the *primary* control over all Mankind. It is wielded unjustly and has negative power over most people."

"In the Golden Age we will have various kinds of work, but also ample time to spend with our families and live life like it was intended we should live it. We will have time to spend with nature and will have totally forgotten about the prior existence of schedules, pressure, turmoil and lack. We will finally be free! Free from all prior encumbrances. Free to express, create positive experiences and enjoy life, All life. *Can you imagine it?* You will find that material things that had meaning in or for your life such as an incredible sound system, 'in' clothes or a deluxe car, will cease to be of any value to you. You will have out-grown the need to have the best, to compete or compare yourself with any other. You will understand how selfish and petty the 'old' world was, and appreciate the 'new' world for the meaning it will convey into your life. Desire to participate in the Golden Age. Desire to fulfill yourselves as the children of God. Desire to accomplish and do the magnificent things that the Masters have done, and to a greater degree."

"Our Father wishes you *all* to experience this fantastic opportunity. To experience what life is really all about, and to experience all that you really are! So cast off the old 'shells' of self-protection, self-images, ego, misdirected thoughts and blaming attitudes. Is it really that hard to simply ignore perceived 'negatives' and refrain from detrimental or limited thinking? Why do we find it so difficult to do and perceive good in everything, especially ourselves? Only the *individual* can answer these questions for themselves. I pray they are satisfied with their answers, because they *will* experience the results of embracing the thoughts they hold as truths as we approach the Apex. THIS, is the time to prepare."

"Share that we should not worry that we might not be 'good' enough, as there is no such thing. Our Father knows our heart, even if others do not. It is what is in our heart that counts... Our care, desire to change, our desire to know, our attitude, our desire to be of service to others and our desire to grow. If the desires are there, if the sincerity is there, if the intent is properly placed, we *will* be successful. No matter the level of enlightenment we *imagine* ourselves to have, the Father's Love will be there to provide us the means to endure, succeed and fulfill ourselves as Children of (the) Light."

"Now... You all have wondered about those crop markings. They are from some of our galactic friends. Some call them aliens, some extraterrestrials. They are creatures of the Almighty, just as we are. Yes, many of them look different from us but imagine how *we* look to them."

"Fortunately, they have a more advanced understanding of the term Man. Alien is such a terrible word to use to describe another intelligent life form... They are our distant kin. They care greatly for us, and all life. Allow them the respect that you would give your neighbor, for that is what they truly are. The set of circular patterns, as some of you have concluded, is our solar system. The extra circular pattern reflects another planet in our system which is opposite us, on the far side of the sun. Sumerian records some 3000 years old tell of this tenth planet. In 1972 an astronomer discovered an anomaly in the orbit of Haley's comet. His findings indicated that it could be caused only by the gravitational pull of an astronomical body approximately the size of Jupiter. He concluded that it might orbit the sun every 1800 to 2000 years or so. It is thought that this planet's orbit is much closer to Earth than Jupiter is, as it swings into it's apogee around us. Some believe this to be the great 'star' seen in the heavens at Jesus' birth."

"There *is* life there. Advanced, intelligent and spiritual life, and soon we will know of them. Soon the scientists will discover this planet's existence. How will we prepare to meet these individuals? *Will* we be prepared? Could we love them as we do family? Or will we fear and attempt to attack them? This remains to be globally answered. The large humanoid form on the other hand, depicts Man in the New Age. He holds the symbol of conception at his finger tips. The symbol of Creative God Essence Energy. The basic building block of all that exists. From this thought plasma comes Light, from this Divine Light comes the electron, from the electron comes matter. These are but a few of the understandings to come."

"The Bible says in the Last Days there will be many signs. Native Americans will soon have such a sign. Previously foretold to them... a milky-colored buffalo will be born at the beginning of the Time of Preparation. When this occurs [it now has] there will be no doubt among any Native American tribe or nation. As to the rest of us, the crop markings are only the meagerest of signs to the world at large. As you are well aware they have appeared all over the globe. This, to cause us to question many things, including recognizing the fact that we are not alone. Within such anomalies are important messages for Mankind, but they have yet to be clearly deciphered as to their true significance. Several display the 'hidden' planet; Can you now draw any hypothesis' from this last statement? As I have mentioned, other presently active signs to watch are the changing attitudes in governments, the world financial stability and the atmospheric climates and geological conditions. Even the concept of a major war is looming as a potential probable reality, this however can be avoided! I will now predict another sign to watch for as the Apex closes in. That will be the rising of at least one large volcano off the Northern portion of Japan. The frozen shores in that area will boil in turmoil as a result of that activity."

THE SIERRAVILLE EXPERIENCE

"This could signal the beginning of the end of that land mass as we know it to be. The Pacific Ring of Fire could rupture shortly thereafter with unceasing activity. Great oceanic storms would thereafter appear and island chains will be deluged with winds, water and quakes, signaling evacuation. Many will not heed these warnings expecting things to calm down. At that point it may actually be too late if we haven't made more spiritual progress."

"As for the well-known unidentified flying objects, they have been coming here for eons upon eons. Some are from other galaxies, some from multidimensional worlds and they congregate around the unique power centers of our Earth. All are from inhabited worlds. Some think it odd that many men of science have the ineptitude to say that intelligent creature life doesn't exist on any celestial body near us. They believe that intellectual life as they understand it must only exist in conditions similar to Earth's. They haven't allowed for other possibilities and conditions. Do you see how they've substantially limited their thinking? If they had the proper 'tools' and instruments, they could easily detect other forms of life on some of these planets. But because they don't think in terms of expanded mind, they only develop simplistic sensors. Then, using these sensors they don't detect anything so they 'appear' to be right. However, they are vastly wrong! There will be a day when they know the truth as well."

"The object that was seen around the lake... That was for me. The BEings within were witness to my being granted permission to come into your midst as a teacher. There are a multitude of craft around that communicate on an ongoing basis with others such as I. We all desired to be of service prior to the Time of Transmutation. However we had to wait for the proper time to begin administering. Even now it goes on in all corners of the world. At first there were advanced entities. Many of these did not succeed in their charter to further develop Man's spiritual consciousness. Later, there came communications from the beyond to various spiritually devoted students, to take up where the others had left off. Then public communication and messages in the forms of books and channeling arose. Now the present spiritual teachers of life's higher philosophy appear. We exist in all forms. Some are school teachers, some ministers, some even, are common street people. All fulfilled a particular position or station in life in a holding pattern, until permission was granted us to become involved in the transformation process of Mankind. Some are very active, some less active."

"We are all involved because of our personal desire to do so, not because anyone coerced us. We love God deeply and desire that others may experience life more completely through spiritually opened eyes and ears. *None* of us came here to be worshipped or idolized. There are to be *no* churches or religions created in our names."

166

"We came only to deliver a message. We came that we might help the awakening masses. No-one knows what *you* need to do to grow spiritually. *That*, is your responsibility to examine. You as future teachers, must avoid forcefully directing the paths or decisions of other's; they must choose their own. Be there for them to help guide, but let them decide. We make our own decisions and create our own reality, be that as it is."

"I and the others are here to help re-awaken in you that which you already know, but have lost touch with over time. Gain your independence from, and power over all other distractive and unbeneficial influences. BE! Believe in God and yourself for you *are* creator gods in the making, or rather, in the stage of 'awakening'. Your *attitude* is the key; what you internalize *will* come to pass. Embrace and apply all that you have learned and will continue to learn from the available sources. When you adopt and use the Philosophy, you reach upwards toward your personal divinity. Divine Mind my friends, is Man reflecting God... As it should be."

"Be meek and be humble. Allowing others, is the application of being meek and humble (understanding), contrary to popular belief. If you can not or will not give others their right to BE, then ask yourself why. What prevents you from doing so? If you can not answer, then you have much to study on. If you sincerely seek, and can find the answers and cause change within yourself, you will continue to grow. Remember, the Changes are coming to allow Man to put everything he has ever thought or done into perspective, not as punishment. When *they* are actively among us we will not have time for pettiness or arguing or wars. We will *have* to turn *inward* for the answers and solutions. Even now some are unprepared for these events."

"I caution you to work earnestly and with dedication. Leave your traditions and beliefs steeped in fear, anxiety, depression, suspicion and control, behind. Re-evaluate, re-program. Go into the Holy of Holies. The place within, that is *your* Source. That is your 'temple', there you will find the Father's guidance. This you can do through meditation. Connect with the Spirit of God (the God Presence within). You have been instructed on many things and I have spoken on the New Age of Man. Enlightenment means to be in knowledge of, in the fullest sense... To know of the upcoming events, is to be forewarned. To be forewarned allows action. It is your decision alone, to act or react. Action infers a positive output of energy, while reaction can only deplete your energy and is based in fear."

"If you choose to hold onto things that have no meaning and that are of no importance, save that you *think* they are and you fail to prepare, then you will experience your unconscious desire to fail in this life plane. Fail, in terms of having gone blindly through this life without rediscovering your greater potential and the reality of God."

THE SIERRAVILLE EXPERIENCE

"You will only react to the upcoming Changes, and potentially with great fear. If that is your choice, that is fine. There is nothing wrong with that choice. But when you sincerely desire growth and embrace spirituality... and LIVE it, then you may very well experience the Changes unscathed."

"My friends you will all continue to grow, ultimately finding that you do not have to repeat a physical existence unless you desire too. *That*, will be your graduation present to yourselves. You can not grow by allowing *others* to make path decisions for you. That is called following. You must desire to DO! Not lead, *but do*. For by doing you lead without resentment from others. You teach by demonstration. You guide others by showing them the Way through your actions. How absolutely divine! The threshold of tomorrow is just in front of us... What in your heart-of-hearts do *you* desire to experience? Dear ones, learn to laugh more often and take joy in all that you do. Seek out the positive in every experience you have, for there IS a positive aspect to each experience if you take the time to look for it. Love one another, love life, love yourself and love God. Embrace each other as family of the Almighty, for *that* is what we are."

Mr. Beckworth calls Tom out of the group. He presents him with his medallion. As he places it around his neck, a tear appears in Tom's eye. He knows too well what this means. "Listen to Tom, my beloved brothers and sisters. He will have more information for you in the coming times... And now, it is my time. I am called to help others in need of further awakening." Many begin to tear. Not from sadness so much, but from their now deep affection for Mr. Beckworth. They realize their purpose... and the responsibility that lays ahead of them, and they want it.

"Blessed are you all and deeply loved. Go now and BE!" Mr. Beckworth stretches out his arms and a vaporous White Light envelopes him... As he begins to transcend we hear his egressing message...

"BEHOLD GOD. . . HE, is with you ALWAYS!"

So Continues The Adventure

JOURNAL 9

"Q and A"

As I compile this special section, I ponder whether or not I'll ever see or communicate with Mr. Beckworth again. I'll treasure my few months of experiences with him for as long as I breath... or perhaps and probably more accurately, for eons longer. Over the course of our many private conversations together, I queried him on various and sundry topics. Although not in any particular order, the following represent a partial, yet substantial collection of the subjects covered within our informal discussions:

Q: "I'd like to know what you think about prayer?"

A: "Prayer is a very important aspect of establishing a personal confidence, trust and relationship with our Creator. Jesus is this world's Lord and Creator Son and our prayers may be made just as effectively to He, Mary, or our protecting Angels because the truth of our vibrations of appeal are presented thereby to the Source, our Father and His Light Workers."

"If you could only see the energy which is emitted from our being as we pray you'd be amazed. Streams of Light flow into the heavens from us to the receiving angels who interpret which to acknowledge first. Brightly glowing and wide beams depict the sender to have intense faith and are gathered up immediately, while the dimmer and more slender beams announce the sender to be of a lessor faith and are gathered subsequently. There are also those that are sent without conviction at all and because they are hollow, empty of faith - as in routine or memorized praying. They are recognized, but remain unattended to by the messenger angels as there is no component of emotion or faith. Only the true prayers of faith are collected and sent onward to the Source for special recording, review and action."

THE SIERRAVILLE EXPERIENCE

"Prayer will always be with us, it is our link to God and our giving over of our *complete* trust in His Power and His Hosts. However, due to certain religious constraints, some of us may have been taught that we can not approach our Father directly. This is indeed a shame. It was written that 'we *must* approach through Jesus' and yet there is a valid argument for this. The heavenly Order exclaims that since Jesus IS our world's creator, we should honor his appointment as our first step in prayer... Giving His name the glory it deserves, and to which He is entitled."

"There is another view that goes hand-in-hand with this one: That we must accept Jesus, as he is our key or doorway into the advanced and higher realms of Life. The term 'acceptance' stems from our understanding and embracing the concepts which He presented to us... not the physical person. Jesus said 'I and the Father are One'... The interpreters at the time didn't understand what was meant, which was twofold. Since they are of the same Higher essence, the relational interpretation presented was that if we really knew and understood Jesus (what he *represented*), then we also knew the Father. Thus, and for most of us, Jesus IS our doorway to the Father."

"Not having discovered that it was not the *man* image we were to seek the understanding of, as much as what his *message* was, it would then be best to approach Jesus with our misplaced focus. Our resonance's (plea's) then, may not have been of the necessary vibrations to go directly to the Father. Our thought vibrations were predicated on a physical persons actions for us (our reliance on and acceptance of the *person*), instead of the *higher* vibrations of *creative Love* (necessary from within ourselves) which if we understood this, would allow us to go directly to the Source. I believe people today are beginning to understand this concept more fully."

"Further, for those without the understandings of advanced spiritual knowledge, prayer may be our only means to effect seemingly miraculous answers to our requests. Also understand that prayers for others in need or otherwise, may actually be in contradiction to their chosen path. If we are in question, we would do better to pray with conviction for the 'right and perfect' solution for that situation, nothing more. All earnest prayers are answered with absoluteness, and in the perfect way for each situation. There are times when our Father or Jesus, or even special Angels do intercede, and these are very special times, but we mustn't forget that we also were blessed with powers of initiating healing and manifestation."

"Realize that with proper intent, spiritual understanding and raised vibrations of (higher) self we can, with these 'right and perfect' conditions, utilize the energy of thought based in love to accomplish for ourselves or others. And remember, prayer without faith reflects a lack of belief in the process, our selves, and or God... empty prayers, yield empty answers."

170

Q and A

"Too often we pray out of desperation, *hoping,* even *begging* to see some etheric based response to our plea... *this* condition is less than perfect. It also exclaims that we, as the initiator of the request for an answer, are not worthy of being an integral part of the process. I would never insinuate that prayer is of a 'lessor' thing, it is a very powerful and positive act, an act of acknowledgment of the All In All. However, we usually place our expectations for results or answers in the hands of the One who desires that *we*, as a precious identity of spirit, experience the creation or manifestation of miracles for ourselves; In accordance with His Laws of course."

Q: "What do you mean by: *the right and perfect conditions*?"

A: "First, let's start by assuming that the praying entity is of the proper faith, love vibration and spiritual wisdom. That their prayer, a projection for 'some thing' is positively based of course, and that he or she is in total and complete alignment with all spiritual aspects of BEing. A state of BEing which is pure and in perfect harmony and balance with Life, Love and the Light, with a solid and unwavering belief in the powers Above and within, having unrestricted thinking, powerful will and believing nothing, *absolutely nothing*, is impossible to accomplish through the Power of God. Then... if their projection does not impede another's progress, interfere with another's will or path, go against their *own* growth, path or assignment in anyway, is based on a need or healing for self or another out of the emotion of love-desire alone, with no thought of *extended* benefit to self, the likelihood of self-fulfillment is probable. If the projection, perhaps unknowingly to us, involves or encompasses attributes of another's purpose or plan, including our own, then when, how or if the projection is to be made manifest, is up to yet 'others' with far better knowledge and decision making capabilities."

Q: "What about an unanswered projection?"

A: "Again, let's assume that all the conditions of the essence of the one initiating the projection are without imbalance, as before. Their projections would be extremely powerful, and certainly acknowledged in the heavenly realms. If the projection couldn't be completed as to *our* particular focus, it would be accounted for, in our behalf, in our personal Book of Life. It is our resonance of heart vibration (BEing), personal philosophy and beliefs in a *structured* Higher power; our awareness of ethereal energies and purposes, our trust in faith, our understanding of proper intent and the appropriate application of Divine Laws, WITH a willingness to turn over our projection or thought of manifestation, *to* this Higher authority, wisdom and knowledge, which directly impacts the formula as to the resultant degree of our manifestation success - in most cases. Jesus said, 'Not my will, but yours (Gods Will) be done.' Only He, knows what is absolutely right and perfect."

THE SIERRAVILLE EXPERIENCE

"This does not inhibit or preclude absolute free will, yet until we more completely understand how ALL of the Laws work together, why they work and when and how to properly apply them, how our projections impact the seen *and* the unseen, how we are guided and watched out for from above, we will be limited to only those results which best fit *our* level of interpretation, comprehension, faith and wisdom. One should not loose confidence if a projection or manifestation isn't directly forthcoming. It is possible that *we* may be doing something not entirely correct in our processing, OR that our prayers or projections may be interfering with a natural state of events which mustn't be tampered with, including our own!"

"We should learn to critique any (seemingly) 'empty' findings, and with a *positive* outlook only. They can only truly be empty if we are insincere or have little or no faith in the processes. In lieu of this, they are all noted. Further, it doesn't mean that any particular directional input from a physical teacher, friend, book or other source on this subject is erroneous. Many may eventually disillusion themselves if they haven't established a solid *foundation* because of their adopting or accepting only *certain* criteria."

"If they use limited information and then see no results, they will most often tend to down play the concepts (even subconsciously) and might never come to understand the 'more' which is involved at higher levels; within AND without! One may then simply fail to 'see' the whole picture as it relates to their less-than-desired outcome, and as a result, question or discount certain important criteria, cease to evaluate or explore other avenues of input; or worse, they may find that their faith is reduced to the point of demanding proof and/or becoming 'grounded' in negative emotion and confusion. There can be no positive results if this is the case."

"Of course, negative energy directly impacts the manifestation process, and confusion or questioning will most likely stem from misinterpretation or a lack of Divine understandings. This is a clue that perhaps more study, faith, persistence or spiritual grounding is required. Also, assuming we apply ourselves in the right way and it *isn't* a dire emergency, (a situation always given first priority) we shouldn't limit the process by pre-determining how (or in some cases, when) the projection or manifestation should occur. Leave that responsibility to those who know better (for all), for their cosmic vantage point offers a far clearer comprehension and determination when all 'things' are taken into account."

"Our contribution, is to formulate the desire and pass it on to a Higher authority for completion. Absolute free will (Spiritually speaking) is gained *only* by our increased growth from *within*, as determined by our application and understandings of the Divine Laws of the Universe as they relate to our Source."

172

Q and A

"When we speak of spiritual free will, we mustn't forget that our projections may affect the Universe to some degree or another. Since it is God's Universe, He (and His Light workers) retain command of the ultimate results; especially if they involve others beside ourselves, or if *we* aren't ready (studied). When we endeavor to apply ourselves faithfully in the right and proper way and can accept the outcome whatever it may be, only then will we be attuned to the Father's will. As someone much learned once put it, 'Thank God for unanswered prayers'... Think about that declaration and how it could truly be a great blessing, in light of what we just covered. Whatever the unseen or empirical results, they are and unceasingly *will* be, the right and perfect answers, ALWAYS!"

Q: "You use the term Soul-Assignment; what exactly do you mean?"

A: "An individual's soul assignment is a path he or she takes to fulfill a life plan or purpose which may or does include some attribute of being of service to others. Deep inside of yourself within your consciousness, there is a cosmic remembrance of why you returned to this plane and what you were to accomplish while you were here. Without spiritual understanding and interpretation, it is almost impossible to identify what your self-asserted soul assignment is. This occurs for many reasons, but primarily because of our learned focus on the physical world as we become adults. We loose sight of, and our conscious knowing of what we are to do. With meditation, evolvement of spirit within, or sometimes at a predestined point in our growth cycle, we sense what it is we are to do or accomplish. An inner feeling develops as we mature *spiritually* which allows access to this prior knowledge, making it available to us to interpret, make a particular decision and/or take action toward that path."

"A higher root of knowing one's self, is the knowledge of our purpose and that specifically, each of us is to love one another and share ourselves with others. Caring for and about another displays love for others outside of ourselves. The giving to another with *no* intention or purposeful thought of receiving benefit other than the deep sense of pleasure in the sharing of yourself, reflects God in action. My assignment is to be a teacher of enlightenment, as is Tom's. He chose to do this before he came back to this physical plane, yet as you know only recently did he become re-aware of his decision to do so. Now he feels it in his heart and it is an intense and beautiful feeling."

"You have recognized within the recesses of your own loving heart, that you are to be a teacher and healer. This is absolutely beautiful. This occurred when you were searching deeply for spiritual truth and became open to energies outside of your normal awareness." I nod.

THE SIERRAVILLE EXPERIENCE

"Your work may eventually encompass the physical or spiritual aspects of others or perhaps both, in addition to having a desire to share the message of God and spiritualism. Yet only you can conclude what it is that you are to do, from that feeling you sense from deep within yourself. I perceive you as a humanitarian, interested in helping others however you can, and I foresee your success at it because I truly feel the sincerity in what you are attempting to do. *What* we do in the name of God and Love is not as important as *why* we do it. The giving of ourselves is unlike anything else we can do for another. Seek to understand more fully what your soul assignment is, and act upon your instincts."

"Allow God to direct your path, go to the Source through meditation and patiently listen. Through His love, His Brotherhood and His Spirit (Holy Ghost), He is available to all. When people listen to their inner voice they will obtain a knowingness, a feeling or a direction for what they are to do. They will know it when it manifests within their heart because the sensation or urge will be in complete harmonized vibration to their plan. It will become an influence they can't ignore the presence of. There will be no doubt... They may not be able to act upon their feelings immediately, which is okay, but the remembrance will never again leave them. Eventually they will obtain the necessary information which will lead them forward on their self-assigned path for completion - IF they desire it so. Unfortunately, if they become trapped in self, 'hardened' I call it, they may never (during this particular life experience) come to full realization and ultimate expression."

"Sometimes information (not always pertinent to our purpose or for ourselves) is made available to us in our dream states. With increased spiritual awareness a person is able to interpret their, or another's dreams more accurately, to find meanings to the symbols or expressions found therein. Most often spiritual guidance or information is made available to us with symbols and symbology, a more complete expression or thought process. Remember, when you 'dream', you are actually in a state of astral oneness with the higher aspect of yourself and possibly others of higher learning. Here knowledge is made available to you on a higher spiritual plane. Make an effort to remember what you have 'seen' or 'heard' while in the sleep state. It takes practice, *everyone* can do it. Many times the messages are insights, answers to our requests, and many times knowledge is obtained for allowing us to continue our growth cycle. It will become obvious with spiritual growth which 'dreams' are meaningful and which are the result of anxiety, or an overactive subconscious."

Q: "One question which is difficult to respond to and which others ask many times is... If God is kind and forgiving, why does he allow us to experience physical dysfunction's, abnormalities and afflictions?"

174

A: "My goodness, why would anyone think that God perpetrates these things? They ask a very sincere and solemn question! God is purity and unconditional love. God does not hand out pain, anguish or lack, we do that all by ourselves; and in some cases as you well know, we've gotten pretty good at it. As it truly relates to their question, I assume they speak primarily of the crippled, the retarded, the deaf and blind. (I nod) Those individuals that are diseased or die young?" "Yes...." "Their hearts obviously go out to them, as does mine, but those situations do not reflect the lack of love or care on God's part. It may be hard to accept and understand, but some of the afflictions they sense may be God's handywork are really Man's reflection of self. You are familiar with the term Karma (a condition WE set into motion to experience) and the Recurrent Wheel of Energy, so I will attempt to explain these perceived inequities for you and the others."

"Ignoring for the moment the souls which transcend from this plane at an early age, the remaining afflictions happen for several reasons. One explanation, is those born of parents who partake of biochemically altering substances, through direct or indirect exposure or application. Our bodies can only fend off dangerous toxins up to a certain level, and for only so long. An unborn child of parents who have been exposed before or during pregnancy, may transmit the chemicals directly to the infant with a great chance at causing one or more birth defects. Such an occurrence can actually be an accident, but more than likely is not. A spirit soul who wishes to reincarnate to continue growth may have priorly projected for or desired physical alterations for their new body; seeking out this character in an infant so they can experience one or more types of dysfunction's, for one or more reasons."

"One reason may be that in their prior life they taunted and teased others of lessor capabilities, or were actually physically or mentally cruel to the less fortunate. The negative energy patterns and thoughts permeate their aura, essence and BEing (and the ether) and eventually come back to them in Spirit, to assimilate. Having recognized their mistaken ways, they may choose to make amends for their transgressions before advanced growth can take place, by experiencing what they formally commissioned or chastised. In order to resolve the negative vibrations and replace them, that person experiences the ever present vibrations set into motion by their own doing. Thus, Karma. 'What goes around, comes around'... sooner or later. We *will* experience what we set into motion, physically, emotionally, mentally, spiritually and all the above. Also, we may have desired to experience a life of less-than to find out exactly how it feels and what meaningful information lies within such an experience, as it relates to our particular plan for growth and spiritual evolvement. Just as we may choose the *kind* of individual we are to be and experience."

THE SIERRAVILLE EXPERIENCE

"I'm referring to the *nature* of our life experience: good, bad, selfish, holy, rich, poor, pacifist, dictator, man, women, long or short lived, yellow, black, tall, short, smart, dumb, blind, sensitive, hateful, creative, single, married... all the many many types of experiences which are possible in one or multiple earthly, or physical lives."

Q: "Choosing to have certain afflictions, is it then possible with enlightened understanding to choose to *change* the experience once in the physical plane? To progress *beyond* the desired experience?"

A: "YES! Although sometimes this may or may not be part of our plan, and healings may or may not be seen or occur."

"Also, some illnesses or afflictions can occur later in physical life as 'attention' getters, and/or, as potential component(s) of our unique plan. Bear in mind that as the incoming vibrations increase, we will observe many spontaneous healings throughout the world. They have in fact begun already. Those that desire wellness *will* manifest those conditions for themselves, and often times without necessarily realizing what they're doing... and it will amaze the doctors who will look for chemical or biological reasons, instead of a spiritually based cause as the correct answer. With the right tools and foundation, even subconsciously, there is unlimited creative manifestation ability of the individual involved."

"As to those which leave this plane early, they are another story, albeit similar with regards to life plan or purpose. Sometimes, we have unfinished business (growth cycles) which need to be completed before we can transcend to more advanced planes of life. In such cases, a person may return to the physical for only a short period of time in order to complete his or her cycle. We may not be aware of our life path because of our usual separation from the knowledge that our Higher Selves (Overselves) retain, but nothing happens to us as individuals without our directly causing it to happen. So rather than questioning certain situations, being mad at God, or saddened by abnormalities or grieving at the loss of physical personages, understand that *we* all make our own path decisions."

"There are the occasional 'true' accidents or mishaps, but they are few and far between. Further, God allows us *whatever* path we need or want to take in order to grow onward and upward in our evolvement as a cosmic individual of the Universe. Illnesses are interwoven and unique experiences. Almost every condition of sickness we know is caused by stress and/or negative feelings. There isn't any real need for illness to exist at all (outside of mandating such an experience for ourselves) but we allow them power by suggestion, negative projections, or allowing our bodies to break down from such things as pressure, guilt, anxiety, fear or tension and stress."

"Negative vibrations will always negatively influence our bodily functions and may precipitate illness or disease. Some of us use disease as part of our plan to come closer together with our loved ones or families before we heal, or exit. Sometimes this is the only opportunity we give ourselves to take the time to comprehend life, reflect on our existence, or make amends with friends or family. Sadly, we may have priorly been to 'busy', never making space in our lives to do so. Then on the other hand, illness can be used as a learning tool. It may allow us to see a bigger picture, exercise a different change of attitude, or take control of our life by utilizing the powers we have available to us."

"I won't suggest that we should ignore the presence of an illness if we get one, but we do have the authority to either succumb or mend ourselves in those situations... By declaring ourselves well and/or by disavowing an illnesses influence over our body. We must remember WE did this to ourselves, no one else made it happen to us. Therefore *we can* undo it! If we claim we are well or healed and *believe* in our statements, then we could see amazing results of this creative energy [of Spirit]... as in the cases of spontaneous healings."

"There, we simply refuse to submit to the illness and eventually it disappears! Our *will* of spirit affects any healing process, without it we could easily wither and potentially, even die. There are many influences (spiritually and physically) as to why and what, if any, illnesses or afflictions we may experience, and just as many reasons why or how they can be uncreated."

Q: "Is physical death, karmatically speaking in terms of the human race, mandatory?"

A: "No! How do you think the term 'ascended masters' could have come into being if this condition were still binding on us? The true reality of physical death is learned. As a child develops they will eventually learn or hear about it or see death occur around them, and because it occurs it therefore becomes permanently ingrained as a reality. Something we have no control of. We learn to accept it and expect it to occur to us eventually. We modify our 'systems' biochemical processes in this manner, and to such an extent that we actually begin dying at an early age."

"Somewhere between 12 and 17 years of age, that's when we have absolute belief in the (un)reality of death. With this unconscious focus and acceptance of thought, we alter our hypothalamus and pituitary glands to no longer produce certain substances which prevent aging and unconditional reforming of the cells and tissues. Thus we create the conditions, which are manifested through *thought*, to fulfill the vibrations we have put into place. The creative brain *absolutely* responds to the beliefs held therein."

THE SIERRAVILLE EXPERIENCE

"A person can 'kick-start' their important biochemical centers by actually giving love to them and talking to them, telling them that consciously they no longer believe in the process of physical death and truly desire that these centers again begin producing the necessary enzymes, chemicals and secretions to prolong life. Thank them for doing so, as if they had never stopped. *Believe* in the process of uncreating an undesirable, and manifesting a miracle in it's place. We can tell ourselves every day that we look healthier, younger and feel better. If we believe it, if we focus on it, it has to happen!"

"We would do well to talk lovingly to the other functions and parts of our bodies as well. A spiritually oriented person is of a great benefit to themselves because they are of the understanding of higher energies and powers, particularly as it relates to infinite possibilities of creative thought and the importance of the removal of *doubt*... An absolute cancer to *all* creative thought processes."

Q: "What of those individuals who are as of yet, unaware of the higher aspects of Life, Self and Spirituality as it concerns the Changes?"

A: "Their subconscious minds may or may not constantly be battling (in turmoil) between the mental/physical aspects of life and self, and trying to interpret spiritual messages or urges it receives. Whether they are or not, they aren't without salvation. The kind of heart, the meek, the gentle, the caring unaware, these souls will be provided for... either by a Higher Consciousness, physical teachers or spiritually advanced BEings when the time is right. The same goes for children; those which haven't *fully* developed a conscience, capability to control their own life (not dependent on others for survival), or understand the concept of assuming responsibility for all their deeds. God knows the hearts of all, and His flock will never be abandoned."

"Concerning adults, what we may see on the outside may never reflect the inner higher self and essence of an individual, only God knows these things. As individuals become conscious of what is occurring and ask for guidance or assistance, His Corps of Light workers will be available to respond to those which *ask* and *desire* it so... Including helping those without direct knowledge of the upcoming transmutation. For the self-fulfilling and self-indulgent unaware, the purposefully and willfully un-enlightened, these people will experience more and more chaos, crisis, emotional distress, mental and physical imbalances, handicaps and in general, dysfunctionality in their lives; Particularly as we edge ever closer to the Apex of the Changes. Of course, this may be part of their plan, but they can modify that plan... whether or not it was part of their original plan to do so. The truly unclean and unspiritual at heart, they may indeed have to endure the 'pangs and lashes' of rebirth to some degree or another."

178

"Unfortunately the Dark Ones, the unlearned, ungodly, unspiritual entities will be attracted to these types of individuals, just as the Brotherhood of Light is attracted to assist those so desiring, on their way to enlightenment and spiritual knowledge. The Dark Forces will precipitate obstacles for us at all opportunities *if* we allow them to, for they desire only to *assist* us in holding *ourselves* back. Again - like attracts like and all it takes is one unspiritual thought to attract their attention. They, as do the Brotherhood of Light, sense their opportunity to work through us by what emotions and thoughts and beliefs we display within our aura, or our cosmic lights, which are known to all etheric BEings. If the aura reflects weakenings of any manner, they can use that dysfunctional energy to gain access to our *emotions* and *thought processes*. It is *vitally* important that you remember this, for to be forewarned, is to be forearmed. Just as the Brotherhood looks for the higher spiritual qualities within our aura to assist in imparting knowledge and wisdom, the Dark Ones do the opposite. You need not fear these entities if you have embraced God and His Principles."

"They **can not** overcome the Power and Light of God, but fear itself only tends to attract them, for it implies weakness within an individual. To truly know God however, is to know no fear... of anything, at any time! These forces of darkness will begin to gather strength and methodically and tenaciously assist in the break-up of business and personal relationships, marriages, friendships and families in the coming times. They have in fact already started their unscrupulous acts. There is only one reason that this is to occur... to propagate disillusionment. If relationships, the foundation of society, are less than cohesive, chaos will prevail. If we are too busy in sorting out our 'heads' and just trying to get through each day, or business, personal or relational tribulation or conflict, or running from life, we won't be able to allot time to our development and spiritual growth. The result will be dimmed Light around each entity so encumbered, and dimmed experiences."

"As for personal [man/woman] relationships of all natures, opposition could begin with simple and insignificant nit-picking. Usually occurring as a result of unresolved conflicts from the past. It might include or progress to possible verbal or other degradation of the 'significant other', with careless ease or (perhaps) no forethought. Eventually one party might find themselves doing what motivates and interests only them, while becoming ignorant of and possibly showing no regard for, or interest in the 'others' feelings. Animosity will precipitate from this. Ill feelings might be internalized by the party 'left' isolated because they may feel ignored and alone, harboring injured emotions of being 'less' important. Eventually conflicts may swell to absolutely unreasonable proportions. Emotions may become so toxic, expectations so high and prejudices so deep, that a split may be inevitable, called for, or possibly occur out of blind intolerance."

THE SIERRAVILLE EXPERIENCE

"Decisions to separate may then be cast in haste and usually won't evolve to be the correct or best one we could have made for ourselves later. We must guard against this by endeavoring to know what is really happening. For many, we won't realize what is occurring to us (even realizing that something *is* wrong) and that we *could* prevent such a circumstance if we applied ourselves. It may just tend to 'sneak' up on us because of various factors, perceived or real, such as past unresolved emotional pains having nothing to do with the present relationship, but *all* negative emotions within us will be amplified by the Dark Ones. We must strive to maintain our relationships through any and all tribulations, for only then can we gain power over those forces which would see us flounder and become isolated. One way to do this is to be willing to discuss the issues at hand - all of them, but not necessarily at the same time. Be willing to compromise and give, be willing to listen and attempt to understand the other persons feelings. People must work together in unity to accomplish this and to resolve imbalances."

"Couples must become as the Tree of Life, solidly rooted in the concepts of love. The 'aware', refer to this as: 'Grounding'. Many people are sadly grounded (focused) in other things in their relationships, such as power, money, materialism, selfish interests, *other* peoples lives and problems etc. Couples most often tend to fail when one or both fall trap to one or more of these unbecoming vices. 'Self' is by far the worst of the bunch. If one decides they are generally more important than their significant other, the 'other' will see or feel that energy no matter how well hidden, and react to it. If one truly feels and flaunts superiority, none of that person's relationships will ever succeed. A relationship must have both give and take... but this must be purposeful behavior based out of love. This simple activity does a lot to insure harmony; understanding does away with disillusionment."

"Some relationships will unfortunately go their separate ways. This however, is how it should be for many. Those truly desiring to advance will choose to let go of those *conditions*, *things* and *people* which would hold them back. They will see the greater importance of the spiritual aspects of life as they seek and find joy, harmony and peace. The 'others' will continue with intolerance, casting blame, producing negative energy, fighting the world, struggling and otherwise only comprehend the painful material world they call their reality. These persons are in great danger of being 'preyed' upon even further. They may never make progress until they are willing (perhaps with counseling) to go back even as far as childhood experiences to resolve various conflicts, feelings and emotions, so they can have a better chance at success in making any relationship as good as it can be. But individually, *we* need to be healed first! If a relationship encounters what seems like insurmountable problems and those involved mutually work toward positive solutions, the tireless effort put forth may be worth the trials and tribulations encountered."

180

"If the relationship is worth something to the parties involved, it *should* be worth fighting for. Has it not been said, 'It is darkest just before the dawn'? How much stronger the relationship will be when the Light is finally allowed in so that it shines through, allowing love to manifest back into their lives and hearts. Once harmony is found, truly found, they will never allow disharmony in their lives again. They will *see!* They will be One."

Q: "Since we are on the subject, in the far and distant past, I twice thought I'd met the right person, but eventually discovered that these ladies were acutely affected from old history which they were very unwilling to resolve. Eventually those pains took their toll in our relationship as they withdrew deeper into what I'll call, their 'real' selves. I hadn't sought out a hurting person, yet I am confused about what other influences could have contributed to my being attracted to these particular women in the first place. There has to be something else I'm not aware of. Initially they showed no signs of any emotional problems, in fact, just the opposite. I saw in them aspects I thought and felt to be important to me, including those of initially being a caring and loving person. I had no idea until several years of being with them that they had so deeply and ingrained past hurts, angers and frustrations. Nobody has ever been able to explain this odd illusion phenomenon of 'perceived compatibility' to me; what did I do wrong?"

A: "Wrong, is inaccurate. They *may* have been part of your life plan, but let's focus on your 'illusion' statement for now. Most couples have the ability to receive and give love if they aren't trying to be someone they're not (in their heart) to the other. Yet at times, because of past experiences, one or both parties can subconsciously become demanding when the eventual 'real' self comes through. Emotional-imbalance looking for a balanced relationship won't work. Emotional balance must be present first. A couple *can* groom a relationship so that it becomes as perfect on earth *as is possible*, but in too many cases it doesn't become a fulfilled reality. We are never taught how to have a loving relationship and many times carry 'baggage' with us into a relationship which can affect the it to the point that it eventually ends, with neither party really understanding what happened. Then having once gone through those losses and tribulations, we may become 'tainted' with adverse feelings. Obviously, these emotional 'mind-sets' set us up for future failure(s). Doing nothing about healing these feelings, we may negatively affect any future relationship we enter into. It happens all the time and it's very sad for all the parties involved because it *doesn't* have to be like that. One must recognize these 'carryovers' and be willing to resolve them. If we don't, we are just kidding ourselves. It will never get better. It usually gets worse as we become more intolerant, impatient, self-centered and unloving. We become exactly those things we *least want to be*, yet through 'hardening' we fail to see that *that* is just what occurs."

THE SIERRAVILLE EXPERIENCE

"When we become willing to acknowledge and resolve these emotions and feelings by wanting to understand them, and work at releasing them, we can heal ourselves and make the best out of any relationship. This can occur even in the *midst* of a 'perceived' bad relationship. But it takes personal effort and far too many people want to hold onto the false image that 'it' is mostly the other person's fault. If we are unwilling to assume responsibility, then we are in denial. If we are in denial, our life will never be better. People in denial tend to be on the move, going going, doing doing, filling their lives with so many things that they don't have to 'think' or 'feel'... they are hiding from themselves, their mates and anyone close to them. Some call these types of people 'distant' or 'removed', or even 'cold'."

"When this occurs in a relationship, it will eventually destroy it because the significant other will usually become a perceived threat to the other's selfish 'survival instincts'. The one 'running' (in denial) knows in their heart that the person in their life is the very one they should be open and honest with. But they *feel* if their special person knew how weak or hurt *they feel* they are, that person may think of them as so, and decide that they aren't worth loving anymore. So people in those positions do not typically share their intimate inner-most emotions or pains. To do so, the one hurting feels vulnerable and that is exactly what they don't want to feel. They may never give consideration to the fact that the other is usually willing to do anything possible to help. Instead, the hurting one pushes them away over time with various methods and excuses, actions and deeds. They may not even be aware they are doing so! The one on the receiving end may have little idea what is going on, but will usually end up feeling less important, slighted, and very hurt at being left out of their significant other's life. When one continues to push someone away, they will probably loose them... sooner or later. The hurting one doesn't really want that to occur, but out of shame or unresolved pain, they (by not seeking new information, getting professional guidance or counseling, and *particularly* by not sharing with their mate) can become so withdrawn that any effort required on their part to obtain insight becomes too much work. They will cause exactly what they don't want to happen, *to happen*."

"A wise one once said: 'Be careful what you ask for, you just might get it!' Many people do not understand the flip-side of this statement. If we focus on something we don't want to actually happen, we can cause it to happen just by *projecting* thoughts on, or towards that subject matter. Conscious or subconscious projections have immense power, particularly in the times we are living in now. Negatively based thoughts do have recourse and can be fulfilled just as easily as positive ones! We need to look inside of *ourselves*, none of us is perfect... *That* is why we are here in the first place!"

182

"When a significant other leaves (from being cast out, or by their own volition), one or both may (think they) feel safe again because they don't have to share or be responsible, they don't have to feel guilt and they can continue a false life - thinking that it is satisfactory, that they are okay, that they can handle it. Absolute denial. Over time, some of these people may eventually believe that they are not worthy of love, and then they will subconsciously insure that it never can, or does take place. These are very empty and very hurting souls. They want more than anything to be needed and loved by another, but are so *afraid* that they shut themselves off. With just the *minutest* pieces of new information, their lives could be greatly changed. Yet, they have to want it; They have to assert *themselves*."

"When the spirit within us dies it can only be revived by *our* personal attention and efforts. If left too long, there may never be a cleansing. If there is no resolve, there can be no love. *Given* OR *received!* I can offer a theorem as to your confusion of thinking you'd found an ideal mate, only later finding that she was emotionally scarred. Since you are a healer, your higher self was in tune to the vibrations of emotion which others have, hold and emanate... all others, male or female, whether spoken or not. In the case of women, you first recognized the facets of importance which you were desiring in a significant other. These being acceptable, your higher self (already being *many* steps ahead of you) and being in tune to naturally desiring to help others and being sensitive to others hurts, jointly affected your decision to form a bond. The latter occurred unconsciously and without immediate knowledge. Because it is in your heart to be able to *feel* and to really want to help when you can, this wasn't a foreign vibration to who you are on the inside. Thus, and again, that action occurred without notice."

"Looking back, you said that you felt you didn't have all the necessary 'tools' to fully groom a relationship, and that you still feel there is more to learn. That's very honest. Many people are unwilling to admit that. We all think we have the proper tools for having a balanced relationship, but very few actually do. Men and women think so differently, and if the other doesn't really know these differences, it can play havoc with a relationship. Men and women need to locate information on the opposite gender to come to a better understanding of how they think and feel. There is a lot of material available today on this, like how we respond to different stimuli, how communication can be made better and how to generate what the other needs. Such as feelings of importance, of respect (they make each other feel that they matter), of knowing the other will be there for them at all times (security) and honor (they are the most important person in the other's life). A couple *must* have *trust* in each other, have *realistic* expectations, and a willingness to say 'I'm sorry', an ability for empathy and compassion, a willingness to bend and to acknowledge, and a desire to be supportive and attentive."

THE SIERRAVILLE EXPERIENCE

"Most importantly they should do these things out of love, not out of falsehood, coercion or force, because if it isn't real (isn't coming from their heart) they will come to detest 'having' to render these things. Those 'tools' as you refer to them, are extremely important for a successful relationship and are greatly enhanced by expanded *conscious* spiritual knowledge, which you now do have. As you continue your seeking out of these tools, your love, your spiritual understanding and your care will make you even more of a healer and loving person. For a relationship to flow properly, one must be willing to work at it. A couple must open up to fully understanding themselves, then the other, *then* what is required in a relationship."

Q: "Why is it that we humans even bother to seek long-term unions with the opposite gender?"

A: "You've heard the term: 'Twin Flame'? This is the *complement* of Light from which we each began. The originating sphere of personality encompassing the Yin and the Yang potentials of the male and female essence, to say it simply. Many refer to it as our soul-mate, as opposed to soul-friend, kindred spirit or eternal companion. There is such an entity for each of us, and that spirit is the perfected other half of who we were when we were created. The love bond is immensely strong and when we part to have our individual experiences, we carry with us an unconscious desire to find and share *that* love and bond with another again. We greatly miss the presence of such a powerful love (part of ourselves IS *actually missing*) and will usually seek out the opposite gender (as they hold the *aspects* of our twin flame which we are missing) in order to create a necessary natural balance and harmony - of completeness within. A desire and search for perfected Oneness."

"That's the largest reason why, when many people experience a relationship go awry... one they have given their entire and complete heart too, they become overwhelmed with immense and absolute pain inside, and to the point they can become deeply depressed and withdrawn, even suicidal. The pain of loss is absolutely real and does so affect the spirit of the person as to be devastating. It goes beyond most onlooker's understandings when they see someone like this. Their first instinct is to think that the person in pain just wants to feel sorry for themselves... this isn't even close to the truth. It feels like a part of them has actually died and they are intensely grieving at that loss. They are not weak people, contrary to what other's might have us believe. They are of the few who truly understand total personal commitment and can appreciate and feel love in the greatest sense. They, like you, may not be aware of all the tools available, may have even become co-dependent, but their natural instincts lean heavily in the direction of desiring solutions and having the capability to love, even when in pain."

"People who do not or can not feel love this deeply usually become hateful or resentful, if not hardened (as their form of expression, release or denial) when a separation occurs with their significant other. The good news is we *will* eventually re-unite with our soul-mate and be completed once again; but in the mean time we must endeavor to interpret and live life in the best and most loving way we can."

Q: "Can you explain why 'time' on the higher planes is not interpreted as we interpret it?"

A: "The reason is somewhat simple. We see things occurring in our life as *multiple single* events, each following another. We apply this understanding to all experiences and aspects of our life, the most influential of these being tasks, employment or work. We live by a clock, so we view time as having attributes of a past and a future, besides the now. In the grander scheme of things, a personality's 'life' experience in any given plane is the only thing that has substance, in relation to the concept of time. The term 'experience' (there) is what is confused with the term 'time' (here), there is no past or future, only the 'now'. Our life in this plane forms a complete cycle, beginning with birth and ending with rebirth. That event is viewed as an *experience*. It is ongoing and therefore has no past or future, no yesterday or tomorrow, just a beginning and an ending, because in between these states we are still *in* the experience. Consider this, an American astronaut circles the earth with his space capsule, going from sun to night back to sun through many orbits, then returns 36 hours later. Obviously he changes time zones and thus dates. You live in India... Between the two of you, did his flight actually start or end, yesterday or today? Did his flight have a today and a tomorrow? It started and ended only once. His trip would be viewed as an *experience* in higher realms, having no relation to a fixed period of duration. Only *we*, add the factor of the passing of that thing called time."

Q: "Can you add more to the potentiality of manifesting?"

A: "The Laws, Premises, Principles, imparted wisdoms, our spiritual understandings and personal utilizations of these, are all factors which precede our success for manifestation. *Every* detail in our life must be right, in balance and harmony, for manifestation to occur in full power and to it's fullest potential. But having these understandings without the fuller comprehension of eternal and infinite Love and the realization that we are of God and therefore without limitation, will deter us from experiencing an expanded reality and it's associated freedoms. Understand however, that we may not witness all of our projections in *THIS* reality. That's not to say we can't, but rather that we may cause certain energy influences on the spiritual or other realms, that can only manifest *in* those realms."

185

THE SIERRAVILLE EXPERIENCE

"Also recognize that due to our personal level of spiritual wisdom and comprehension, that our projections may not manifest as *we* wish them to, nor in the time frame *we* expect them to. There are Higher reasons and influences beyond our grasp and understanding that are involved in results expected or experienced. If we feel we aren't succeeding, maybe there is yet more for us to learn or become aware of, before becoming accomplished with this gift. Also understand, that when we allow God's Will *priority* over all that we project for, there is *nothing* that we can not accomplish in His name. *Every* projection based in love for another is taken into account and duly noted."

"Whatever the result(s), they are for our or another's best good. Remember, we are part of a larger, more complex picture. I can only say, we must be sincere in our projections and base them in love. As it relates to attention for ourselves, we should not desire more than we actually need. There is an unending supply and this we must have faith in. Projections do not have to be a one-time thing, this Jesus demonstrated over and over for us. Project for others out of care and love only. We must do so in the right and proper ways, for the right and proper reasons. Our deep and compassionate heart-felt emotions and proper intent allow our projections the energy to become reality in this plane or perhaps, in other higher planes to be realized later."

Q: "What happens to our attributes when we do physically die?"

A: "That is a good question... Let's start at the beginning. When we leave here, we get to review everything that happened during our lives. We get to see how our thoughts are like the ripples upon the waters, and how our thoughts and deeds impact and affect perhaps many others. Sometimes a 'backwash' (effect) is much larger than we could or do imagine. We also get a chance to feel not only what we did at the time of our actions, but the feelings of all involved, clear down the line."

"This gives us a true picture of what impact we had on ourselves and those individuals, including animals and other life forms, both positively and otherwise! Then after our review, we may decide on a new plan and what to experience, and or what to correct. When or if we return, all prior deeds are left in spirit so as not to affect our present purpose(s). If, as spiritual entities we advance however, our less positive attributes are usually done away with so we are left in a more pristine state. One, more in harmony and balance (of vibration) with the plane we are entering... We may remember the negative attributes and experiences, but the energies are no longer part of our subconscious essence and makeup. Our higher aspects of self and what we have done for others is what we will take with us."

"Our reward to ourselves is heightened spiritual advancement, and this only occurs in the planes after the physical. Advancement is based upon our true nature of BEing and the heart of our spirit. The aspects which depict the character of self and which are rooted in the essence of that spirit."

Q: "Is everything we experience day-to-day a part of our plan for spiritual growth?"

A: "In the most strict sense? No... Overall... particularly as we interface with others, yes. There is a section of our lives dedicated to becoming a learned individual within the physical dimension. How to tie our shoes, how to speak and read, learning a profession, etc... These are experiences mandated for the physical environment only. They have no bearing on the spiritual realm other than one concept... to learn to live together, hopefully in peace and harmony."

"We have full latitude as to what we can experience within the physical world, but to comprehend the spiritual is to vastly increase opportunity and overall experience. We have a plan when we come into being here, certain things we need to or want to experience. Other experiences are 'fillers' and may or may not be part of our plan at all. Like a grape vine, each vine has multiple branches with multiple stocks, each bearing multiple heads of grapes. Wine made from that vine will taste the same whether or not all the grapes are used. The wine being the result of pressing the grapes to extract the essence. Our (wine) essence is the result of what we did with our life; who we became (on the inside) and what we did (outwardly) with our experiences or knowledge. Not all of our experiences will affect our ending review however."

"Incidental experiences like choosing where to have dinner, what color dress to wear, taking a different route to work, choosing when or where to shop or what party to attend, these types of experiences have no affect as to growth. Incidental experiences add flavoring and color to our lives. They are simply lessor experiences we choose to have as a part of being physical. *BUT*, how or why we do certain things may indeed contribute to growth, or cause us to back-step. Intent and motivation are the attributes of self which weigh heavily upon who we a. ., color our essence and highlight our level of spiritual growth. With active exertion on our part and depending on what growth we have left to accomplish, we can make such progress (spiritually speaking) that we need not return to a physical existence, circumventing the need for the same by adding to the present existence, those things perhaps we would have waited to be or do. This accelerated growth may also not have been a part of our initial plan, as we usually don't bite off more than we think we can accomplish, but the potential is always there to *exceed* what it was we set out to do. This again, is our choice..."

THE SIERRAVILLE EXPERIENCE

Q: "Being the inventor type, will you discuss the term invention?"

A: "Invention is considered to be a materialistic (physical) improvement on or in our lives. It is an improvement, technologically, whether the function is a new type of broom, or a new computer. Let me say that concepts, and ideas for concepts, are originally developed in the realms of spirit before finding need or placement in the physical plane. Although it is true that an earthly scientist or inventor is a unique person, we all have the ability for technical innovation."

"It's just that some are more aware of this inner trait than perhaps others. Being more aware, they utilize *expanded* thinking and take opportunities to investigate or explore *possibilities* eluding others. Their minds are more open to seeing *beyond* the contemporary. Due to this, they may reach certain vibratory *states of mind*, creative mind that is, which puts them in a sphere of vibrational energy allowing transcended thought to permeate their subconscious, bringing with it the precipitation of revolutionary thought."

"Even if the new idea is an outgrowth of existing (known) physical concepts, which incidentally is the foundation from whence all creation came... modified step developments from older ideas, it held spiritual form first. All creation starts with a single thought, one which may be well expanded upon before completion, but it all began in spirit. On the physical realm, we can draw upon these cosmic ideas and energies, and utilize them for our benefit when we apply ourselves appropriately. We, have never developed anything which wasn't already conceived to one degree or another in the higher realms. We may modify some of these ideas, perhaps even improve on them, but they belong to the cosmos."

"Spiritual inspiration can and does course through the very veins of those inclined to invent. Through these multiple energies and focuses come wonderful and advantageous ideas. We unwittingly then claim invention on them, and to a certain degree this is accurate, but only as it pertains to the here-now principle."

"They were never ours to start with, *and* you will notice that we never 'invent' something which exceeds our needs, requirements or technology as **proof** that we get only that inspiration which is applicable at the time. Take the silicon chip, or integrated circuit as an example. It began with the development of the transistor in 1947. *Our* conception of functionality only saw this new design as a signal ampifier, then later, as the concept of a solid-state electronic switch. Nobody envisioned microprocessors or multi-functional 'smart' electronic components at the time... These evolved slowly, never exceeding where need or science was."

"As Man continues to spiritually evolve and comes to a better understanding of the Universe at large, even more meaningful and beneficial technologies will come into existence as an outgrowth of mind expansion and awareness. Some of these concepts will take large leaps beyond present understanding, but with cosmic interfacing all that is required to develop these ideas will be made available, actually *bypassing* certain physical steps of mental and physical evolution."

Q: "For some time now I have had interesting thoughts of a telepathic nature concerning new energy developments utilizing the electron and crystals... These thoughts must also be from the beyond!?"

A: "Yes. However they are not exactly the same concept. Concerning the electron, the major point of interest is the vibrational spectrum of the element itself. Science will learn that the effects generated by the associated frequency, velocity and energy, present exciting advantages as it relates to gravity and anti-gravity control, propulsion, communication and fusion. There are various corridors of different types of energy throughout the cosmos. The electron dwells within one such channel and is of very great significance."

"Crystal designs operate in a slightly special manner. The vibration of the crystals' atomic structure itself offers another, yet different channel. As you know today's lasers are focused and extremely brilliant light. This light is 'bounced' back and forth across the length of a polarized, man-made crystal. When allowed to exit the end of the crystal, the light having become even more energized (amplified) is then released with a very precise pattern. We appropriately use such applications for scientific and medical purposes. This is a *passive* use of crystals, not an active one. The *active* form of usage will come about by coupling certain vibrations with a crystal to produce an energy field which will result in communication, healing, light, higher forms of electricity, or even a shield of protection."

"Some of the coupling will be the result of our... I'll use the term 'physical' but only as a reference, interfacing directly with the crystal; others by the influences of the fourth or other dimensions, within and without. Setting up a resonance within it's structure, it will be possible to amplify this 'input' creating a mode of output which far exceeds the casual input. There will also be created, a method for controlling the intensity of the output as this development comes into being. Modified electro-magnetics will also play an important part in one aspect of new energy sources."

Q: "Concerning visualizations for remote healing, can you describe such a process or give an example?"

THE SIERRAVILLE EXPERIENCE

A: Remote healing begins with a desire to help a person who has sustained an illness or injury; the process could simply be: Obtain a relaxing position, close your eyes and engage the White Light. This Light substantially raises the cosmic and creative vibrations around you and amplifies the heart-mind-soul link or love consciousness energy associated with your Genesis Ability. Then ask, if it be His will, to allow God to work through you to heal your entity of focus. This action acknowledges your belief in HIM, and HIS Power. Then send your healing projection to that entity as if you had been granted HIS approval."

"Projections based in Love, will always gain HIS approval. Then visualize that person, perhaps laying in a bed and send him or her a feeling of calm and inner peace. You do not have to know what that entity's bedroom looks like, you already know how these items (generically) appear... indeed, they aren't as important as the visualization of the one in need, which you probably do know in detail. Then send the White Light to them. See it move down, into, through and around them, as you normally would do for yourself. This puts them into the same vibrational atmosphere as yourself, etherically and spiritually connecting you, them and the Source TOGETHER... it is an important and vital link. If you know the location of the illness or injury, visualize that area becoming instantly healed by focusing on the normal physical condition, operation or appearance of that area. If you can, (definitely not a requirement) visualize a bright clear-green light moving in, over and through that area after you have completed your projection for healing. This light may be called upon for cellular healing."

"You may even want to pursue this action with an all encompassing (around your friend, or the one in need) vivid pink light for global healing [emotional, physical, mental, and spiritual] and overall protection of that individual. Or in severe illness or injury, project a bright clear-red for a restored and healthy life-force energy around your friend. The additional projections of the Lights of Life I speak of are not required for the healing process, but these Lights certainly can not impair your effort."

"For some afflictions, you may want to even visualize internal organs, pulsing with vitality and life... it is not necessary that you have the knowledge of a doctor of internal medicine. Visualize and allow only the perception of healthy, glowing cells. Broken appendages (bones) can be healed by the same process. Or in the case of diseases, perhaps you may want to visualize white blood cells that are chasing down and overtaking, even dissolving any intruder cells. Whatever you can visualize for any given need you can make materialize... If you have faith in the process, and it doesn't upset the balance of natural events. By that, I also include the others desire (will) to *be* healed or helped."

190

Q: "How about hands-on or hands-off healing, how does this work?"

A: "The healer has usually prepared by bringing in the White Light and calling upon God, Jesus, the Powers of Heaven or others of the Light for assistance. Whether or not a healing is successful, is primarily predicated on the will and belief of the one of need, as well as what life plans are to be carried out with the involved individuals. A healer knows without doubt that he or she can be successful, as they understand they only initiate a projection, and realize that the healing, if it is to be, is generated and accomplished from a Higher Realm. As healers raise their creative love-harmony vibrations, these energies precipitate through them via the energy vortices of their hands, to be applied on the one of need. Touch isn't mandatory, only proper vibration of Spirit. If the vibration IS proper, it can overcome the stricken vibrations within the individual of focus, bringing their vibrations into balance and harmony. By harmony, I mean the 'normal' state of vibration of healthy cells and structures within the body, even if the affliction had been a life long characteristic or disease. Understand that remote or hands-on healing are identical in the energies which are used. Neither is less capable than the other."

Q: "Concerning the Changes, does the age of the person make any difference as to their ability to take part in the New Age?"

A: "Absolutely not. Excluding innocent children and others and those who are finished with their path on this physical assignment, it only depends on desire and the effort put forth by those now present. Age in general, has nothing what-so-ever to do with partaking in these events. *Every* soul has the possibility of participating... but so many will look the other way thinking they can slide by. It just won't happen that way. No strain, no gain. By that I mean: No effort, no reward... No giving, no sharing!"

Q: "Can any of us totally avoid the approaching changes?"

A: "Not unless you transcend beforehand. The process which is taking place is not an option any longer. All will be changed. The planet, and all things thereof, including those who now inhabit the planet.

Q: "Will you comment on what is referred to as the Rapture?"

A: "This period of time, at least at the present, includes two potential processes: evacuation and ascension. Evacuation would occur as a physical process, as and if the changes are to end up being catastrophic to life itself. Special entities and vehicles will be available for this, to help us into the next realm of life. Ascension is the etheric process where the body as well as the Spirit is lifted into the next dimension of life."

THE SIERRAVILLE EXPERIENCE

Q: "Will the physical now still be physical in the New Age?"

A: "You and I and the others? No. The density of all matter will be modified. Our vibratory states will be of the fourth or possibly greater dimension. We will have abilities much like the original Adam and Eve BEings. Yes, there were more than one... We will see, hear and feel with heightened states of awareness. Much more than what you would call psychic awareness. We will have an immense understanding of the numerous energies around us, what they mean or offer, how to communicate with these energies, and powers of manifestation will be abundant. The necessity for the things of the physical past will not be required, *nor missed!*"

"This includes the necessity for food as we know it. Our primary sustaining energy will come directly from our Source. It *will* be a very different world than this one, and a very exciting one at that. I haven't begun to elaborate on the unique differences from this one, but I can't give it all away you understand; it wouldn't be fair on my part. Beside that, I have no permission to do so. That would greatly exceed my charter and purpose. I *can* tell you that it *will* be worth the effort!"

Q: "Various writings use a term called 'Rays', is that a pseudonym?"

A: "Yes, it is used in a multiplicity of ways to mean one or more unique (separate or collective) channels of: dimension, color, thought, sound, intelligence, Light and/or frequency... particularly, and best understood as *vibration*. The term vibration still hasn't been clearly understood or embraced by the masses yet, so the terms: Ray or Rays are used as a mind-picture 'tool' to attempt to covey some special thought or concept to the reader.

Q: "Can you put into a nut-shell, a definition of: Brotherhood of Man?"

A: "If everyone at one time could see what we were OF, our exquisite bodies of Light, and the purposes of physical and extended life, one would immediately see no further need for negative types of emotions, deeds, thoughts and feelings. Experiences once perceived as negative would no longer be interpreted as such, nor ever needed again. We ARE brothers, even closer than that. We are cosmic family... The Bushmen, the Aleuts, the Indian, the Chinese, the Black, Red, White... We are interjoined at the root of our very being by the *exact same essence.*"

"Experience is the only external 'thing', and our heart the only internal 'thing' which separates us! That is why we are to love our neighbor as ourselves. In the infinite understanding, they ARE we! Can you comprehend that last statement? Not too many can..."

"If everyone really understood that we are all here to learn and grow, we'd be helping each other out the best we knew how or could. Why? Because we'd be helping ourselves, discretely (individually) and globally (Universally). Our individual and jointly made cosmic plans and lives would coexist in complete harmony, speeding spiritual growth quadratically for the whole. Soon transgressions, crime and other anti-persuasions of life would be eradicated."

"But people left to their own devices will develop limited concepts of self and life and with these then make judgments toward life in general and others, unable to see past the reality of an infinite life, the greater self, and why we are here now and what it is we are to accomplish. We become stuck in the quagmire of 'just living' in the third dimension. Sad situation isn't it? We are each Lights of a grander Light, *identical* in essence."

"Our 'outer' natures are developed out of the physical environment we become acclimated to, and they don't (necessarily) reflect the 'inner' us. We then tend to operate from a basis of shadowed-self, ignoring our higher attributes, connections and purposes. Division begins here. Losing touch with the spiritual, focusing on the material, judging another, *or ourselves* keeps us grounded in unrewarding energies, experiences and sometimes, lives. That is part of the reason for the Changes. We need to develop focuses beyond just ourselves and come to realize just how un-different we all really are!"

Q: "How do the vibrational shifts affect those of lessor beliefs, or those without knowledge of what is occurring?"

A: "Those 'tied' blindly to the physical will wonder if they are getting sick at times, and at the very least, become confused with and about these odd experiences - especially as the vibrations increase in intensity. There is no way to escape sensing these step-changes, nor is there anything anyone can do about them. There is no medicine one can take to alter the conditions one is feeling, and if one 'fights' the feelings, they will only intensify them (in a negative sense) within themselves, perhaps actually to the point they *make* themselves sick as a subconscious response to the conditions. Being sick is acceptable, tangible and seemingly real. So if they alter their systems to such a degree that sickness prevails, then that situation is better understood, even acceptable, but they have missed the proverbial boat... Yet perhaps they were suppose to... *remember?...*"

Q: "Are there any other odd side-effects which may be noticed by us during the present vibrational shifts?"

A: "Yes. Remember that the density of all things is changing. The vibrational frequency of all matter is rising. Cellular changes are occurring."

THE SIERRAVILLE EXPERIENCE

"This precipitates an effect of physical 'lightness' many times, as well as perhaps the unduly 'heaviness' of certain situations or emotions. People may experience time passing more quickly than before, or that they feel an urge to know more or do more, or have trouble making decisions. Also episodes of momentary Higher Illumination may occur. What one may experience, is a brilliant White Light and a magnificent presence of Love. During these moments these people will be totally oblivious to the physical world, entirely swept up by the etheric experience. Important knowledge or information may precipitate during such an experience which may be relevant to the one in the experience, or it may concern others, or even the world."

"Also, one may occasionally experience (peripherally) seeing flashes of light(s), shadows or movement where nothing *should* be; witness white columns of light(s) during the day or night, distantly rising from the ground into the heavens where there should be no lights, some of these columns may be quite wide and even contain one or more soft colors; feel a coldness and/or an electrical charge in the air that passes through them, or which they pass through (which is not stationary) and comes and goes; feel flutters or earthly tremors or movements which others nearby fail to sense; and hear low, or mixed low and high frequency sounds which are akin to a frieght train slowly passing in the near distance (possibly with a whistling 'wind' sound effect) where no tracks lie... and the sound can never be pin-pointed. Another interesting sensation will be the occasional ability to sense energy, or vibrations from all manner of objects, including other people."

"Expect to witness many wonderful and amazing things. When they occur, one should attempt to shift his or her focus beyond the physical effect(s), they should try to become one with the energy... by opening up to it at the moment it is sensed. There is much to be learned and beheld. Raising our vibrations by immediately focusing on the White Light may allow visions or glimpses of the extrodinary world(s) which surround us (all the time). Sensing the unique vibrations and energies (which are going to vastly increase in individual observance in the future) will prepare some minds for transformation, by broadening their belief systems via personal experience! Yet, if we get too engrossed or preoccupied with the unknown or spiritual 'effects,' we may miss the lessons still awaiting us in this fading dimension. We *should* however be paying intuitive attention... *Expecting* to have new experiences, increases the opportunities to *have* those experiences, by belief that they *can* happen... Left brain reprogramming. We must live in the present, continuing with our normal lives, but be cognizantly aware of, and open to the changing energies around us and potential input from the universe. Although it is much easier said than done, we should attempt to maintain a balance between our physical and spiritual interests for a while longer; we *are* still physical, yet we will discover how to mix these energies as we expand."

194

Q: "What do you see as being 'in the way' of the many desiring something different today, desiring spiritual growth?"

A: "We usually learn how to be self-sufficient, yet we typically grow up in a co-dependent society. It starts with our parents. When a child asks a question, the parents have all the answers, even if the answers aren't what the child wants to hear. The child will learn to embrace much more external information than he or she will ever learn to develop from within. There arises the attribute of seeking answers from someone other than themselves. When it comes to the spiritual, they MUST learn to seek answers from within, how to listen *for* their inner-voice so they can respond *to* that information... Then the educational teachers fill in the next steps of our co-dependency. I'm not casting slings and arrows here, just trying to show how we may loose sight of, and possibly confidence, in ourselves."

"As adolescents, we shift, to typically get our answers from outside of the immediate family and our instructors. We start becoming independent, yet still search for most answers from other sources. As adults, we perhaps get too many of them from books, articles, peer groups and friends. We are trained by this time to be focused at finding 'truth' from outside of ourselves. This 'fall-out' may attribute to some of us being less emotional (having at best, shallow emotions) because we have never spent time developing these attributes... by taking time for ourselves - to 'find' ourselves - to 'feel'. Many may never take the effort to derive answers from within, and this is the *most* important thing we can do for ourselves concerning spiritual growth. The answers are always there, but we must get accustom to searching *internally* instead of externally. Reading or going to a medium or others can definitely help in the information obtaining process (*IF WE ARE READY*), but if knowledge is just given (taken) without the experience of achieving (earning) it, it will more than likely be useless, impotent and therefore remain distant and untouchable, perhaps even unbelieveable. Pure truth will come from within and be ushered forth by spiritual development and evolvement."

"People expecting spiritual knowledge to be handed to them on a 'silver plater', then expecting proficiency with it, will be disappointed... Nothing much will come of such information. Giving someone the equation for 'Pi' would be useless, unless they first understood what it meant, and then what they could do with it. The same principle works here. Also, many will need to work at changing their view points, personal and emotional attributes, as well as learning to respond to input from their higher selves. Growth, expansion, wisdom, insight and abilities come from earnest labor of the heart, mind and soul. Further, cosmic truth and understandings manifest with an honest commitment to exceed the concept of the Me-Me, I-I self. Man in general, needs to learn to reach down to help others by teaching and sharing, instead of soley reaching up to others to expedite only his knowledge."

THE SIERRAVILLE EXPERIENCE

"Another stumbling stone of spiritual growth concerns power. When will common man quit being so stubborn? We stand alone and growth stops when we declare that: 'only I am right concerning this...' Dominance and struggles come about when our personal ideas, theories or concepts 'rub' with anothers immovable point of view, by our forcing them on another. Intolerance and impatience usually follows. Some forced 'notions' will be crys for attention from insecure individuals, as negative attention is better than no attention in their understanding, but the majority of such situations arise from some not having the ability to accept new or different methods or information without judging who is more right. If some people can't properly deal with physical world debates of 'rightness' or better, how can they hope to deal with the *vast* concept of the spiritual world, let alone find truth?"

"Also, people can no longer ignore the various facets of their lives which generate feelings of unhappiness, incompleteness or which leave the impression of being 'quagmired' or experientially immobile. When a person is dealing with such emotions, the result is that those emotions will affect *all* the other areas of their lives, including both the desire for, and actual growth, expansion or change. They should resolve all areas of contention before striking out on a new path, *whatever* that path is. Thankfully, more and more people are seeking support groups and supportive environments so that they might mend themselves, as well as finding camaraderie in the ever developing area of spiritual awareness. Keep in mind what is occurring with the changes... Transformation brings with it, the leaving behind of the lower emotions and attitudes of physical Man, and urges the replacement or enhancement of those attributes with higher, more spiritual states of awareness, concern and consciousness."

Q: "Today more and more technology is being made available to ease our lives, what does this 'movement' represent to you?"

A: "I feel this movement, as you refer to it, began eons ago... Once there was a generation of spirit-beings with cosmic and powerfully creative minds, and thought alone could produce whatever results were necessary for co-existence of the Spirit in the physical domain. When Spirit transitioned from the higher realm, eventually becoming rooted in the physical, we misplaced that creative or genesis ability. Misplaced, not lost, by our intense focus on ourselves as absolute, within our now physical environment. Creative-mind manifestation remember, represents the finest (highest) type of creative process, while the physical development of 'tools' or conditions represents the lowest creative process (labor intensive, cumbersome, densest, imperfect). At one time we could simply 'think' a thing, condition or process into being, fully developed... then after the Fall, as you know, we were left to our own to try to accomplish."

Q and A

"It was a physical world, and therefore we had to develop physical processes. The modern-day gadgets of these times, represent material and temporary replacements for creating conditions of what was once able to be accomplished by the power of the creative mind; physical simulations of etheric processes or effects. We push a button on a device and something happens, instead of thinking of a desired effect, and it occuring... It's somewhat humorous when you see the larger picture. We have buttons for light, music, cooking, automation, door openers, environmental conditioning, communications, alarms, etc, etc. yet we aren't even close to a midway point between the vastly different processes of physical labor, and applied creative mind, to accomplish some 'thing' or task. Think of the wonder of being able to create a soft rain shower outside and the floating scent of gardenia or jasmine at your home, or manifesting a wonderful piece of art, or enjoying pleasant music flowing all around you with the non electrical lighting set at any level you desire... all by the power of creative mind! We are headed in that direction by evolvement and transformation, even now!"

Q: "How can a person tell the difference between: receiving input of a higher nature, and our physical minds' activity, when we get a random thought as an answer to some question, or as an urge to do some 'thing'?"

A: "Messages from our higher self, or even spiritual entities contain emotions of peace, harmony, balance and resolve. These messages may also bring the initiation of some form of action on our part which will be the right or proper course of action. Remember physically speaking, our minds are used to relating to physical stimuli and experience *only*, and therefore can become confused as to the proper course of action from a random thought, especially if there is a factor of spiritual energy involved. We very commonly misinterpret spiritual input and resolve to take some other, less effective course of action. The physical (logical) mind [left brain] can place limitations on best using the data obtained by weighing it's potentiality, impact, method of implementation, urgency or reality. Our logical mind will try to analyze most, if not all messages, and this may lead us to ignore certain input, take no action or make erroneous choices."

"The logical mind may also create mixed emotions, causing confusion as to a direction we should pursue, by taking in to account only the *potential* physical effects of a *fulfilled* random thought as *we* think it should be fulfilled or as *we* see the ramifications, ignoring the possibility of spiritual involvement altogether. If we aren't open to the spiritual, we won't 'hear' the most proper course of action. A spiritually based thought, no matter whence it originated, will always contain the right answer, proper course of action and cause no confusion... unless we analyze the input as to it's merits, or reference it to our physical world of reality and knowledge."

197

THE SIERRAVILLE EXPERIENCE

Q: "If the future hasn't happened, how can one 'see' into it?"

A: "We all created, or set up conditions for our particular life path prior to coming here, and continue this creative process while we *are* here. All creative thought energies are in the ether and may be fully or semi-developed. The probable 'future' holds all of these conceptions... developed by ourselves, singularly, and collectively. New ones are always added, old ones modified. Some remain as was previously conceived, some fall away. They are always able to be sensed, viewed and/or interpreted by any number of individuals, including ourselves. The 'future' is a particularly hard thing for most to comprehend. It is a *probable* reality, I believe I've already shared that; It has various avenues of being realized because people can and do change, thus possibly altering the planned, subconscious or foreseen event(s)."

Q: "What of the near future, like sensing something is wrong and avoiding a 'situation'?"

A: "You just said the magic word - *sensing*! One aspect of your developing higher self is that it acts as a cosmic antenna, sensitive to all thought activity, particularly to that which is counter to your essence and even your path, and therefore it may warn you to avoid, IF you're paying attention. This has nothing what-so-ever to do with 'seeing' into the future."

Q: "Jesus once said 'In my Father's house, there are many mansions' and, 'I am in this world, but not of this world.'... what did he mean by these two statements?"

A: "He was attempting to confer knowledge. Think about the era of all His wonderful messages and how difficult it would have been to make Man of those times understand the higher principles of *non-physical* Law. He used the only verbiage he could in an attempt to let them 'see' a bigger picture. As to the first statement, He simply shared that there were vast and differing communities of spiritual beings, within vast and multiple planes of extended life, that life continues on and in many realms; that it does not stop here, and there is far more awaiting us as we develop our spiritual awareness and lives."

"As for the latter statement, He was exclaiming that he was not absorbed by the physical environment, so as to become 'stuck' or 'blinded' by it's activities or effects; that He recognized his higher purpose, plan and origin. Jesus also recognized that being a transcended BEing, He was sharing experience on this plane for a fleeting period of time, as we ALL are. Our temporal shells, or bodies, are composed of earthly compounds, our souls of etheric Light... Our physical form houses our cosmic essence and eventually returns to the earth, yet our soul, our personal essence lives on. We also are, in the most comprehensive sense: in this world, but not of it."

Q and A

Q: "What is the most dramatic social effect these times bring, as it concerns each of us as individuals?"

A: "Society balks at different, progressive or conflictual thought. Persons rendering information which 'tips' the boat of acceptability, or which rubs against standardized thinking are many times labeled activists, trouble makers or radicals, among other defamatory names. The great and awesome spectrum of Spirituality is and will continue to cause many waves within society, especially from those of un-enlightened authority. People in general are afraid of what they do not understand, and as history has shown time and again, they will attempt to verbally or even physically squash those involved in any unorthodox activity. Resistance to information which brings 'power' to individuals is even greater when either the Church or the government is involved, so it is possible we could witness abuses of the spiritually inclined in the future. I suggest that everyone pray for this world and their fellow man, that his consciouness be elevated to know higher planes of thought, that cosmic understanding comes to him that is without, and that Divine Love becomes a fundamental attribute of those lacking it, that Spirit may be embraced by those failing to know of it."

"These times bring with it, the drawing together of like-minded souls, whether the impetus is for light or dark energy, thoughts or behavior. There is a parting of the planet taking place, a division occurring between the ranks, and it will continue to grow as the concept of Spirituality takes even a stronger foot-hold. This is a natural divison, and as it should be... for many here today are not necessarily going to take part in the New World tomorrow. We are not without conflict yet, and this will be of the last we are to endure. Many could lose friends, family ties, jobs and freedoms while pursuing the spiritual aspect of life. Yet, sad as it may outwardly appear to be, they will be losing nothing. They will in fact be gaining everything the universe has to offer!"

Q: "What is your greatest concern of these last days, as it were?"

A: "Firstly, the charlatans which will come out of the woodwork... 'Know of them by their deeds' said Christ. Those attempting to gain control of peoples lives and resources by promising that which they can not deliver, or telling them what they want to hear if they give up everything and 'follow' them! Those who make a mockery out of Spirituality by knowingly taking advantage of others earnestly seeking answers. Those jumping on the 'band-wagon' for the sake of a dollar and sensationalism only. They have no concern for their fellow man and yet they will sway many before Truth reigns again. This is where people really need to ascertain whether or not the information offered is in their best interest. There is only one God, and he makes no deals, charges no dues and controls no-ones life!"

199

THE SIERRAVILLE EXPERIENCE

"Granted, many 'sharers of the truth' (writers, teachers and practitioners of the holistic/metaphysical/spiritual) are very spiritually adept, grounded and focused, and have all of humanity's best interests at heart. I don't refer to these individuals by any of my previous comments. The living they make is by *helping* others at *reasonable* charge, not by taking advantage of them by demanding outrageous fees or forcing the fulfillment of inequitable obligations. Buyer be wary: Truth is serene; Hesitation, may be a warning."

"Secondly, the growing movements of those focused in hate, intolerance and power. These people feel that they don't belong or that no-one cares about them, so they've sought out others of like-mind to form a 'family'; Somewhere to go, something to believe in and belong to. All they really want is to be accepted and to feel as if their lives matter. Unfortunately, they've been blinded by wrongful motivation. Humanity has enough conditions to correct without the additional problems of this inner-societal cancer... Starvation, health, employment, energy, pollution and the extinction of animals and fauna. Imagine what good they could render in the world if they put their overzealous energies into one or more of these fields."

Q: "If in the Golden Age, Man is of a higher vibratory state and no longer being physical as we know it, how will babies be made, or will they?"

A: "Yes, there will be creation of the young, although not necessarily by all 'couples'. Conception will be a highly spiritual act, the intense union of loving personalities, utilizing their higher creative energies only. There will be no need for bearing or delivering them, suckling, for internal evacuation or any other requirements now mandated for the physical process. The young will come into being at a more developed stage. Not the infants we now know, who need constant protection and attention, who must have everything done for them. The Golden Age young will be able to carry on for themselves, and very well I might add. Family will still be family however, this will not change, yet the relationship *will* change somewhat. People will understand where they came from, and what they are of. Children, as it were, will no longer be viewed as belonging just to the family into which they were 'conceived'. In fact, no-one will feel this restriction any longer. Of course there will be the natural bonds of a 'typical' family environment, but the isolation between entities, families and others will have been done away with. Everyone will feel integral to the larger and more loving 'picture' of belonging to the *family* of God."

Q: "Will *you* be among us in the New Age?"

A: (He coyly grins) "*Perhaps...*"

And So Ends My Experience

JOURNAL 10

"TABLETS OF LIGHT"

Author's Comment: I have seen the odd metalized tablets, heard the voices and witnessed the visions. The many messages offer insight, wisdom and guidance (instruction) for experiencing a transcended world. In a way it's sad that this knowledge has not been presented sooner, but perhaps since the world is suffering and looking for answers, maybe now we are really ready to examine information which is in our best interest. Knowledge which will allow us to expand beyond ourselves, ushering forth a spiritual homecoming with our Creator. Will Mankind take heed of the precious knowledge contained herein? Will we use it? That remains to be seen, but an enhanced world must begin with each of us, and I believe it will come whether or not we individually pursue our own growth, or learn the greater meaning of Love.

What I am about to disclose, was granted to me to do so only because it was felt that the *masses* must now have access to this information. Priorly retained and shared among only small assemblages of spiritually oriented human beings, these messages were kept secluded by them as it was recognized that the information would surely cause great disharmony in many religious sectors and philosophical circles of 'educated' Man of the time. This measure prevented the revered information from being subjected to blind and or purposeful ridicule and possible interpretation as dissension. The bearers understood that in *general*, Man wasn't ready to hear or work with this material yet. Now, whether or not we are ready for this knowledge, I was told it must be presented. As accurately as possible, we have recreated, assembled, and contemporarily edited excerpts from several of these accountings of knowledge for you. A few tablets felt to be of immense value and importance were left in near-pristine format and verbiage.

THE SIERRAVILLE EXPERIENCE
TABLET 1

Vibrations of Alpha VII, Book of Oneness:

Behold WE say unto you. Imagine your cosmic assemblage of Lights as all you know to be of yourself. You are without particular form other than the radiant essence of your BEing. That you have immense powers of creativity and latitude therein, answering only to yourself for your creations. You have thereby, the ability to perceive and manifest your creations in many ways and upon many planes. You as an overseer, must maintain position on the uppermost realms of vibration, yet you at one moment desire to experience the many diversified other realms.

Would you not if you could, send a creation of thought to be made manifest in those other realms, therein to experience what you have created? And would you not if you could, create multiple sub-forms so as to extricate even more experience? Would you also not give free expression unto your forms that they may operate without direct intervention, thusly enabling variation upon your themes. Would this not cause joy and excitement within yourself? This, the Father has done; and many many times it has been done by his seed. All Humankind and Man throughout the cosmos originated from the same mortar. Derivations generated only as to Divine Plan. All personalities are of the One. All of the same consciousness, yet free as to expression. You, dear ones are of the most extremely gifted and distinguished entities in all creation. Accept your rightful station and awesome essence. Radiate as threads of Life then, a garment of Light of the greatness whom you are, in your Creators name.

TABLET 10

Vibrations of Alpha I, Book of Remembrance:

Brethren of this wonderful sphere, rejoice in the knowledge that you are not alone in the Lights of the cosmos. That which fills the void of the everlasting with a vastness of creation on many planes. On this plane, you have unto to each of you, powers and capabilities transcending the physical world which you interpret with unknowingly clouded hearts and minds.

WE, called the Fifth Assembly of Voices of the Celestial Books of Truth, are at all times available to you as counselors and mentors. What WE impart, is Light. That, which ascends the darkness of melancholy manipulation of the Laws. WE are with you even now.

The pristine physical form from which you began, brings with it all manner of creative phenomenon. These abilities are not bound by temporal restrictions and are administered by free will. There many times occur, chasms in the webbing between Truth and manifestation. Separation of Source by intent. Creation comes into being which limits functionality or purpose. Ultimate detachment from higher vibration is inevitable as a result of tampering with selfish motivation. That characteristic energy of self, which vanquishes the Divine ethereal residue from the essence of Terra-Man. Especially recognizable in that which dilutes the Spirit by means of self importance.

WE make hail to you, that you might come to understand all which you have brought upon yourselves. Neglect of Truth, neglect of the Laws, neglect of purpose. Neglect of the Light. Where indeed, are you? Lost you are, in the tides of self righteousness and indiscretion. WE appeal to you, How many aeons will it take until you truly see, until you truly feel, until you truly BE[come] that which binds you with the consciousness of the I AM?

In your sorrows and in your grief you look in directions which can bear only transient solution, if [even] that. Seldom is there recognized a Higher Cause. [And] when sought out, you call upon a Source you no longer know. The misplaced wisdom of your ages has tarnished this perception and connection. Have you so soon forgotten of what you are? Of whence you came? Of what you are to accomplish? Of what is the purpose of this life?

You, dear entities, have been witness to the creation of many universes. You have walked among angels and communed with celestial bodies of paradise. Do you remember nothing? Can you not feel, if only occasionally, the inner tugs of higher self? Those wails of etheric knowingness which desire to guide [you]? Crying out for [your] request to do so... Can you not hear them?

Can you not see beyond your own shadow? Your own personal condition? The conditions cast upon the face of your Earth by your own hand? Do you not see where it is leading? The signs are all around you, yet you are blind to them. All that through the ignorance of Terra-Man, has he done, he can undo! It is in respect of your forgetfulness that WE leave these panels.

Do not be remorsed, WE are not among you to judge. WE come to bring remembrance. WE come to free you with knowledge misplaced. WE come with extended hearts that you might seize this opportunity for growth.

WE come that you can not say in the twilight which edges ever nearer, that you did not know.

THE SIERRAVILLE EXPERIENCE
TABLETS 12-24

Vibrations of Alpha III, Book of Means:

You have in your grasp, the answers. But first you must recount your steps. You must remember that you are indeed greater than your physical world and revere the I AM, the Source of All That Is. In That Which IS, you have been given marvelous powers of manifestation. Yet you must reembrace faith. Faith in the seemingly unimagined, unknown fields of vibration, in God and of course, yourselves. WE unfold for you the elements known as Universal Premises. Give no attention to the order WE confer them to you, as [the] order is not important. Only their messages have substance for you.

The first WE shall speak of, is called **The Premise of God**. What or whom is God? Are you also, creator gods? The Supreme One, the I AM, is understood best as a Universal and Spiritual Thought Energy. He is neither male nor female, yet both... and greater than either. The term HE is commonly used by you to refer to that Great Presence, so WE too will use it.

This Presence does not sit in some great chamber, upon bleached stone waiting for you to arrive so He can issue judgment. He is a collective and superior thought energy who's vibration does however reside and permeate throughout the entire Cosmos, or Super-Universe. HE is the epitome of Pure Love. All giving, all understanding, all compassionate, all allowing, all knowing and all powerful. HE simply IS.

HE, is Divine Consciousness of immeasurable wisdom, peace, harmony, and creativity. HE exists far beyond your interpretation and comprehension, much like your ancient Man would feel if standing next to you; yet HE is beyond physical limitations in all aspects. The radiant and cosmic Love energy emanating from His BEing is so powerful, that you could not look upon Him directly. This is because you have yet to grow spiritually enough to be able to behold or be in close proximity to that type of dynamic love energy.

Your collective vibratory fields are now so removed and distant, not in a physically measurable length, but rather the quantitative type of energy from each other, that third dimension physical Man at your present growth level would simply be overwhelmed by the intenseness and power of that Divine Love Energy. His radiance is vastly superior to anything you can imagine and simple words alone can not fully explain the end result of such a meeting, if one were to take place. You, as well as WE, are extensions of his ISness and creation.

He does indeed work through lessor, but accomplished spiritual entities termed creator gods, which in turn work through and for the benefit of others below their established abilities and energy levels. How many levels there are is beyond even our knowledge, yet they do exist. When HE created the Super-Universe with it's many tributary sub-universes which team with abundant and magnificently different life and environments, He instilled part of his consciousness, HIS ISness, into what He called Man. The creation of Terra-Man was eventually proposed and adapted from prior conceptions. That special order uniquely created and destined to experience all realms ushered in by His breath. In all creation, no other life-form has been so wonderfully privileged. Not even WE.

Man is not limited to what you have been taught he is. He exists in many forms throughout the Super-Universe. Some look very similar to you, some appear quite differently than you, with many existing in physical bodies and many having other forms beyond physical limitations. But each is adapted to his own world perfectly, by design of the Grand Creator. Are you also creator gods? Yes you are, but you fail to accept or recognize that facet of yourselves because of your distant separation of Spirit.

The abated term god, by no means presumes absolute likeness to God, the Almighty. Rather, it boldly announces the fact that you are divine creatures, made in His image, ratified by your Jesus and thereby, do have similar abilities as allowed for by your level of spiritual wisdom and comprehension. Man does have dominion over all things, which includes abilities of manifestation. This attribute is rooted in that essence known as your Body of Lights, or your Higher-Self forms. To use this great gift, one must employ interpretations of infinite mind and pure consciousness, with the results only being witnessed to the extent that you believe this gift is available. Most of you have lost this direct knowing and learned to believe that you can not and do not have such a capability.

The second fundamental axiom is called **The Premise of Divinity**. You [Mankind] are all Divine creatures, blessed with extraordinary talents and capabilities. You are god-like, being conceived in His image. You are in fact, cosmic creature creations or lessor deities of the Supreme One on an upward path of spiritual growth, with a deep subconscious yearning to go home. Yet you discount these inner feelings, even hardening yourselves against them.

To many, these words will be as a verification. Others may refuse to acknowledge this distinction and possibly call it blasphemy. This is indeed sad. To disregard and ignore your God Presence is to accept that you are less than you really are, to renounce yourselves; inevitably, renouncing God.

THE SIERRAVILLE EXPERIENCE

WE do not suggest that you are on a level comparable with the I AM; God exists above all else. What WE expound is that you are of God, and thereby through HIS Great Perfection and Love did He grant and instill into you, like abilities which empower you to accomplish in similar fashion. In order to utilize those gifts, you first have to believe you truly are made in His image and believe that these abilities were instilled into your bodies of Light, or your spiritual life-forms. As your true life-form is etheric, or spiritual, when you incarnate into physical form you then develop mental processes to maintain and control that form. But the physical form is only a structure which temporarily houses part of your consciousness. This form allows you to experience this dimension and express creative thought in this plane of life. Nothing more... without a better understanding. Yet, there is more!

All you need do to experience it, is refocus your thought energies, adjust your convictions, have faith and exert yourselves, and you must WANT to. If you could but only remember your true essence and from whence you came, you would each behold yourself as a great being of Light and creative intelligence. You are all of this coding and design, there are *no* exceptions. You would witness your true divinity and see others for what they truly are. Divinity is always yours, and always with you. The extent to which you experience divinity on the physical plane then, is only up to you. Your growth toward expression of your divinity in the physical is achieved through spiritual understandings, utilization of Universal Laws in the right way, and is solely your responsibility and choice.

The third axiom is called **The Premise of the Overself**. Your Overselves are of the etheric consciousness from whence you came, your true cosmic identity. One extension of your Overselves, is your mind. A reality conditioner, interpreter and controller. Your conscious minds are of transcended thought which at or just prior to birth, become one with those physical bodies that they might have intelligence and share in the wonders of this plane of existence, with capabilities and powers beyond this plane. Without this Overself capacity, you would be little more than a physical body created by a physical process... truly no more intelligent, capable or expressive than an automaton. The greater part of your Overself exists in the etheric. Always part of you, yet non-physical in nature, so removed from your normal awareness. When you sleep or in many cases of meditation, you may reconnect with that greater part of your consciousness.

Yet for the most part, you may remember nothing of the experience[s] or fail to recognize that it has occurred. With effort however, one can consciously reconnect with that superior part of yourselves and remember. Your Overselves retain all knowledge of past lives and of life beyond.

If you would give credence to this and make an effort to directly communicate with your Over-Self, you could bring important spiritual knowledge and wisdom back with you when you leave your meditative states, or awake into the physical again. Others have done, or actually do this, and with practice you can also. To be truly cognizant of that higher part of your Self, is to be directly in touch with the reality of your God Presence and His cosmic endowments.

The process of reuniting, results in Awakening. Yet certain Divine gifts, such as manifestation, are not allowed full potential of power by the simple desire of purely mental and physical entities, as there is no spiritual understanding which allows structured and proper utilization of these wonderful and awesome capabilities. Only through the continued process of enlightenment and BEcoming, are more of these gifts made available, and in a more unrestricted way. As you grow spiritually, you will often times get glimpses of your abilities. Such as consciously or subconsciously manifesting into your lives something you need, or in the successful and unexplained healing of another. These capabilities grow as you grow, that is a Cosmic Law. Your objective then, is to become god-like in all that you think, do, or say. Doing so ensures you full potential of your Divine Rights as Sons and Daughters of God, as was granted you from the Beginning.

The fourth, is called **The Premise of Genesis Ability**. This super-creational, elevated-thought, matter-manipulation ability has been referred to as The Breath of God. This is synonymous with His breathing life into what is called Man, or even the heavens. His calling into being, a thought. This super-etheric protoplasmic phenomena is an immaterial cause and limitless effect action of the super-consciousness of mind. A fantastically real process stemming from the manipulation of creative thought energy.

You also have this capability but slightly differing, now partially extinguished, due to where Man is in his Spiritual evolution. Consider the process as focused thought, which controls the etheric-formulation of the necessary cosmic-elements; Which, by the action of drawing together and the binding and manipulation sequence, allows for a completed expression of a given thought. One level of expression then, may be for a physical result. Of course, the finished expression isn't limited to only the physical domain. The dimensional realm for completion is decided upon by the creator of any given thought.

Genesis Ability is a qualitative thought-energy capability the Creator endowed various beings throughout all levels of the Super-Universe with, which if applied properly, can bring together the hidden essences of the necessary atomic or other elements required to fulfill a manifestation process.

THE SIERRAVILLE EXPERIENCE

This action is the creative foundation behind everything born of the Super-Universe. This divine creative ability also allows one to alter events based upon time and space elementals, physical conditions seemingly controlled by physical processes as well as providing for healing, or other positively oriented needs. This ability is that thing, from which substance is created from nothingness with, and it's utilization has no limitations as to results. The process can never run dry or be depleted, it simply IS. Through positive power of thought one can animate or bring into being from the unseen, a finished result of creative thinking.

It is one's properly focused faith-consciousness-projection, released to transcend dimensions of vibration, which is the catalyst that commissions the cosmic forces, if it be one's desire, to create a physical, or other thing. Genesis Ability is forever available and anyone hearing these words, can utilize this Divine gift through love-thought transmission, for the purposes of creation, healing or manifestation. However, you must first understand the principles behind thought projection, how to engage the process properly and most importantly, believe it exists for your use.

The fifth concept, is referred to as **The Premise of I AM**. *I AM*. This is a powerful statement. It absolutely proclaims that you *ARE*. You typically only know yourselves by who you see in surface reflection, what you think about yourselves and possibly what others express about you. This is all locked into the now in physical, mental and emotional terms... the least important aspects of who you really are.

The concept of I AM reaches far beyond these simplified ideas. You are a spirit-being on an individual journey, on a path of BEcoming... learning to BE. That is, to fulfill yourselves as Divine entities which emanate love and joy, and utilize the knowledge and wisdom of your God given abilities for the positive and spiritual advancement of life, free from the leg-irons of the concept of SELF.

Experiencing all that you truly are, infers a firm understanding of the concept of Infinite Mind or truly unrestrictive thinking, and linking up directly with the God Presence within you. When you have fully attained mastership over your perceived world, you cease to be limited by any physical handicaps, you need not age and you can control every aspect of your totality. You can even escape all known physical laws and move in and out of other dimensions of life by will alone.

Of course, these abilities are developed and evolve over what you refer to as time and are predicated on such things as love, wisdom, and the desire to transcend beyond the limiting and shallower concepts of the: I for ME, self.

Routinely affirm to yourselves, I AM... I AM Love, I AM Light, I AM Peace, I AM Harmony. I AM Balance, I AM Joy, I AM Compassion, I AM Gentleness... I AM Truth, I AM Divine, I AM Foreverness, I [AM] exist[s] beyond space and time. I AM, I AM, I AM. Reiterate it until you understand how powerful and important the statement of I AM is, and believe it. Then state it even more. You are a part of a larger and most Divine scenario. You are not limited to your physical bodies. The breadth of your ability to perceive, acknowledge and believe, are the types of mental conditions that will either hinder you, or allow you total freedom to share expression in the greater meaning of BEing.

The Premise of Truths, is the sixth axiom. There are a great number of learned, terra-bound truths which you all hold as real and meaningful. These are considered to be Personal Truths. Cosmic Truths are those which are consistent, transcendental and fundamental spiritual realities based in Divine fact. Whereas personal truths may or may not be based in fact, which is perfectly acceptable. Cosmic Truths are unwavering, strong, reliable and repeatable... they simply ARE. Cosmic Truths are forever and contain the wisdom and knowledge which allow you to understand what Life is really all about. Many Cosmic Truths can be used to form the premises for living a Divine life. Each entity learns about life in their own way, formulating their own truths and then ultimately, you express these beliefs through some form(s) of action. Action is the doing, the expressing and utilization of your accepted truths. To know and not do is a travesty, the intimate lessons have not truly been learned.

What each of you embraces as a Cosmic or Personal Truth, is done with your own understanding... As it is meant to be. What you hold as a truth, is important only to and for, you. You can all share truths about a given subject, yet all of your truths might not be the same when compared; this also, is entirely acceptable. You demonstrate both a collection of both Cosmic and Personal Truths, yet typically rely only on the provisional evidence of the physical plane. Any embraced truth implies a belief in a thing or concept. The interpretation or outer expression of that belief, is not [near] as significant as the belief itself!

What you must carry out, is examination of your personal belief systems and the truths you hold dear to yourselves to determine which truths are best for your spiritual growth and which are truly meaningless, or Self serving. This may not be [an] easy [thing] to do, for it means that you must review and possibly judge yourselves. However just believing in spiritual truth does not insure your development. Belief without action is fruitless, meaningless. You must not only believe, but you must express those beliefs in all that you think or do.

THE SIERRAVILLE EXPERIENCE

There is only one correct path as it concerns this axiom... continual personal demonstration of the spiritual truths or beliefs you embrace. Become an example for others, as the one termed Jesus demonstrated.

The seventh concept is called **The Premise of Cause and Effect**. This is a Universal reality, a cosmic law concerning energy-imaging. This premise if embraced, can be used to coordinate peace and harmony in your lives and is one of the basic components of manifesting. Each of your thoughts can be described as an initiator or Cause, and the resultant circumstance or condition, tangible expression or manifestation of the thought, is then termed the result or Effect of such thought. Every thought you have, along with the emotion you hold to it, creates.

They can create conditions for you, or be expressed in physical terms, or even more than these. All thoughts make a kinetic impression on the creative and causal energy associated with your Genesis Ability. This energy medium is then motivated or activated, to become some 'thing' by your thought action, consciously or even subconsciously. The experienced result[s] then, reflect your most inner thoughts. As it relates to how you perceive your personal environment, the [time] developed declaration: What you think is what you'll get, is absolutely true.

Many people negatively respond to conditions in their lives instead of looking within for a cause, and then finding the cause, seeking to understand how the outcome positively impacted that experience... even if you only learned of some concept, it was positive. Circumstances which happen in your lives are reflections of how you think. If you expect negative things to happen to you, they usually will. If you find joy in life and expect good things, you find that your lives are much richer and more positive circumstances tend to occur in your lives more often. You alone, create your personal environment, and usually without even giving it a second thought. Tangently, accumulation of certain thoughts by the masses also affects your terra-sphere.

Looking back then, many of your situations may have benefited, or the results been modified, by having used different thought projections or approaches. Hindsight is a wonderful term. It is pre-supposes self-reflection and if one is truly honest, one may immediately see where one can alter their future thought patterns and yield different results. It would be very beneficial for you to be aware of your thinking process, especially before acting, by insuring you generate only positive thoughts and deeds predicated on concepts such as balance and harmony. Take pause to analyze whether or not the message you may want to transmit is just and proper, and whether or not it is in your or another's best interest. What you sow today, is what you shall tomorrow reap... Is that not how you term it?

The eighth thought concerns **The Premise of Miracles**. You will all eventually evolve, by the process of learning to BE. You will learn that you are vastly greater, referring to spiritual composition and abilities, than anyone has ever told you that you are, because you ARE. You can, and many do, actually perform what is called, miracles. What is a miracle? Some might suggest Divine Intervention, an unexplainable demonstration of faith, or simply a coincidence of events.

Miracles in general, are inappropriately labeled as such. Although that does not preclude the possibility of God or His Light Workers becoming involved with the outcome under extremely unique, or very special circumstances however! Miraculous experiences can only come about or be witnessed by the use of Universal Laws in the right and proper way. Miracles are [typically] identified as wondrous and amazing.

They are indeed; and are the end product or result of action taken on your part to create a condition or circumstance beyond your normally limited and logical three-dimensional thinking capacity. Therefore, when miracles occur in your lives, you look to and thank God for their manifestation, which is very much the proper thing to do. However, you choose not to accept that your being had anything to do with them occurring, but rather that some Higher power did; and of it's own volition.

This is simply not the case. You are sorrowfully instructed, that only a Higher Source of Illumination and Love provides for miracles, and that you can not manifest [initiate] them for yourselves. Indeed, this is misleading and erroneous input; generating personally restrictive thought... barriers to freedom of full expression.

The power of God works through you, most often without your even realizing it. When you generate a desire, a personal request relating to a need, and then project for its fulfillment, through your convictions and beliefs in a higher power, your faith in it occurring, your emotional intensity at the moment, and the right application of Universal Principles, you can manifest that desire. Based on your awareness of the preceding conditions, some of your desires may manifest slowly, perhaps even over years. Some can be instantaneous, and some may never be totally or physically witnessed due to special cosmic circumstances.

The projection for the manifestation of an end-result does not, and should not, be a lengthy or draw out procedure. Focusing with love-emotion, on the immediate need or result is all that is truly necessary, and you needn't necessarily incorporate specifiers or conditional statements into your projection[s]. Sometimes these only restrain how the result can manifest, and you certainly do not want to place any restrictions on that special process.

THE SIERRAVILLE EXPERIENCE

The ninth axiom, is **The Premise of the Recurrent Wheel Of Energy**. All creation is composed of energy, and there is a vast multiplicity of energy types, levels and functions. As you may know energy constantly moves, it is not static, and is constantly re-organized as certain influences play upon it. From the physical to the super-etheric, as one thing passes away, another may be formed. Thus, the concept of a recurrent wheel of energy or life-forces; a progressional transition without end, incorporating the seemingly finite and the infinite.

All things advance through a cyclical pattern of motion and some of the simpler patterns are very easily witnessed... such as your seasons, migrating animals, tides and the orbits of your planets. Each function has a beginning and an ending, then the process starts afresh again. Many advanced life-forms call this process: transition... birth and death. Your diminishing ancestors of the Northern Hemisphere refer to such a cycle as a Sacred Hoop.

As for what is termed reincarnation or rebirth, it is a seldom understood concept by you which has been in place from the beginning of the Beginning. This is your process of spiritual evolution which sadly, many do not believe in. This too, is a Divine gift which goes unacknowledged [for the most part]. After the Fall of Terra-Man, you found yourselves isolated from the God Principle of living life. You, as is the tendency of many Man-forms, make erroneous choices. The largest oversight was the separation of God from your lives and the ignoring of the God Presence within you, eliminating or reducing your spiritual growth and understanding. When you leave this physical plane, you will have an opportunity to evaluate your prior life cycle[s].

The cyclical patterns experienced for intelligent life are alterable and can be either or both: horizontal, meaning delay or stagnation, or vertical, interpreted as expansion and growth. Understanding from the next advanced plane of existence and knowledge that you can not skip any [of the] steps to spiritual advancement, you usually and ultimately choose to reincarnate, not necessarily here nor on the physical plane, in order that you might continue your spiritual growth in an enhanced or more refined fashion, with amplified wisdom or vision.

On the other side or the next higher plane, you are afforded a time of rest and reflection, then spiritual guidance and a time to review on your level of growth. You gather a greater understanding of what you need to do, in order to advance. You may even choose to bring these ideas or thoughts with you, back into the physical, or alternate planes, as components of reference. However once removed from the spiritual plane, you may soon forget what you came to accomplish. Many times this is due to social guidance, your environment or teachings given you, or restrictions placed on you as a child which continue into adulthood, but your Overselves remember!

Perhaps in your physical life, you may feel one way or another about certain things, which might be brief or faint memory lifts from the path-decisions you made priorly, or perhaps guidance from your Overselves. These can be sensed as an inner knowing that you should be doing this, or not doing that. If you have experienced those kind of sensations, [then] you may be perceiving some of the data you should be working with. Give close attention to those thoughts, for they are the footlights on your path to enlightenment. Thoughts [incidentally] are also cyclical in nature. You may consider thoughts wheels within the wheel of consciousness. What emotions and feelings you project about any given thing termed the beginning, will return to you, termed an end result, of your thought to complement your projection. These can be positive or negative in nature. We share, cling only to the positive.

The Premise of Cosmic Vibration is the next concept. Everything seen and unseen in the Universe vibrates with energy. Stones, water, distant galaxies, the planets, your sun, all atomic structures, atoms, electrons, and the sub-atomic particles within all molecules, even what you will call free space is in motion. But do not confuse this concept with orbital oscillation, which is caused by other factors and influences. Sound, light and color are also composed of vibrations. As the finer units of matter oscillate they generate an electrical charge by their continued movement, thus vibration of energy. This type of energy is far more advanced and refined than common Man is able to create, and vastly more significant. As matter vibrates, it emits one or more celestial timbres. Also, within many of these types of these vibrations, there exists intelligence and even the ability to communicate. All creation is based upon vibration, at one or more levels.

Even the physical structures within your physical selves oscillate, or vibrate, as do your thoughts. Creative thought, a capacity of the higher orders of life, is the most refined and powerful function of cosmic vibration. Your spirit-selves, as partially witnessed by your Body of Lights, also vibrate with divine energy. This energy is composed of pure thought. Thought is of Super-Universal significance and an interactive form of communication. The thoughts that Terra-Man emits can affect not only yourselves emotionally, physically, mentally and spiritually, but situations and others around you. This is why you should strive to entertain only positive thoughts and emotions. Thoughts of non-positive natures are known to be of lower vibrational energy, thus lower spirituality; whereas positive thinking creates higher vibrational states of energy and spirituality.

When you grow towards spirituality, you increase your overall vibrations. Not merely in field and strength, but in what is termed frequency. As you do, you may find that you are attracted more to certain life-vibrations than others.

THE SIERRAVILLE EXPERIENCE

This includes people, places and things such as color or sound. In time, the aware may also find that they can utilize more of their Divine gifts by learning to sense higher vibrational energies in and around themselves, by earnestly projecting for harmony, wisdom and Light, within themselves and for others. The higher you raise your spiritual consciousness, the more you become of Divine Mind, the easier it will be for you to sense and even communicate with other forms of cosmic life.

Also realize, that the higher and the more pure the vibrations of self become, the need for continued physical experience is reduced or overcome. This leads to ascension. A truism, whereby the physical is atomically transcended into Light.

The eleventh premise, is called **The Premise of Vibrational Patterning**. If Man could witness creation of anything from an elevated vantage point, he could observe an etheric matter counterpart, that being one or more energy fields, to all things created. This energy imprint is due to the residual creative thought energy pattern from whence these things were originally conceived. Nothing exists in the cosmos which does not have a prior etheric thought form or mold being associated with it. The more refined and intelligent life-forms have additional features to their thought forms. [Some of which were discussed in Premise Three.]

These life forms emanate an intense energy field which can be projected and sensed by others, and if witnessed, dynamically displays thoughts or emotions through what is called a veil of Living Lights, or your Auras. These Lights are an adjunct part of your Super-Consciousness and will always reflect the kind of person you tend to be, or are in terms of spiritual growth, as well as indicating your mental activity and physical well being. You as individual personalities, have certainly experienced meeting another for the first time and sensed something about that entity. Maybe good, maybe uneasiness, or possibly you might have had mixed emotions.

You sense these feelings from the other's auretic energy. What the other individual is, which is the outer expression of what they think, is impressed in their aura. You can sense, or temporarily absorb these vibrations because they make an immediate impact on your consciousness, especially if you are sensitive to those particular vibrations. When a person thinks and projects good thoughts or gives off good vibrations, you can sense the peace and harmony.

Like will draw toward like. You tend to associate with others of like-mind, because it is more comfortable for you. Sometimes however, you may find yourselves in situations where you can not physically escape others of different minds.

As an example, if you were around an individual who generated negativeness and you weren't aware of the vibratory conditions being created by that individual, you could emotionally sense, internalize, or even outwardly reflect their negative vibrations of emotionally transmitted thought-patterns or projections; even if you were truly of opposite thought convictions.

You can guard against this possibility, by projecting only positive thoughts and emotions and ignoring the negative influences around you. You don't want to internalize [anyone else's] negative thought energies. It's difficult to rid yourself of them once you internalize them; and you may, and many times do misinterpret them as your own. There is a difference between sensing them and internalizing them.

Sensing them allows a conscious interpretation of the emotions you are picking up. You may then unemotionally decipher them as to their meanings or intent.

Internalizing however, allows you to emotionally *feel* the conditions of vibration because you have permitted them deep into your sphere of consciousness. They may feel as if they are your own, and many can be uncomfortable. By continually projecting Light around yourself, you provide a strong extra-sensory shield against any unwanted or negative energies. In fact, your positive vibrations might very well influence a more negative entity's thought patterns, possibly making for a better personal relationship.

Or perhaps the entity might avoid you altogether; because harmony and disharmony don't mix well. Each type of thought is powerful and creates, so you must be careful what you think. Your aura emanates all that you think, and your thoughts are therefore available to anyone else, at any time. Keep in mind that what and how you think, generates vibrational energy which will return to you through one or more means. Therefore, it is imperative that you hold only good and positive thoughts. [As we see from Premise Seven.] If a person is deceitful, you can feel this energy because you can sense the foreign vibrations if you are paying attention.

When you think a certain way, you eventually develop an affinity for similar vibrations. What kind of person you are, or tend to be, will draw or attract similar people and circumstances into your life, so be careful of how and what you think. Take the time to review your thoughts, especially the hasty ones, to see if they are in your or another's best interests. Particularly ones whom you do not even know, or circumstances seemingly beyond your control. Thought energy is cumulative and will amass. Absolute Truth about an individual, is perceived through that entity's auric vibrations. Auric activity will first be discovered and witnessed by a simple invention utilizing a corona discharge [Kirlian] process.

THE SIERRAVILLE EXPERIENCE

It will be considered crude in operation, but will prove a useful tool. There are multiple layers to a complete human aura, but WE will discuss only three as a collection of those for simplicity sake. The [Kirlian] method will show only the closest aura, the corona or auretic sheath, available from yourselves or other life forms. This will be captured on a plate [picture] and will tend to represent the physical element and the most basic life energy of the object being studied.

For Terra-Man, it is your residual or primal animal instinct energy. An energy which is essential for three dimensional life forms to exist. Basically a spiritual-less, non-creative energy. This energy will be observed anywhere from less than one, to three or four of your fingers from the subject. There is another general auretic band approximately four fingers wide over the first layer. It is a composite of the spiritual layer, or the outer layer; and the primal layer, or the first layer. Higher and lower-order energies exist here to help maintain balance and order between your simultaneous physical, mental, emotional and spiritual existence's.

The most spiritual aura flows around the composite aura. This is where your God Source is based. It is an awesome and powerful life-cause energy, the base of your souls. It reflects more accurately, your true-self cosmic-life evidence of BEing. This is also where you obtain spiritual information, where you communicate by thought, where you draw energy from to manifest, and where you can sense and communicate with the ISness of God or others around you. This aura can be very thin in undeveloped or non-spiritual personages. It can extend for cubits or beyond, depending on the nature and spiritual development of the life force associated with it. It has been said that your Buddha's aura extended several leagues from his physical form.

The as yet unfamiliar terms of [telekinesis], or the ability to move objects through the power of thought alone, [clairvoyance], or the ability to understand and interpret vibration, psychic ability and extrasensory perception as well as other spiritual phenomenon or God given abilities, are rooted within this energy. Some sensitive humans can see auras with their physical eyes, some with their mind's eye, or what in other societies is termed Third Eye.

Most of you however, will not be able see anything until the invention and with the aid of special instruments. One day there will exist a special device which can capture this spiritual energy or aura on more highly specialized material [pictures]. On the material, specific colors will be seen to any given aura. The colors will represent your spiritual nature or stage[s] of development, or capabilities, or where you might have been focused at that moment the plate was processed.

216

Your aura is always undulating and changing, to reflect your thoughts and energy levels, or spiritual connections at any given moment. The plates [pictures] will be fascinating to view and provide much in the way of knowledge, to use to your benefit if you choose to do so. It will be a useful future tool for those on their path of self-awareness and enlightenment. When available, having a series of plates [pictures] taken over a time period, allows you to see how and where you are developing. In the future you will need, or perhaps more accurately, desire physical evidence to help impress your subconscious, and this process will offer an excellent source to do so.

Recall Vibrational Patterning, OUR elucidation about the drawing-in of circumstances. How many times WE have heard the excuses... That fate or predestination was the cause when something unfortunate happens in a life. There are no such things! If you project a particular pattern of thought, you must be ready to receive back the cosmic echo, or vibrational effect of that thought. You do bring to you, by your projected thought patterns, what you project. Whether you are aware of it or not, so WE suggest you become very aware.

As WE have said before, like attracts like. The term magnetic personality will be developed with this understanding. If you are a delightful person, you will usually have many delightful associates, if you are quiet, you might have many quiet associates. If you often think or say I hope something doesn't go wrong, chances are great that it may. Sooner or later. You can actually call to you the very thing you desire not to happen by giving those thoughts energy, by thinking them not to occur.

Sustained thinking puts emphasis on an undesirable thought projected, giving it an equal chance at success. When you think one way or another, you attract to you conditions that best reflect the nature of the energy projected from your being. Your aura is a super-vibrationally conductive energy-field. This field, through your power of thought, can transmit and receive energy patterns. It is actually one ability-element of your composite life-energy capability. Holding a negative thought or emotion to you, however well hidden from others, invites negative energy to manifest into your life by drawing similar energies to you. Loose all negative emotions and thought patterns now! Seek and express only positive thought energies, for if you do, they will also manifest into your life.

The twelfth axiom is known as **The Premise of Enlightenment**. Enlightenment means to develop a working knowledge about cosmic principles and yourself, as you relate to a Higher Consciousness. The ability to manifest as an example, is an expression or a demonstration of being awakened to who you are, and being spiritually adept and learned; or what will come to be referred to as being spiritually grounded... focused. Centered in thought.

217

THE SIERRAVILLE EXPERIENCE

A result of transcendental authority over perceived reality, stemming from proper utilization of supreme spiritual wisdom and applied scholarship. Limits thereof, depend on your faith, spiritual awareness and knowledge, your intent and what emotional intensity you put into a given desire. When WE implement the term spiritual, WE do not refer to religion in any sense of your word. Religions and their associated messages are ideals generated by Terra-Man. Spiritualism can become a religion if you wish, though in this case the term would simply mean an embraced practice. Spiritualism, is an edict for a method of living life as a by-product of being linked with your Source. Enlightenment then, is the self-realization internal path you take to grow towards spiritualism.

The last premise WE shall speak of is called **The Premise of Transformation**. Transformation implies Change. Man, as everything else, evolves or develops with time. Evolution, is the accepted scientific term now used for the physical process. To develop spiritually however, you must develop from within your heart-soul consciousness center. When you grow spiritually, you can only do so from the inside out, not the other way around. One outgrowth of spirituality, is the learned comprehension and insight which allows you to interpret circumstances that occur around you as to their higher meanings, without the need for exercising your lower emotions. Emotions of anger, loss, less-than, retaliation, denial, why me and numerous other concepts which you have unfortunately developed. Eventually you need not use any emotion outside of Love with which to examine your life experiences. This is but one aspect of self-transformation. If one just mentally, emotionally or physically reacts to life's seemingly unfortunate experiences, one can not grow. In fact, one might substantially regress.

Instead of responding with anxiety to undesirable circumstances, one should entertain only positive attitudes, look for the good and strive to create better life conditions, giving the lessor alternatives no mental consideration. Create new reality from your power of positive thought. This activity ushers in more personal freedom if you allow yourself no limitations as to what you can experience. Internal transformation is not an instantaneous process, you can not rush it. A lifetime of embraced thoughts, emotions, habits and other learned behavior and programming can not be rendered harmless, impotent or ineffective overnight.

Tragically, you think you've been accurately taught what things are true and what things are not, of your reality. And you are mostly comfortable with yourselves and these concepts. But many of these abstractions have been the teachings of the finite mind of Terra-Man, and many of these concepts are in gross error. You must come to question and understand why these things that have been taught, are slanted one way or another, or bear investigating for hidden truth[s].

218

Having accepted most if not all of your prior teachings and experiences as truths, you must unlearn many of them so that you might consciously and spiritually grow. Ethereal science, or spiritual science is the real study of and sincere desire to understand Cosmic Truths.

Science will soon prove that what you believe to be a single mass termed brain, is actually two independently functioning, yet intertwined orbs. They will also show that what you have empirically learned or truly believe to be real, resides in your left orb without question [as fact]. The right orb creates and passes to the left orb, the understandings [facts] you will ultimately hold as true. What you can do to usher in further development, is consciously reprogram your left orb accepted truths by utilizing creative [right brained] expanded thought. This allows room for possibilities beyond left orb thought, promoting personal emancipation.

Most of your conclusions concerning reality are held in a rigid box within your left orb. Can you not see, that if no latitude for intangible concepts are allowed, creative expression and expanded experience can not take place? This process is made easier by seeking to experience spiritual growth. Recognition and acceptance that the Source is the only real and true origin of all knowledge, reality and possibilities will nourish your efforts. Know that that relationship is there for the asking. The more you take to heart, believe and make use of this information, the faster you will reprogram your left orb into spiritual activity and action.

If you don't believe you can do a particular thing, then you won't be able too. This also, is a reality [fact]. Your left orb controls the emotion or belief in the reality of a thing occurring. However, if [on the other hand] you could allow no limitations to your thinking, you might eventually embrace the concept that nothing is impossible. If you believe you are instrumental in the process for initiating a miracle, or that you can truly create or manifest a desire, then it MUST manifest. If you do it in accordance with the Laws, it always works.

So to transform yourself, you must go inside and start building the foundation by first knowing that you are of God. That He has blessed you with dominion over all things. You are a co-creator, nothing is truly impossible for you to accomplish, but first you have to believe it!

Once you firmly accept your partnership with God, then you can apply the Principles [following next to be shared] to evolve your spiritual growth so you can create and do wonders not unlike the entity known as Jesus did. He expounded: Even greater things than I, shall you do.

Is this not cause for excitement, and therefore inducement to experience all of the gifts bestowed unto you? WE charge, that it is indeed!

THE SIERRAVILLE EXPERIENCE
TABLETS 29-41

Vibrations of Alpha IV, Book of Ways:

WE have come bearing insights and methods, used for developing that thing called self-awareness or personal enlightenment. Many disclose how one can effect positive changes within ones self, others offer strength. They are considered elementary and fundamental aspects of Universal Consciousness and are not difficult to incorporate into the attributes of your BEing. WE disclose there have been countless messengers of the partial collection of truths and axioms which WE are sharing with you, and many more will follow. Their individualized elaborations and explanations may seem to differ slightly, perhaps even utilizing different approaches as to composition or structure; this is quite normal and to be expected. However, the conceptual content, parallelisms, genuineness and importance of their unique and stylized messages remain the same... They all speak Truth.

WE now share and expound on a series of important Principles for you. They are but a few of the available concepts which will allow you as individuals to actually use these conceptual tools to apply Universal Law, in order that you might become further aware of enlightened thinking processes. These are not theories, nor are they suppositions. They are embraceable wisdoms and obtainable aspects of self, which are essential to advanced personal expansion and comprehension, and very much the acquired understandings and attributes of the spiritually accomplished.

The absolutely most significant concept is called **The Principle of Love**. Do you really know what unquestionable, undeniable love is? It, is the foundation for the Divine Way of living life. This kind of love has no restrictions or conditions placed upon it. It expects nothing, and asks nothing in return of it's being offered or given. The entity known as Jesus emanated and demonstrated this kind of love, over and over while he was physically here on your earth. It does not encompass such folly as loving the scent of flowers or baking bread, particular colors or animals or those impractical physical things you retain and so treasure. It has nothing whatsoever to do with trivial salutations, or an affinity for the opposite gender. Nor does it imply fondness for your mate; although this compassionate love might come closest to this concept, if given without limitation.

The powerful and dynamic love WE speak of, is reserved for the concern and care of and for life... All life-forms, and all beings within your life that you may have occasion to come across or interface with, whether you personally know them or not. It should never be withheld, for any reason.

220

This kind of love is what should be extended to, and felt for others outside of yourself, offered from yourself without reservation. Genuine, heartfelt love IS a life-force energy in and of itself. Extremely potent and a most vital expression of BEing. When you can feel this grand life-emotion for and in all life, at all times, then you can see and experience nothing less than God at work.

Evolved love-comprehension generates many by-products, one of which is the internal wisdom and understanding that all the seemingly good or bad life experiences you encounter, are actually events cloaked in positive revelation. This may be quite difficult to understand, especially when the events seem to be negative. Yet, as you grow toward cosmic realization and infinite mind, you will learn to seek out these at first seemingly hidden positives, instead of focusing only on, or reacting to, the negative appearances of an event. You may recall from Cause and Effect, that many times less than positive situations are created by you; and can be truly for your own benefit and spiritual growth if you would only take the time to examine all the conditions from whence the event took place.

Seeming tragedies of your lives are perhaps the most difficult to comprehend as to their positive meanings. In many cases when you loose someone you care about, the concept of love seems to quickly disappear as intensified emotions of loss, anger, frustration, hate or even revenge replace it. You begin to question all nature of things, including God. Why did HE let this thing happen? Why wasn't it me? you may ask. Why would you immediately throw away all the kind remembrances, the times of joy and the wonderful experiences of having known or been associated with that entity? Who are you to know what that entity's life plan was to be? Why do you believe that who they were, somehow belonged only to you? You and WE are all from the same cosmic Love Source, all related and intertwined. The many are in actuality, One. Together we are family, hence the passage Love your neighbor as you would yourself. It's important to recognize that when once you displace the vivacious love presence from your BEing, you then open yourselves up to the substantially reduced and subconscious energies of the Me-self... The lower mental aspects of mind.

You may only comprehend Your losses, display pity for Your selves, imagine the things You will never experience, and so forth. These emotions can destroy you if you allow them the opportunity. Love can and does overcome all situations. Love can and does provide for infinite understanding. Love is eternal and always a source of inner power. As for any feelings of sadness or sorrow... these reflect within you that indeed you have loved; yet these too shall pass... if you will but allow them to. Holding on to pain would serve no purpose if you truly understood the nature of Life.

THE SIERRAVILLE EXPERIENCE

There is magnificent strength in the knowing that there is a Greater Love, and that life continues from your physical plane, in advancing stages of grandeur and glory. You must know that you are not forgotten, nor even removed from your loved ones simply because you can not touch them in a physical manner. They have escaped the limitations of this reality and moved on to wonderful new one. You should be excited for them and the opportunities that lay before them.

Extended grieving can only keep them from moving on to their awaiting experiences. If you realized the impact, you would be quick to alter your emotions. As a result of intense grieving, they feel concern and obligation to stay near you. Would you knowingly desire this limited situation for them? They can always be contacted, at anytime by your thoughts of love. You haven't lost anything... Truly, you have gained from personally knowing them.

Yet bear in mind, from their new vantage point they will not advocate any emotions which may be based in wanton negative vibration... For they fully understand the significance of Life, cosmic law and such things as the importance of harmòny, balance, peace, and of course, love. They truly comprehend how negative vibration of thought or emotion suspends or degradates spiritual growth, and how these energies can and do find recourse; resulting in potentially solemn consequences, and manifesting repercussions at, or on any realm in which you may be participating.

As it relates to personal interaction with others, if each entity loved unconditionally, you could not hold emotions such as hate, jealousy, denial, revenge, or feelings of torment, pain or lack. It wouldn't be possible. For with true love, you would find the understanding and compassion necessary, which would allow yourselves to be at peace, while sensing that all entities are free spirits and walk on their own paths of life as they imagine they should be walked.

As you embrace the concept of true love, it allows others total freedom to BE who they are and the wisdom for yourselves, that it is natural and proper. You see, if you could learn to love as Our Father does, there would be nothing that could occur in your life that you would not fully comprehend or find resolve in. Insight based in Love does provide answers.

If you could but grasp the majestic and larger concept of Eternal Love as a foundation of wisdom and strength, a Power without limits, then perhaps you can discover the higher meanings to the term: Life, itself.

Absolute Love is a prerequisite of infinite mind, or that condition of love-wisdom and comprehension which allows spiritual interpretation, allowance and understanding in, of and for:

Seen and unseen realities, tested and unknown potentialities, imagined and unthought of possibilities, tried and unexperienced personalities, and the true meaning, significance and purpose of Life. It is that supreme thought process which is without discord, without limitations, without judgment; founded in the exercising and scholarship of everlasting Love.

The next axiom is referred to as **The Principle of Allowance**. WE do not speak in terms of monetary, bargaining or trading situations. To allow others, is to understand that you are all on a life experience called Learning to BE. Each developing entity of mineral travels along his or her life-path, learning, making decisions, acting and reacting, which includes carrying, displaying and actualizing thoughts and emotions, feelings and opinions. These concepts are important to, and meaningful for each individual entity, as are the beliefs you personally embrace. How could any entity suggest to another, that what that other entity embraces as a truth, is less than it appears to be? Your opinions and feelings are special to you, and rightly so.

Allow others to express and identify with that which makes them their own individual. You are not replicas. You are individual identities, with individual convictions and ideals, understandings and comprehensions. That, is what makes you appropriately unique from each other. Further, you do not know what another's life path is, or should be. That is why you should never judge another. If you have to judge someone, let it be yourselves. How are You doing!? That, is the only question of importance and truth. There is nothing wrong with gently sharing your thoughts with another, but there is if you do it out of anything but love-respect.

If some entity should disagree with you on a subject, so be it. After all, it is their right to hold onto what they believe to be true. Do not become annoyed or upset, demanding or impatient. It serves no purpose; save that you feel disharmony and your vascular system compresses, or your abdomen becomes knotted. Understand and allow each entity to be who they are, which must not be confused with who you are. Could you imagine your world with nothing but multitudes of identical you's in it? Everywhere you turn, every face you see is yours? Consider that thought... How unnerving an existence that would be... if you, were all there was.

Terra-Man makes 'allowances' for children because he knows they are in the process of learning. Yet somewhere along the way, he has forgotten to make allowances for those past this age... Why?... You all continue to learn about life, and at your own rate(s). Some at different levels and understandings than your own. So why should another be less correct than you are about a subject? To them, they may truly believe that they are right and you are wrong about a given subject... What is wrong with that? What might you believe they are doing to, or against you?

THE SIERRAVILLE EXPERIENCE

Are they making you feel unpleasant by not agreeing with you Insulting you? Why would you even allow those emotions to grow within yourself? Must certain entities always be right? What happened to the rights of the other entities? What if you are wrong? There are interpretations other than your own to consider. It is infinitely better to hear them out and silently disagree, if you must, than to demand that they accept only your view. However, if you find yourselves disagreeing at all, then perhaps it may be you that haven't accomplished much in the domain called allowance. When you allow another to BE, then you are expressing care and love, tolerance and patience. Are these not better ideals to cling to? WE say that they are!

Within these messages, WE are processing and sharing what WE believe to be critical information for your individual development and spiritual growth. You have the option to choose to accept it, or reject it. Some of it, or all of it. That decision is yours as an individual entity, alone. WE will not allow ourselves to feel poorly, nor will WE be upset at you if you decide to disregard any or all of these messages for WE understand that that is your right and privilege. WE are simply offering this information to you, for your benefit. If you choose to denounce it, WE will be at peace with your decision; If you wish to use it, then you will derive the benefits of your efforts. WE would only pray that you at least examine it all before coming to a firm conclusion.

The third thought discusses **The Principle of Will**. Terra-Man is a will creature. You make no decision without will being involved. Typically, you entities don't consider that will plays any part of the process to make a decision, yet a decision could not be reached without it. Many times your level of will goes unnoticed, particularly as it concerns simple or routine decisions. The more complicated the conditions, the more will becomes predominate, thus noticeable.

Strong will, is the inner emotionally driven force observed as tenacity, behind an urge or a desire, which renders a powerfully active or at times, a supercharged decision to do or perhaps not to do, a given thing. By your own volition and motivation, persistence and decision, you go determinedly onward toward a purposely chosen, and hopefully, well defined goal.

The term called: freewill, means the internally generated motivation and conscious decision relating to a path or direction you allow for, which encompasses a course of action interpreted to be the best method to successfully obtain a goal based on your initial desire. Will does not mean desire in a passive sense however. Although will is composed of desire, which is constructed of such concepts as intent, focus, and emotion, it also encompasses a sense of personal authority over a situation.

You alone, establish the terms of what is acceptable, or unacceptable, as it relates to the pursuance of your desired result. The will to do a thing, can be weakened say, as in a result of emotional battle but is typically based on passion or very strong emotion, and may take into account a multitude of feelings and other factors which allow you to precipitate a decision as it relates to a definite goal or result. Will proceeds activity.

Have you not heard the expression: It was your, or another's will-power which allowed some special personal accomplishment? Will is a power, and of immense latitude. It is that personal force one uses to overcome serious illness, or to strive for excellence. To do what perhaps, none has done before. To do what perhaps, is a 'thing' you might never have considered you could accomplish [before]. When will is associated with a manifestation process, it becomes a declaration, a causal command over the situation, circumstance or event. Will proclaims the serious intention of activity and completion... You declare: I will, do this thing!

It is an absolute and a powerful condition of thought, leaving no alternative but success. Intense will, can not allow a condition that would impede the conceptualized process, the fulfillment or the outcome. Will is one of your unique thought-emotion abilities which allows personal control and freedom over perceived or perhaps imagined conditions, situations or obstacles. It is a powerful attribute of personalized thought, which lends itself to purposeful behavior. This focused energy to do, is not limited to the physical realm by any means. Consider the following thoughts: I will become master of my reality; I will overcome my limitations; or My will, is greater than any earthly influence. Will is a formidable tool... The assertion of Causal Mind over Matter.

The fourth axiom is referred to as **The Principle of Attitude**. We are talking of mental and spiritual temperament and disposition, or demeanor. Your attitude on life, among other influential feelings, is the fundamental determinant that decides how you base your thoughts or deeds, how you act, or react, and directly impacts what you will experience. Also, an attitude may have one or more emotions attached to it for any given circumstance, what you call: good or bad. WE strongly suggest your attitudes should be for the betterment of yourselves or others... For success and accomplishment, and that nothing is truly impossible.

You've heard or said yourselves: He or she has an attitude... It could be positive or negative, but nevertheless you notice it. [don't you?] Which is more comfortable to be around? Which protocol would you suppose creates an enhanced and substantially more healthy life-energy? Try to maintain a positive attitude toward everything and everyone.

THE SIERRAVILLE EXPERIENCE

Negative attitudes lead to dissolvement of spiritual growth and divine capabilities. Disharmony within your vibratory systems and spheres caused by negativity can even lead to illness or disease of the physical mind or body. Learn to project only positive thoughts, and be ready to experience how your lives do change for the better. You can decide through strong and positive attitudinal energies, what you can or will accept, do, believe, try, accomplish, experience, overcome, realize, or control.

If your attitude is weak or negative, then you allow limitations, indecision, failure, disappointment, doubt, vacillation or other constricting and self defeating results to manifest. Why would you consciously let yourselves be controlled by emotions that have absolutely no beneficial energy?

Attitudes begin as a conscious thought decision based primarily on experience, belief or opinion. With time they can become what you call: personality traits, whether perceived by others or whether they go unnoticed. They can make you resolute, or cause you to become ineffective. The positive ones will definitely be noticed, possibly even admired. Your power to control your reality is everso predicated on your personal attitudes.

The next axiom, is **The Principle of Projection**. What is a projection? It is a mentally focused thought. It could be compared to how you throw your voice, as in a call. In times to come, Terra-Man will develop what is called: film [motion pictures] of many earthly subject matters, including history. A process where [translucent pictures] plates are animated and viewed on a remote rampart [screen]. A strong light fixed in a mechanism to be termed a projector, is positioned behind the [pictures] in order to send the images through the atmosphere to the rampart. Your mind would be synonymous with the mechanism of such a projector, and the [screen] would represent the ether around you. A mental thought-energy release called: projection then, is concentrated thought-energy moved or dispatched consciously or possibly even subconsciously from your creative mind to the ether. It contains intense focus as to some condition, thing or result.

A projection contains the totality of what was conceived and is either [1] extended from yourselves as in how a stone ripples the water when thrown into it, or [2] released in it's entirety like an arrow, completely let go from your consciousness - to permeate the intangible energy realms of dimension, space and time called: the ether. The resultant effect of any particular projection, is regulated primarily by the foundational structure of that particular thought.

The term called: structure, includes such concepts as: the overall polarity [positive/negative] of that collective thought-energy and the magnitude of that energy, together being further comprised of such things as:

226

The type of benefit [for others or for self], the attached emotional conditioning [love or anger, etc.], the amplitude of sincerity [serious or trivial], emotional intensity [strong or insignificant], purpose [gift or gain], conceptual energy [focused or confused], symmetry and balance relating to harmony [peace or discord], thought concentration [pronounced or fleeting], attitude [know or wish], importance [substantial or meager], emotional intention [kindness or malice], desire [creative or destructive], and need [now or later].

WE pray you grasp what WE are sharing… There is an unlimited set of factors which can be involved in a projection. Further yet, a projection can be sensed by other entities by what is commonly referred to as vibrations, or the extended projections of emotion or thought released from your or another's being. It often times is generated with the purpose of manifestation termed: released projection. WE pray it ultimately becomes evident that it is wonderfully more advantageous to concentrate on positive aspects of projection. Harmonious thoughts and positive thought projections will always create beneficial life-circumstances for you.

The opposite condition, if not obvious, is also quite true. Both forms of thought can generate an equal amount of energy… and they can be equally successful. EVERY thought projects, and these projections of thought will be manifest to one degree or another whether or not there is visible evidence. Projections can be positive or negative, conscious or subconscious. Always project for the good, for the positive, lest the energy return to you in a less meaningful way. Greed, lust, revenge, retaliation, retribution, selfishness, the hunger for power and ill-gotten gains are all forms of negative intent and are spiritually unworthy, and personally dangerous projections. These types of projections reduce your vibratory field, and certain projections will keep you from ascending.

If any of these types of energies should ever become part of one of your projections, be forewarned and be prepared to experience inescapable, potentially unpleasant, and possibly unannounced circumstances at some point in your life. Negative projections are detriments for you as individuals in any theater of reality; They virtually attack the entirety of your essence.

The more one has such projections, the more that entity is removed from the Light, and the harder it becomes to regain positive flux! It is also possible to become ill from embracing the darkness of such energies as your physical forms, made up of life sustaining spheres [cells], are depleted of Life Force Energies and begin to fail. A term to be called: stress [self-generated and imposed emotional pressure] is also associated with negative energies.

THE SIERRAVILLE EXPERIENCE

If you understood more of what is termed: Life Experience, you would understand that there is no need for stress. Stress comes about through such things as worry or guilt. It is those undesired circumstances or situations which seem unresolved or overbearing and are held within the consciousness of your minds. You feel you can not, or for whatever reason will not, seek resolution. You feel the pressure of holding these emotions within you, yet you do nothing outside of perhaps complaining. The result is negative energies abound within your being causing catastrophic damage to your immune and other systems. This can lead to premature physical death. As it relates to thoughtful love-projections for others, typically they are successful. Yet there is an interactive element which many may not be unaware of, and it has to do with the entity you are focusing on, and the energies they are generating as it relates to their particular condition or circumstance.

The will of an individual is never allowed to be overcome, no matter your best intentions, unless *they* willfully allow it. If they have chosen to give up, or tend to believe the worst, you must immediately pray for them and ask for spiritual assistance in spiraling their emotional energies to the positive. Then you may project for them, and with vigor. However, you must be prepared to accept the outcome... and if it is other than desirable to you, it doesn't mean that you failed, but that that individuals will prevailed. If on the other hand their thoughts should run along more positive lines, your projections can benefit them greatly. This is because you are substantially adding to the positive energies within and around them, you are in harmony with them. You aren't combating their perhaps hopeless feelings of potential doom, or lack of options.

As for the well-meaning projections for others by initiates, [a *positive* term used to identify: one in the beginning process of learning] if you don't have a full understanding of what you can do, or why and how to do it, or are aware of the unseen influences that play upon these situations, then you have a kind of cosmic fail-safe mechanism to protect yourselves and possibly those others.

All conditions necessary for healing or manifestation must be right and proper. If you have the best intentions, yet lack the required understandings or wisdoms, there may be no tangible results noticed. This is not indicative of failure, nor is it a negative thing which has occurred. Understand that the outcome is always what is best for all involved... particularly, as it concerns the one of center focus. However, if as adepts with expanded comprehensions, you hold no other attitude but complete success and your faith in the process is beyond reproach... even to the extent that you know the end result is obtainable and will be [IS] AND all other conditions have been satisfactorily met including the attitudes and will-energies of the recipient, beneficial projections founded in love can always be realized.

228

What you think about any entity, subject, thing, situation or condition projects into the ether. The ether being those vast and multiple dimensions of unseen substance, causal energies, unknown intellects and sources of power which exist in and around you, and throughout the entire Cosmos.

Remember, your thought energies play vigorously upon your Genesis Ability, and the associated consequences are usually governed by what is in your heart. The Principle of Projection exemplifies the fundamental criteria for manifesting your desires. In order to manifest, a sincere, positive and well defined projection of thought, typically enshrouded with an intensified emotion, backed by unwavering faith must be presented by you, releasing it to the ether for completion. The Principle of Projection has an interesting condition placed around it however, referred to as: Intent.

The Principle Of Intent then, is the sixth axiom. This principle can work for, or against you. Intent is the purpose, meaning or motive behind your focus, projection, request or desire. It may be a weak conditional energy or it may be a substantial and far reaching, deep inner-feeling or emotion. Your intent[s] should be for the fulfillment of a real need [for yourself] or initiated in the name of love for another, and be based on total unselfishness. It should be purely honest and extremely positive in nature.

To have intentions which would not be in your or particularly another's best interest or desiring another have a negative experience, is very detrimental to your spiritual development. Ill-intended desires directed toward others can not manifest to their total potential. However they can and eventually will return to you with undiminished vigor. You must be careful exactly what you ask for, especially in haste. Through vibrational energy-reflection, you just might be the one to experience what was asked for!

Be spiritually motivated with your intent as it concerns personal desires and projections. Always give thanks for what you already have, no matter how insufficient you may think it is, and for the receiving the end result of your desire. Giving thanks for what you literally haven't received yet, promotes the concept subconsciously, that it WILL manifest.

Expect your desire to manifest by believing that it already has [IS], whether or not you see the immediate results. The physical or non-physical manifestation of your desire can take many paths, and may come into being in a most unexpected way. If your intent is properly placed, don't be concerned how it appears... KNOW, it is in the ether forming even moments after the release of your emotionalized thought!

When you desire something in or for your, or another's life, focus with vigor on that particular request.

THE SIERRAVILLE EXPERIENCE

Concentrated well defined focus allows projections ever more power to create whatever you desire; now, and in all other planes of existence! You must have faith that it will manifest. Faith is a firm belief in the unknown and supreme processes outside of [Above] yourself. A lack of faith will always impede your projections. Never allow fear of failure into your thoughts, it will offset your positive thought action. This particular type of fear is not uncommon for the initiate, nor is it detrimental to your spirituality.

However, spiritually improper, wrongful or selfish intentions are indeed detrimental and will almost always produce fear, resulting from anxiety, apprehension, or guilt. Either from worry of being found out or from the ever-present spark of Light within you, warning or urging you that that was a wrongful thought energy. It is from your higher subconscious awareness, you call it: your conscience. A projection based upon non-spiritual energy has little likelihood of successful realization, but you never know... OUR advice... Do not tempt those energies.

The seventh axiom is called **The Principle of Visualization**. The strongest mechanism you can use for manifesting a desire, is termed: visualization. This is a personal process of seeing in your mind, what it is that you desire to manifest. Every entity can do this, yet not all will do it the same way... perfectly fine. Some of you can visualize without any problem, and some may encounter difficulty because you are not accustom to this type of a thought process. It may take practice, and one form of practice is to take an object you are familiar with and study it in detail. Begin with a simple, uncomplicated object. After you feel you know this object, put it down, relax yourself in some sitting position or perhaps laying down, and close your eyes. Now, recreate that image [object] in your mind. See exactly what you saw with your eyes open. Don't necessarily try to focus on color as yet, you can incorporate color visualization later on when you are more comfortable with this new thought process.

Try to envision the object in a three-dimensional form, even rotating it or turning it in your mind to see other aspects of the object. If it has moveable parts, envision these parts flexing. Not wildly or without purpose, but as it might move when activated or controlled by normal physical means. As you find the increased ability to visualize simple things, gradually move on to more complex items, and to envisioning color schemes.

Attempt to visualize in three dimensions [height, width and depth]. Although this is not an absolute requirement, it is because you are animated in a three dimensional plane of existence, and your desires must typically manifest into this dimension to be of utility. In some cases for a physical thing, you may want to later incorporate the ability to not only dimensionally visualize, but taste, smell or feel that thing of desire.

230

These accomplishments are performed from within your mind, not from without. In cases involving healing for another, knowing that they *are* being healed is usually enough... one needn't visualize in three dimensions. Many beginning the process of visualization include a useful mental-endorsement utility, one called: an affirmation.

An affirmation is a simple, yet concise statement describing what your request or end result is to be... your desire. It should be restricted to only positive needs or objectives. The preferred method for initiates of the future physical plane would be the symbolic or written affirmation. [with acceptance of the process, a verbal or mental causative will suffice later on] Compose and draft any one particular affirmation, in groups of three at a time. Attempt to feel the significance of each utterance as you set your words forth. After you have scribed an affirmation at least three times, which impresses the thought[s] to your subconscious, read at a leisurely pace, that series. Reading aloud, try to perceive [feel] the tangibility and power of each word.

Your affirmation should now be simple to recall with eyes closed. Relax, shut your eyes and let your mind's-eyes go blank for a moment. Attempt to see only a blank void of perhaps emptiness, or perhaps what you call a writing [black] board. Try to allow no unrelated thought[s] into your mind. Then consciously open your heart center. Project love-emotion, kindness or peace and harmony, and prepare to surround yourself with a beautiful, emotionally cleansing and energetic White Light. Bring this Divine Light into the top of your head, knowing that it comes from Above. Allow it to flow through and over your entire physical body. Filling every sphere [cell], cavity and structure within and without you with a brilliant Cosmic Love radiance. Know, at least attempt to emotionally feel, that you are connecting with the God Presence within you, and beyond [the physical] you. Slowly and with feelings of intense conviction, repeat your affirmation three times.

Be gently advised, do not present any emotion of demand. One can demand no-thing, but one is always free to declare it. Wait a few moments, allowing yourself to sense your conviction and more importantly, your connection with a higher power center. You may have feelings of being enshrouded with a tingly energy, or of light-headedness or being physically there [wherever you began this process] yet mentally removed, or sensations of weightlessness, or perhaps even feel that you and all the elements around you have become immaterial. The focus on your connection however, is vastly more important than your sensations of the surrounding conditions.

Repeat the affirmation three more times, but this time SEE the end result... your desire. Visualize in your mind, the effect you wish to cause or see occur. See it in great detail, and in completed or finished form.

THE SIERRAVILLE EXPERIENCE

This action further impresses the subconscious mind with the tangibility and reality of the desire coming into being... making it even more authentic to your mind than you might otherwise allow for... Doing so gives the projection ever more energy to Become. When you have gone through this process many times, and to the point where visualization is easy for you and you have come to believe in the reality of YOUR potential to make a difference, then the symbolic or written affirmation process may no longer be required. At that point, simply obtain a relaxing posture then visualize the desired manifestation as you offer your projection, allowing latitude as to success and insuring first that you are of proper emotional condition and have priorly brought in the [your] White Light connecting you with your Source.

The eighth axiom is called **The Principle of Acknowledgment**. This is a very, very important concept. The power of God works through you, not by you. You are never working alone whenever you project a desire for manifestation. Yet, it is you who have the power to initialize the process. You begin the process, whether in your or another entity's interest. A manifestation process will not occur from the unseen, unprovoked. They can not come into being without a beginning-energy input, and that initiator is you.

Once you have released the projection for actualization, other energies and actions become involved. Therefore it is spiritually proper, even obligatory, that you offer thanks for what you ask of the Greater Cause. This action prepares the consciousness for the reality of receiving a desired result. One should include the words: I give thanks for this 'thing' of request. One may also wish to include the statements: total and complete or right and proper somewhere in their request. Such as, I give thanks, I have total and complete physical health now; I give thanks, I have right and proper affluency now; or I give thanks, I have abundant love in my life now. The term: I Give Thanks acknowledges the gift, or blessing from Above.

The term: Now gives the statement a term of immediacy for action to take place. The term: Right and Proper means, that from a spiritual stand-point and your present growth cycle, you expect and more importantly ACCEPT the spiritually Right and Proper, or perfected result independent of the conclusion YOU may desire, as allowed for by a Higher Authority. Feel enthusiasm with each of your projections. Visualize what you desire in your mind.

Make it as real as you can. Smell it, touch or feel it, hold it... SENSE, the realness of your desire, as if it already WERE. This is very important, because the more real it is to you, the better the thought projection will interface with your Genesis Ability and the higher realms, to manifest. KNOW that what you desire WILL manifest.

Eliminate from your mind any and all doubt. Doubts are considered a depletion energy and they WILL affect your results. Your projections should not be executed nonchalantly, casually or with mediocrity. Render them with joy and anticipation, exclaim them with vigor and excitement, and EXPECT results!

Acknowledgment is also accomplished by prayer and worship. Prayer done in earnest allows one to connect to the Source, and exclaims faith in that Source. You should pray for your development and spiritual insight. Doing so opens channels of the mind and soul for spiritual input and comprehension. Worship, is the act of ultimate praise to your Source. It projects without doubt, that you accept your relationship with God. It is this adoration, devotion and reverence which glorifies your Source; it offers Love to the Creator.

The ninth law, is **The Principle of Faith**. Faith is perhaps the easiest understood, yet hardest implemented facet of your BEing. It seems easy to have faith in others, yet hard to have faith in yourselves. Spiritual faith, goes beyond believing in something physical or empirical. It implies unwavering strength and comfort, and a special knowing that a spiritually superior love-force exists. True faith exudes and exhibits a powerful and positive attitude, while questioning on the other hand, generates only restrictive energy.

When you feel stronger about your ability to project and come to desire something in your or another's life, think it, bless it and release that thought to manifest, do not dwell on it. Dwelling may keep the thought-energy grounded in the here-and-now. The thought must be released from your consciousness to actualize... you must consciously forget about it. Holding it to you for a prolonged period of time can prevent actualization and may indicate apprehension [a lack of trust or faith] in the process. Loose thoughts of impatience, worry, anxiety, or the lack of self-confidence. These are all fears. Relax, know in your heart and mind that what you desire WILL manifest, declare it [your desire] to BE. Include unwavering positive emotion, or intense passion in your desire.

Don't wish it to be, don't hope it will be. These [middle-of-the-road] thoughts only give the desired thought projection two poor choices. Manifest partially, or not at all. The focus must be, that it WILL BE! That it IS. NOW! Imagine it SO. Believe it SO. Don't fall into the trap of saying or thinking: I can't understand why it doesn't work, or I don't think this is possible, or It hasn't worked yet, so I'll just give up. This type of thinking WILL preclude you from enjoying total success! What you think, IS what you'll get. How many of you have drawn lots for some purpose or thing believing that you'll probably not prevail?

THE SIERRAVILLE EXPERIENCE

How many of you have then actually prevailed? Why is it seem it always another entity who does so? Do you suppose that [just] *perhaps*, they might have a different perspective or utilize a different set of thought projection patterns? WE do not refer to focus on self, but that those entities might declare with absolute conviction [in their mind], that they see themselves as a victor. Think about the possible ramifications in other areas of your life if you were to be filled with such a convictional power of mind.

The next concept, is referred to as **The Principle Of Harmony**. To experience harmony means: to feel at one with, enjoy compatibility with, emanate peace with, have an accordance with, share balance with, be in agreement with or feel a positive attunement with others, yourself, and or your surroundings. It begins as a thought process termed: attitude, and can be realized internally, externally or both. All harmonious thoughts produce increased positive vibrational energies, in and around you.

Terra-Man oftentimes finds difficulty in retaining happy and harmonious thoughts about all the experiences he encounters daily, especially the ones he considers to be negative. It takes practice, but it can be done. This principle is important for your spiritual growth. Creating personalized harmony, by using a positive thinking process, raises your spiritual vibrations to a higher plane. You become more in tune with the unseen spiritual energies when you make a concerted effort to maintain harmony in your life at all times. This practice is also extremely beneficial for your mental and physical well being.

The spiritual hosts promised by Jesus, or the Brotherhood of God sometimes referred to as the White Brotherhood [of God], are with you to assist in your spiritual development. Their thought vibrations and life force energies oscillate at a much higher frequency than yours normally do. The higher you raise your vibrations and conscious thinking as a harmonious entity, the easier it will become to communicate with and be aware of these counselors for spiritual guidance and wisdom.

Any time you become condemning or critical of another, feel anger, aggression, frustration, or think in retaliatory, possessive, or envious terms, you reduce your creative vibrational energy and the ability to make positive changes in your life. You immediately generate destructive and cancerous vibrations in the ether around you and ground your subconscious in negative energy.

These ruinous vibrations of thought will severely impact any given projection and can be sensed by another entity, or absorbed by the object of your focus. Even if your focus was subconsciously involved, this anti-energy still resides in the ether and your aura. All thoughts create, absolutely. This, you must come to understand. It is absolutely the most vital and crucial lesson you can learn!

234

If you hold negative thoughts or entertain negative emotions, you may cause one or more spiritual energy pattern defects, imbalances or dysfunctions within your vibrational energy field, your aura. This happens whether you are aware of it or not. Terra-Man can make himself sick and create illnesses this way. These energies can also affect others unknowingly. Do not pursue negative ways of thinking. Do not hold or create any negative thought, for ANY reason.

The eleventh postulate is referred to as **The Principle of Humility**. As you grow spiritually, you will recognize that humility plays a big part in your constructive growth cycle. To be humble reflects humility and the instinctive desire to respect the feelings of others. Would any entity consciously be willing to subject itself to a personal situation which might be considered self-threatening? By self-threatening, WE speak of those conditions you create, based in ego or that image of yourselves which you guard to the highest [Nth] degree, and with veracity. Many entities have generated thoughts such as: How dare they ask me to do this or that... that's below me, or I'm better than that, get someone else to do it!...?

What exactly is it, that allows some entities to feel more worthy, important or better than another entity? It arises from once obtaining a status position, real or perceived, and refusing to go what seems like downward. They tend to feel there is a great and unacceptable personal cost involved, or that they loose something called respect. Somehow their image gets tarnished if they bow down before others. They fail to see that beside being of service, they demonstrate harmony and humility, which are superior assets and strengths.

A humble entity is reserved yet self confident, acquiescent yet proud, submissive yet strong and emanates total allowance for others. He is unassuming and judgmental toward nothing and no other. Humility is a virtue that comes with growth. Just because an entity may have more knowledge in a certain area, it doesn't give that entity the right to cast down on others who do not. Often times one tends to place his worth higher than another's, forgetting that he too, began at the beginning. Therefore, through ego he might justify his feelings of superiority. Yet it's the lack of understanding and comprehension that all are spirits on INDIVIDUAL paths of evolvement.

With this supposed evolvement should come discipline, wisdom, and knowledge. Somehow along the way however, many of you become judgmental. This leads to a state of altered self-image, or ego. Ego is typified by what you call: self-esteem, which is not a negative concept in and of itself. It's when you compare yourselves with others, that misaligned viewpoints and energies come into being.

THE SIERRAVILLE EXPERIENCE

Was it not the entity Jesus who washed the feet of His disciples? This caused great consternation within many of the minds of those present. How could one of such distinction and authority tend to such a trivial duty which would have normally been left to one of less stature? In answer: Before one may be of service, he must first serve. Before he may become a teacher, he must first be a student. He was demonstrating that no entity is above another, none is more righteous than another, and that service to others is necessary for growth. To be spiritually evolved, is to live and be as meek as children. There is great strength in meekness, contrary to popular belief.

Humility, is to live the life of a humble person, one who knows his or her capability, but has no need or compulsion to display their knowledge or ability. They sense that they should continue to walk through life as quietly and as unnoticed as possible. However, there are those that feel a need to feel important, and they feel that that image can only be gained by command of others, by whatever means available. Humility is the recognizing that you have nothing to show off and indeed, no reason to even consider doing so. An overzealous ego [Edging God Out] can get in one's way... many times, totally unintentionally. WE would ask you to give unrestricted consideration to others, that you also, might experience the same. You will know when you must draw on your powers and knowledge. You will also know that the timing will be right, as well as the intent and purpose. Humble yourselves before others then, let them feel worth and meaning in their lives. Allow them to BE who they are and share with you and you with them, and learn to appreciate the modest side of life. What purpose is there in flaunting whatever capability or knowledge you have?

Perhaps the most misunderstood concept of humility and humbleness, is as they relate to the doctrine Jesus asserted... Become like children. He was making reference to the difference between the inherent natures of men and children. Men, have misplaced the ability to hear and see as innocent minded children do. You too often have closed and hardened your hearts, taken up blinders and drawn into the concept of self. What then do your progeny learn? The innocence of children precludes them from prejudging or analyzing. They exhibit tenderness, expressive love emotions, unqualified sharing and accept others as being no different from themselves. They demonstrate balance and harmony. They accept on faith what is shared with them... and more importantly they take it to heart. There is no idea of: Better Than, or Self; these abstractions are developed later through close observation of adult interaction. What Jesus was sharing, was the concept that if you can return to the innocent constitution and character of children, you can propagate temperance and modesty... qualities of BEing infinitely more becoming, important, beneficial and conducive to the true nature of Spiritual Life and the Love-Essence of God.

236

The twelfth axiom is referred to as **The Principle of Dominion.** God gave each of you wonderful authority over your personal world. This doesn't mean power, in the sense of ruling others, but total command and influence of and over your environment and over what you perceive as your reality. Creation is the outward [possibly physical] expression of thought. It is the producing of a situation or thing, accomplished by applied focus and will. Your mind may create a thought and the manifestation of that thought can be substance. All creation is based on a thing being generated, from the thought given them. Therefore, if you should dwell on any negative life experience, your thought patterns could manifest into the physical world in whatever terms and by many means, negatively.

Conversely, if your mind dwells on the positive aspects of life, then you may experience goodness around you instead; mental, emotional, physical, or spiritual goodness or any mixture thereof. Your mind is not your brain incidentally. Your brain is only a mortal part of your physical shell, it is only a discernment [bioelectrochemical] organ. It assists you in your basic physical senses and controls, and shares space with your mind.

Your mind, as a global definition, is that intangible apparatus which allows interpretation of your reality, the use of your extended capabilities, and is directly linked to your Higher Self and your God Presence. It is a mediator between the mental/physical intelligence and the spiritual intellect. It is non-physical, pure energy. IT, is the creator. The obvious commodity of the mind is easily recognized as thought.

A product of thought then, could be substance; but more importantly reality, as you believe it to be. Reality can be physical or intangible, or both and even more than these. You alone are the architect and designer of the thoughts you create or hold. When your thoughts are formulated by desire, and depending on the energy put into the thought, you may experience the effect as a physical manifestation, a solution to a problem or a resolved condition. These are all considered substance. You bring forth a 'thing' in response to a given thought.

You have two fundamental aspects of mind, the conscious up front deliberator and the subconscious behind the scenes motivator. Your conscious mind is the decision making part of your self. It has, as allowed by you, free will to do, or not do, any given thing. The conscious mind in turn, impresses your subconscious mind with conceptualized thought beliefs, which are then stored, manipulated, re-examined, re-evaluated, energized or acted upon.

Your subconscious mind never makes decisions based on the thoughts given it. It can not reason good or bad, it just responds to the types of energy given it, by thought from the conscious mind.

THE SIERRAVILLE EXPERIENCE

It can hold onto any given thought forever, or until another thought replaces it, as well as continuing to work on, modify or mold any given thought input. It can also take a thought, through the action of projection, and transmit it into the etheric-matter domains to become wholly manifest; assuming you have diligently met all the criteria in the right and proper way.

It is very important to remember, that the energy vibration behind your emotions does influence creation. Your emotions typically run strongest at times of emergency or crisis, but you can learn to intensify your emotions under normal circumstances and with practice. Understand that negative [-] or positive [+] feelings affect the thoughts to be made manifest, because of the potential [electro-motive charge of: - or + energies] attached to the projection BY the emotion. Realize then, that when proper and strong emotion is present, the greater the manifestation or materialization probability. If little emotion is involved, then perhaps nothing may be noticed due to the possibility that the thought projection might be Universally understood as: The initiator is not really serious.

You can utilize manifestation, properly structured of course, to alter and effect change in your lives, or others' situations, for fulfillment of particular needs or better conditions and circumstances. But one must remember that you do not act alone when you invoke the manifestation process... There is a cosmic hierarchy of Love which is involved as well. Therein lie checks and balances, weights and measures and supreme realizations which exist beyond your limited understandings, and are best comprehended from the Unseen. There exists a Greater Counsel of Interpretation, as it concerns cause and effect throughout the etheric strata of the Super-Universe and the interrelationships of the affected life forms, which includes the potential lessons learned for all involved.

The thirteenth postulate is referred to as **The Principle of Service**. Outside of Love, this is perhaps the most important criteria for spiritual growth. Service to others is usually regarded has having what you call: duty [strings attached]. You might say: If I do some 'thing' for you, you must do some 'thing' for me.

It is an accepted practice, a reward system or an expected attribute of a particular relationship, whether business or personal. The Principle of Service has nothing whatsoever to do with the requirements mandated by Terra-Man in the physical realm. It is predicated on the immaterial and ethereal aspects of life. It exemplifies the spiritual qualities within yourselves as it relates to caring, sharing and doing. It is the personal desire to help others without any need for compensation, reward or glory. It's being there when you are needed, and being available if such a time should arise.

238

If ever there were a time for you as Mankind to entertain this concept, it is now. You have little future remaining to enhance who you are, or who you can become in and on your present plane. WE do not suggest that there are certain times when it is more or less appropriate to offer of yourselves, for this axiom has no limitations or constraints associated with it... unless YOU allow them. The problem is, Man in general has! Ignoring the spiritual aspects of life and making excuses within the confines of the mental/physical plane, you tend to look only for the tangible benefit[s] of what YOU might stand to gain, as opposed to what might be gained by another entity receiving your help or guidance. With this insensitive blindfold on, you further fail to see the invaluable benefit to yourselves, in terms of spiritual comprehension and growth... the spiritual evolvement which takes place within you as you wantingly and freely give of yourselves.

The entity Jesus declared that: It is easier to pass a camel through the eye of a needle, than it is for a rich man to enter the Kingdom of Heaven... You may wonder what the term: a rich man, has to do with the concept of service? A rich man in this illustration is best understood to be focused only on [his] self gain. The concept of service plays no part in his behavioral makeup or philosophy. He has purposely become ignorant of the gentle and caring aspects of living life, thus dissolving his potential for growth toward divinity, self-realization, spiritual understandings and the associated and enhanced vibrational energies which come with that process.

Instead, he seeks power, control and riches; and of the variety only HE understands... for HIS pleasure, and in the PHYSICAL dimension. By doing so he unknowingly removes himself from ascension possibilities as an enlightened man... a truly spiritual entity or personality. He looses sight of the fact that the physical realm is only temporary. There is no internal quest for what lies beyond his limited scope of vision and selfish reality, either because it is for him conceptually, intangible, thus loosing it's importance and significance, or because he really doesn't care... a sad side effect of physical grounding.

WE use the term grounding to mean that condition, place, thought, energy or reality that you allow yourselves to be intensely and perhaps emotionally focused on at any particular moment, or even in general. Spiritual grounding is required for growth, WE pray you understand this everso important and powerful personal attribute. WE can not make this clear enough, nor strong enough... You must remain grounded in positive energies, deeds and thoughts. You must strive for excellence and harmony. You must become Love, and all the attributes it IS. Service unto others, is an exhibition of that Love comprehension. There can be no true spiritual advancement without service being an intrinsic part of your BEing.

THE SIERRAVILLE EXPERIENCE

WE will not coerce you, nor is it OUR obligation to direct you into spiritual evolvement. This process must be your choice, unto each of you alone. WE will however, guide and assist you whenever you should ask, as will others of the Light also do. Please allow US and yourselves the opportunity when, and if you have a need or desire to expand your consciousness.

TABLET 11

Vibrations of Alpha II, Book of Correction:

It is with your hands as to your very destiny; as it is within other similar realms. When once great entities of Light and knowledge cast forth question into these realms of consciousness, precipitating into being a focus of exalted significance of Self, it was then that a separation from your Source took place. Countless attempts have been made through the aeons, to bring Truth back into your and other realizations [other worlds].

All save a few hear, all save a few see. The discord which grows quadratically, and emanates from your and other affected planes have caused serious imbalance in the vibrations of the Universal Spheres of Life. The Overseers have been patient, waiting to find metamorphosis occurring within that of those of affected consciousness, yet it has failed to manifest to the needed potential. That potential which outweighs the darkness. Give heed, the vibrations of the Spheres must be made to align once again.

It would seem apparent, that many affected entities are unable to cast off their shells of self and attain a vibration [biosphere] based in harmony, by and of themselves. For this reason, certain vibrations in times to come may have to be released to aid in the termination of the ongoing stagnation of the affected growth cycles if declination continues. In your sector [some vast portion of the cosmos] an outcome may have to be exacted. Activities on many planes would be involved and would continue to be, if and once released. The vibrations held to be set loose, shall cause many ramifications. Of particular importance, will be the shift and division of entities toward firm implacement of their beliefs.

Up until the final moment of alteration, the decisions of all entities will be given free latitude as to their choice of direction. Should a majority vibration of Light be witnessed from your Sphere, the Cleansing Vibrations shall then have little impact as to effect. However, the accompanying Light bearing vibrations shall cause extensive and positive atomic changes within your particular system. These changes shall be as a commencement into knowledge and peace, predicated on your developing a desire to attain a higher plane of existence.

Should the necessary Light not be witnessed from your Sphere, the Cleansing Vibrations shall cause to take place dire disruptions within your strata [ecosystems] and physical plane. The negative influence of energies must be purged before the metamorphosis into Light can be made final. WE bring this information as a warning. There is time to reciprocate.

The efforts of all entities are being noted, as found in the aura surrounding your biosphere. This accumulation of energy is the outcome and result of the creative energies you have collectively poured forth into the ether. It is a saddening sight, yet not without prospect. It is because of your separation that you can not see this, nor understand the operation behind the impacts of the potentials of your individual and collective thoughts. You, are the solution. You, can undo the fragmentation. Yet should you look the other way, it shall ultimately be done for you in the name of higher principles.

This sector [local Universe] is at risk. It is liken unto a cart. If a wheel thereon looses a spoke, it will travel only so far before it collapses. A lack of action will eventually impede the mobility of the cart and disrupt the flow toward its destination. The sector WE speak of is approaching that situation even now. Therefore a repair may be eminent and must be accomplished before a collapse is allowed. It would occur not out of punishment, but in recognition of the requirements of the whole. Creative love vibration must be maintained... and in the name of love, ordered where purposefully absent.

WE petition you: Examine your options. Once the Vibrations of Order and Harmony are released, they shall not be recalled. They will seek out all affected planes and make known their presence. Be ye best prepared, and least surprised.

In closing,

Our continued and positive soul expansion is extremely important. In order to progress however, we may require various forms of input or guidance to assist us in our journey; yet balance within, is mandatory before growth can occur.

This path is made much easier when we first choose to resolve various issues we may be holding onto from our past or the present, by making sincere decisions to modify or change our thought patterns, behavioral or other attitudes within ourselves, as necessary, by seeking out positive influences and vibrations while letting go of any negative ones, and by opening our hearts to the gentle and perfected love-direction from above.

Consider what you could do with even greater information about who you are. You ARE important, and very special to the rest of us. Imagine the wonders you could experience, by giving yourself a chance to do so with further development or refinement of your unique spirit and capabilities.

Investigate all avenues of spiritual knowledge. You never know when you might come across those very special people or pieces of information which will reveal greater truth for yourself, and which may allow you to appreciate and understand how infinitely grand (ego not included) we all really are.

I wish you well in your self-awareness travels and pray for your spiritual awakening. Make an effort to find quiet times to be by yourself. Open your mind and heart to receive. Then patiently listen... you *will* find the personal guidance you require if you desire it badly enough. May God bless you.

LUCILLE SNYDER

Lucille began to get deeply involved with the spiritual aspect of life when she was only 15 years old. Dedicating her studies to all aspects of holistic healing, she is now professionally regarded as a Reiki (pronounced Ray-key) Master. She utilizes an Aura Camera in her Reiki classes, to monitor the progress and triune life-form changes (spiritual, mental and physical) in her clients, for both the clients' specific validation of the healing process(es) and professional evidential documentation.

She is also well known for her work as an Holistic Health Therapist and a Certified Massage Therapist. She utilizes Color Therapy, Vivation Breathwork, Hypnosis and Creative Visualization techniques in her counseling of holistic healing.

In her work, she has traveled extensively throughout the United States and other countries. In London, as an example, she has done much research with AIDs and cancer patients. Her findings prove without a doubt, that given the right information and tools, a person *can* affect positive changes from within their own being and cause healing to occur.

In the last two years, she has primarily shared and demonstrated the holistic and physiological utility of the Aura Spectrophotometer 2100 at spiritually and holistically inclined meetings, conventions and seminars in the United States. In her travels, Lucille teaches holistic techniques, heals, and informs people of their own personal abilities and potentials.

With her camera, Lucille personally interprets such things as *special talent(s), communication ability, emotions, spiritual capabilities, health, spiritual awareness, grounding, open channels (Chakras), energy vibrations and patterns, intellectual and spiritual growth* from the special pictures of her clients.

She sincerely believes that the use of this type of camera, in conjunction with proper holistic instructional techniques, will greatly benefit medicine as we know it today. Many others also share in her vision, of one day seeing more of these fantastic tools made available to qualified interpreters; and particularly physicians, due to the medical community recognizing the vast benefits provided by this type of equipment and knowledge.

Wherever there is a need for personal healing (physically, mentally or spiritually, or a combination of these) she connects with the Source, to identify for the client the specific areas to work on, and what needs to occur in their lives to allow that or those specific healings to take place.

LUCILLE SYNDER

She notes: "Wherever we look in spiritual study, we find multiple references to *light* and *color* with respect to the inner nature of Man. The 'aura', is the external indicator of the well-being and development of one's potential, spiritual connection, and vibrancy of one's own soul. You may not always be able to *physically* (un-aided vision) see auras, but just being aware of the reality of their existence, ***especially our own***, is an important aspect of becoming 'centered'. Those viewing their own aura for the first time by camera, are usually very excited about what they are witnessing."

"The information offered by a personal reading allows an individual a fascinating look into who they really are and they seem to joyously share every detail of the interpretation with others. For many of the individuals, it is an enormous release and validation of their emotions, feelings, visions and talents. Many others continually return to obtain further pictures to monitor their own development and growth. To watch these people heal themselves and spiritually evolve, is personally satisfying and exciting."

Lucille is dedicated to, and enjoys helping people get in touch with themselves for the creation of healing from within, to achieve their highest possible potential and in aiding with their personal transformational journey. She is in the process of writing an in-depth book on the subject of Aura Photography, which includes viable ramifications relating to human wellness.

Lucille is available to personally counsel at your home or business with an advanced and pre-arranged appointment when she is not traveling. She and her Aura Photography equipment are also available for workshops, lectures or fairs. Call for details. (Taking personal notes or tape recording the aura interpretation is permitted and recommended.)

For more information contact Lucille, presently at:

Universal Energy Awareness
2891 Herbert Way
Sacramento, California 95821
Telephone number: 1-916-484-6875

BASIC AURA COLORATIONS

Reader Note:

Coloration of *your* specific aura, and where the colors appear, have a unique and special meaning for only yourself, as an *individual*.

The aura is dynamically 'alive' and constantly reflects the thought energy you are generating at any given moment. Therefore, it is actually possible to obtain several consecutive photographs, each displaying different patterns and colors, associated with the various thought-energies you may have held during each picture taking process.

A person can *not* generate a particular color image by simply thinking it however; a person has to *be* emanating that (particular) energy at the time the picture is taken. In other words, a false picture isn't possible to create... The camera, like the aura, never lies.

The following color definitions are *examples,* and reflect only that... *possible and generic explanations* of often seen pigmentations in the auretic veil. Do not assume that these descriptions are cast in concrete, they are not. They only represent typical definitions, based on thousands of auretic studies by various individuals, and can be used as a common, but well founded basis for developing an interpretation for any given auretic energy pattern.

Only through the guidance of a *qualified* interpreter, can an individual gain proper insight to what the colors truly mean for themselves. As an example, a certain color appearing in one person's aura, may have an entirely different meaning for another person also having the same color in their aura. Each picture with it's specific coloration, is as unique as the individual it is of.

The colors which appear are infinite in spectrum and range in *contrast* from dull and muddy, to highly refined and luminescent; and from *appearances* of ragged splotches, to bands and veils, to Living Lights in motion.

Lastly, and as a supplementary point of interest, it is estimated that only around one percent (1%) of our spiritual-self energy, or astral body, is visible as our aura! (The remainder resides as our astral counter-part or our overselves, which lies beyond present physical-examination techniques or abilities to study.)

Our astral body continually interpermeates our physical bodies during all waking hours and is the vehicle least understood and yet most representative of our true life form.

The following pages discuss the basic colors associated with an aura picture:

iv

BASIC AURA COLORATIONS

B L A C K S

Black can often mean emotional self-protection or shields, or indicate physical, mental or spiritual imbalances. Black coloration appearing as auretic 'holes' or auretic 'tears' can also mean you were abused somehow or that you may be an abuser. (Abuse is not limited to only the physical.) Black 'clouds' often indicate hatred or malice, or that you may hold, carry or otherwise have hidden secrets which you would be embarrassed over, if they were made public.

B R O W N S

Brown coloration's can indicate areas of *physical* abnormalities or indicate problem areas of the physical body. They can also mean that you are establishing new 'roots', or experiencing new growth. Further, browns can indicate your desire to accomplish, or that you have industrial or organizational abilities. Lastly, they can indicate physical, mental, or spiritual *energy* imbalances.

P I N K S

The duller or 'muddier' the shade can indicate immaturity. Pinks can also indicate modesty, a new love, compassion, purity, joy or the love and appreciation of beauty, or the arts, such as music or literature. It is also the color of female creative energy. Vibrant pink is the color applied for overall (mental, physical, emotional and spiritual) healing.

R E D S

Lurid red can mean sensuality, scarlet can mean irritability, dull brown/gray red can indicate selfishness and rusty red can mean a desire to covet or greediness. Crimson reds can indicate selfish love. Purple/reds can indicate great passion or will, with the darker shades indicating a need to overcome something. The 'muddier' shades can reflect feelings of being misunderstood, a requirement for sympathy or an overbearingness.

Bright reds can reflect exuberance, high emotions or determination. Brilliant reds (sometimes tinged with lilac) can indicate unselfishness love or spiritual love. Rose colors indicate love or affection and bright, clear reds can indicate dynamic life-force energy.

Muddier red spots, streaks or splotches can indicate imbalances, nervous energy, aggression, anger, resentment, unresolved negative emotions and or conflicts, or even misplaced passion. Certain reds around the edges of the aura can indicate that a person is getting ready to let go of something.

BASIC AURA COLORATIONS

ORANGES

Orange can indicate health, vitality, or the ability to manifest or that the person is adventurous. It also represents creativity, healing capabilities, courage and open socialness or that the individual is in the process of 'doing'. The duller the color is, is a good indication of ambition or pride.

YELLOWS

Yellow energy in general represents the emotions, the ability to sensitively 'feel', or absorb knowledge. Pale yellows can indicate awakening psychic abilities or optimism. Clear yellow often means mental activity, wisdom or intellect.

Dingy yellows can indicate jealousy or suspicion. Brown yellows can infer anxiety, worry, depression, frustration, mental stress or negativity. Orange yellows indicate strong communication capabilities.

GREENS

Bright green, moving towards the blue spectrum, can indicate healing capabilities or abundance. Clear greens can mean vitality, growth, transition, change, prosperity, regeneration or cellular healing. Emerald greens can indicate ingenuity, versatility, or resourcefulness. Dark green can mean envy and olive (drab) or duller (muddier) greens can indicate cunning or deceit.

BLUES

Lighter blues can indicate that a person is recognizing their abilities and are opening their creative channels, intuition, creativity or imagination. Darker blues can indicate devotion or control. Aquamarines can indicate learning, growth from within, transformation, nobility or spiritual idealism.

Dull or muddy blues can indicate a person is feeling 'down', has border line depression or that an individual is saddened. Powder blues can indicate male creative energy.

Blues (typically the clearer the better) can reflect regeneration, spirituality or sincerity and royal blues tend to indicate honesty. Blues with a hint of violet indicate either devotion or affection, with the more lilac/blues indicating higher spirituality or spiritual aspirations.

BASIC AURA COLORATIONS

VIOLETS

Violet most often represents high spirituality and proper understanding and use of Universal Laws. Violet can also indicate artistic capabilities, intuitiveness or psychic or spiritual capabilities or understandings. Violets can also indicate personal independence, warmth or transmutation.

Further, they can indicate your practicality, 'worldliness', or the blending of the physical and the spiritual (heart and mind). Paler violets indicate humility or spiritual awareness. Indigo colors can indicate wisdom or integrity.

Ultraviolets can indicate the higher and purer developments of psychic abilities. Purple indicates the love of humanity and understanding of Divine Principles.

SILVERS

Silver is the color of creativity or evolving *creation*. When silver specks or lights can be seen within other color patterns, it can be a clue that something very beneficial is close at hand to occurring. Lighter silver colors can also mean intuitive abilities, spiritual illumination or imaginative capabilities.

(It has also been suggested, that the aura of a pregnant woman may emanate bright silver orb-like flashes, which attracts the attention of a soul who wishes to re-incarnate. That soul then, having become attracted to the new mother, can assess the family members and environment to see if the physical, mental and spiritual patterns and conditions coincide with what that soul needs for proper and continued soul-growth. If the data meets that souls criteria, it may attach itself to the child prior to birth; if not, it will seek another opportunity elsewhere, giving some other soul desiring re-incarnation a chance to evaluate this situation.)

GRAYS

The darker shades of gray may indicate various imbalances within your being, a secretive personality, or possibly that you enjoy the 'lone-wolf' way of life. It can also indicate depression. The more livid the gray is, can also indicate active fear. It can also mean that you are in motion toward the releasing or utilizing the innate capabilities within yourself.

Gray is also the color of the 'initiate', or new-comer (spiritually speaking).

BASIC AURA COLORATIONS

WHITES

White indicates a strong spiritual connection to the God Source. It indicates pure intellect and spiritualness. Whites also indicate overall purity or the 'cleansing' and purification of ones self, as well as the emergence or awakening of greater creativity. White is the color of truth and balance.

White colors can be hidden or 'drowned out' by other colors when a person is busy using other mental or physical energies. When a person is feeling spiritual peace, meditates or prays, the white colors become noticeable, expand and become clearer, brighter and 'sharper'.

Infants and young children often have only white in their auras, as they still represent absolute purity. They haven't been subjected to the ways of negativity or knowledge of self or other less-spiritual learned behavior or thinking patterns.

GOLDS

Gold is most distinguishable around the crown chakra, or head, as in the case of Jesus and other highly evolved entities. A dull shading can mean you are in the process of your spiritual awakening. The brighter the shade can indicate you are coming into your realization and utilization of your power.

Golds also indicate strong enthusiasm, inspiration, harmony and devotion. Gold colors typically represent dynamic spiritual energy.

AURA PHOTOGRAPHY

The Aura Spectrophotometer 2100 Camera

The Aura Spectrophotometer Camera was developed by Reverend Scott Salmon, a psychic minister and scientist, over an eight to ten year period. The Aura Camera is a State-of-the-Art camera and is the newest technological development in the field of Aura Photography.

The study of the human aura (the electro-magnetic energy field around the body) is of great importance in this day and age. More and more people are taking to heart the reality of, and are desirous of investigating, the fascinating energy field that surrounds them.

All living things have an aura, even the Earth herself. The human aura is to the mind of man, as his bloodstream is to his physical body. Vastly important and basically inseparable. As with all things, each is made up of energy and vibrates at its' own level, as proven by Dr. Einstein. So it is with a person's aura.

The revolutionary camera designed by Reverend Salmon incorporates the latest micro-technology in electronics, software and electro-magnetic energy sensors available today. The sensors are located in a specialized hand plate, which enables the highly specialized camera computer to translate the levels of the vibrations within the aura, to corresponding colors and patterns.

The camera and related electronics actually measure the electro-magnetic energy field through a persons hand, as represented by the energy meridians, based on the science of acupuncture. The energy sensed at each of these meridians vibrates at different frequencies, and thusly is represented by a unique color for each frequency sensed.

These colors and patterns are then reproduced on a high quality color Polaroid photograph, and are seen located around the person having the picture taken. The color images of the aura in the photograph, reflect *that* individual's personal and unique energy fields, at *that* moment.

One or more colors will be noticed, as smudges or splotches of color, veils of color or possibly extremely defined patterns of 'Living Lights', or even a combination of these. Sometimes spiritual symbols, as well as other spiritual entities are seen within the picture.

AURA PHOTOGRAPHY

The photograph is then interpreted by a studied and competent color therapist, to obtain the maximum amount of information from the auric data. The colors captured on the film and *where* they are located, have special meaning only for the person having the picture analyzed.

The colors can reflect much in the way of information, as it relates to our physical, mental and spiritual selves. Further, the colors can (and do) change from minute to minute, depending on where our *focus* lies at the time the photograph is taken.

After interpretation, the Polaroid picture is presented to the individual to keep. It should be noted, as an individual, you may want to bring a small recorder with you, in order to have the interpreted information at your later disposal and for review.

PIT RIVER INDIAN NATION

Based on recorded facts, the Pit River Indians were first discovered and documented by Peter Skene Ogden and his exploration team, in 1826. Mr. Ogden was the leader of Hudson's Bay Company, which based their enterprise on the trapping and fur industry. The Native Americans they came across not far from Mt. Shasta, were as then unknown.

The unlikely meeting between these Indians and several of Mr. Ogden's scouts unfolds as almost humorous. Two Indian boys were out in a wooded area by themselves and came across two white men on horses. Stunned with fear, the boys stayed in the cover of the brush and watched in horror. Horses were an unknown animal, as were white beings and the sight of a two headed, multiple limbed monsters left the young men feeling that they had uncovered grotesque and sinister entities.

The riders wore clothing very different from what the boys were accustom to and it was thought that this was their skin. The riders' eyes protruded from faces that were heavily bearded and accompanied by long hair. The boys trailed the scouts until they stopped for a rest, then watched in shock as the entities physically separated. *"What manner of beings can do this thing?"* *"Surely they must be evil ones"* the boys thought.

The scouts then began to prepare a meal for themselves and later sensed the boys hiding in the ground cover. The men called out to the boys in an attempt to offer them something to eat. Eventually, their extensions of friendship were answered. Feeling inquisitive and now somewhat relaxed since the 'beings' had made no aggressive action towards them, the boys slowly ventured into the scouts' campsite.

The men generously offered them plates of bacon with rind and beans. Never having seen such things, the boys' imaginations ran wild. The beans must surely be from the insides of a living thing, maybe a man, and the rind appeared to them as human skin. The boys felt these white beings had to be cannibals. They took the plates and ran off, quickly burying the food (for spiritual safety sake) and speedily made their way back to the elders of their Indian nation.

Based on what the elders learned from the boys, it was suggested that no other contact be made with these strange and possibly dangerous beings. Therefore, few sightings of these Native Americans were ever made by Mr. Ogden's party.

PIT RIVER INDIAN NATION

It was later concluded, that these people had a special means of hunting game, particularly big game. Since the Indians were aware that various animals gathered along the closeby rivers for water and food, they dug pits along the river banks in order to entrap these animals. After they had dug the pits and prepared them, they would cleverly cover and camouflage the openings.

At the bottom of many of the pits however, were many pointed stakes seated into the ground. As the animals fell into the pits, they would be caught upon the stakes, securing them and keeping them from escaping. Some of the pits were shallow, for smaller game, some were very deep. Deep enough in one case to have caused the unknowing Mr. Ogden, to completely loose a valuable horse and rider into. The rider was pulled from the pit unharmed, unfortunately, the same could not be said for his horse.

Thus, Mr. Ogden inventively named the river the 'Pit' River. He would then proceed to document it so future travelers and explorers would not fall prey to the well hidden traps. Eventually, the name given to the local inhabitants was the Pit River Indians and has held to this day. The adopted name seemed quite natural at the time, due to their hunting methods and the location of their settlement. This Indian Nation is actually known as the Ahjumawi. Ahjumawi (Aw-joo-maw-we) in native dialect means 'Where the waters fall together'.

The Pit River Indian Nation has a symbol which is very meaningful to them. It is an upside down triangle, with a dot in the middle of it. Historically, it is interpreted as follows:

In the beginning, there were many great spirit beings before there was an earth, or life on earth. During creation, the first land-mass was formed from the material and foam tossed around and up by the great primordial sea. As they deposited, they formed an island in the shape of an upside down triangle upon the waters. As time went by, this land-mass enlarged and became a super continent. Eventually, this super land-mass split apart to drift and become the various land masses we now know today.

The great creative spirit father, Hewisi Tahkahday Hadachi (Hey-we-see Taw-kaw-day Haw'-daw-chee) is remembered by the upside down triangle symbol with a dot in the center. The symbol represents the One Above and the World's Heart (or Center). The prophecies left behind in the petroglyphs in Northern California for other peoples who came into the world, are left as a reminder that they must never forget his teachings or him.

Miscellaneous Note:

Across from the Big Dipper and the North Star in the night sky, is the constellation of Cassiopeia. If you look closely, you will find three stars that form a bright triangle. A fourth star once resided brightly in the center of that triangle. In all nations and religions of peoples, there is a proclamation which reminds us of the spiritual and physical connection between Man and his God, many will recognize it as simply: "As above, so below".

The Ahjumawi, as all other intact Indian Nations, are highly spiritual people. As an example, they feel that no-one owns any part of Mother Earth, and that She and Grandfather blesses all with the necessary gifts which enable life to be enjoyed and sustained. A person of such knowledge would never take from Her without first asking permission, and then, giving thanks for what they had received.

There are many ceremonies which various nations use to communicate with their spirit providers and protectors, to ask for blessings, healings, and offer gratitude for examples. Rain Dances are real, as are Medicine Men and Women, or those in whom exists great metaphysical and spiritual knowledge and inner wisdom and understanding. Sadly, as many Indian Nations fade away, others struggle to maintain and teach the knowledge of their ancestors for future generations.

What was originally taught by weavings, paintings and mostly the verbal word to only a special few to perpetuate tradition, is coming to an end in many circumstances. More than not, the young inner-tribal 'chosen' have taken other career paths and in many cases, the tribal history and knowledge has been entirely lost (because of the lack of interest within the young of the various nations) when their aged Shamans passed on. Only now is great awareness and effort under way to understand and preserve their ways and teachings through the written word, and audio and visual tapes.

If you are interested in knowing more about any particular Indian Nation or their history, I would urge you to attend the public Pow-Wows and spiritual ceremonies in or near your area. Talk with the Elders, each nation's history is impressive. Seek to understand who these unique people really are. They are no different from any other nation on earth, save that they perhaps enjoy a fuller comprehension of who they are and their relationship with all other life, here in the physical and beyond.

SIERRA HOT SPRINGS

In the Sierra mountains, 25 miles North of Truckee, the pine trees of the Tahoe National Forest spill down to the edge of a spacious and broad alpine valley, and the community of Sierraville. Just to the East, lies Sierra Hot Springs, a holistic place regarded for centuries by Native Americans, as sacred healing grounds. Hike, camp or explore the 600 acres of secluded forest, or you may relax in the various mineral waters, with temperatures ranging from 96 to 108 degrees. Experience massage and other health treatments from certified practitioners.

The New Age Church of Being manages the Springs and are the proprietors of the associated property. They are a non-profit, spiritual organization dedicated to the preservation, renovation and protection of this cherished and sacred land, while ensuring its availability to the public. Non-denominational weekly gatherings, monthly Full Moon ceremonies, as well as Equinox, Solstice and other special gatherings, are open to everyone.

The office is open from 9 A.M. until 4 P.M. Monday thru Friday, and until 6 P.M. on the weekends. Lodge and Dormitory rooms are European style and it is advisable to make reservations one week in advance. Day visits and campers are also welcome. Work exchange programs may sometimes be available, so ask about them. Yearly or life-time memberships are also available for those so interested. The restaurant serves buffet-style vegetarian dinners on Friday and Saturday nights. A vegetarian brunch is served on Saturday, Sunday and all holidays. For traditional meals, there are restaurants in Sierraville (a 2 mile drive) and Loyalton (12 miles away).

Smoking is limited to the smoking area next to the parking lot and alcohol is not permitted by the Springs. Pets are not allowed in or by the Springs area in consideration and for the protection of the wildlife found there.

From Truckee (Highway 80), go North on Highway 89 to the Sierraville stop sign (the roadway "T"s), and turn right. Drive approximately 1/2 mile to Lemon Canyon Road and turn right again. Turn right (the very next right) on Campbell Hot Springs Road, which ends up at the lodge, about one mile away.

For more information or reservations,
Call: (916) 994-3773 during office hours, or write to:
Sierra Hot Springs, P.O. BOX 366, Sierraville, California 96126.

Among many intriguing experiences I've had, a simple but perplexing thought was delivered to my heart-mind consciousness in the summer of 1971. This particular thought held the understanding of: "You are to generate a meaningful written work, yet not at this time; It awaits a foundation." This input was accompanied with the emotional feeling that it would be based on a spiritually oriented man. I warmly and excitedly embraced the thought, but questioned it due to the fact that non-technical writing was not of particular interest to me, I understood the term spiritual to mean vigorously religious, and I was not a historian of such things. And what exactly did the expression 'foundation' represent?

Although I was raised in a religious environment (believing in a Supreme BEing), I was still *spiritually* 'unconscious'. That is, even though I felt I had a spiritual heart, I had not yet been presented with certain mind expanding material which would impart to me certain information on spirituality which I was lacking. Being aware then that there had to be more to life, I deeply wanted to know what it was; but where would I find substantial, if not absolute answers? The fact was, as much as I earnestly wanted to know I just wasn't ready yet. The foundation *was* absent...

Twenty-two years passed, and my life had taken many turns. Answers *were* eventually revealed during this time, and thus allowed me to become spiritually *awakened*. During the course of one ordinary work day I was suddenly moved and mentally urged to put everything aside... Clear my desk and clear my mind. I did as instructed, as I was now able to 'hear', or more appropriately, 'listen'. The long forgotten thought of a written work suddenly rushed back up to the forefront of my mind accompanied by a strong mental impression: "It is time; You have the necessary material." At the time I had no idea exactly what I was to do, but I picked up my pen and contemplated the many experiences I've encountered and the multitude of insights I had gained.

I tried to invoke several scenarios, but nothing came. My note pad remained conspicuously empty of content, for three challenging days. I then embarrassingly remembered, I (as and of myself) could do nothing of a spiritual work. All blessings come from *Above*, as does the basis for **all** spiritual guidance. So I acknowledged my untiring spirit counselors and asked them to work through me *if* this project was in fact suppose to be.

I prepared myself to receive and the direction to "just start typing" came through. My fingers began moving over the keyboard without my consciously directing them. A familiar narrative immediately unfolded, so I collected some old notes. The work contained events and information I had been shown or witness to in the areas surrounding Sierraville from many trips there.

AUTHORS STORY

New or expanded data also came forth as I (we) sat at the computer. I became more excited. I knew then that I was being assisted from the etheric planes of thought! There was an 'unseen' heaviness on my hands as the words came. At times there was a even sensation of a band of pressure about 1 inch wide over my eyebrows, from temple to temple. Most noticeable over the area of what is referred to as our third or 'inner' eye. I now know this to be the 'signature' of Wantanka.

When it seemed the writing was finished I had an unexpected 'guest'. His stay was brief but quite inspiring. My visitor appeared as a six inch or so ball of bright White Light that arched down from mid-ceiling, over my computer and printer; then "*he*" dissipated upward. It was as though he came to say "I AM with you" and "We are not done with this project, there is yet more to do." Directly after that moment came the concept for some other material.

After I had documented those thoughts, I generated the appendix for the present material. As a final step, I debated with myself as to whether or not to include certain events which had transpired prior to the creation of this material. I decided that it would be better not to share the mitigating circumstances; after all, who on the 'outside' would really understand? Thusly, my first rendition was void of particular entries.

For some time afterward however, there persisted a sensation that kept bubbling to the surface of my consciousness: "*They* (you, the readers) *need to know!*" I couldn't shake this feeling... it was ever present.

In months of labored retrospect I concluded that perhaps without the true and factual prologue and the inclusion of various transcripts, one could not share in my enthusiasm nor could one appreciate the value of the material given me to distribute. Wantanka was right, we *weren't* finished! So to those whom might be touched in special ways on various levels of intuitiveness, for you, I (we?) have resolved to include the supplementary material.

In recalling Shakespeare: "There are more things in Heaven and Earth Horatio, than are dreamt of in your philosophy." I have often wondered, what other information did this remarkable man have access to that he didn't know quite how to share, interpret or disclose...?

My hope, is you the reader, can develop a higher sensitivity and understanding about yourself and others so that you might be able to experience more in your life and possibly even recognize the special spiritual personalities around *you*. Truly, there are many such beautiful and waiting entities among us. In my heart I believe the enlightening material and wisdom offered in this book to be accurate and extremely important for our *collective* spiritual growth and the future welfare and development of Mankind on Earth.

AUTHORS STORY

With ever more information now available to us to teach us how to live spiritually, interpreting it and *doing it* still seems to be somewhat complex. Especially when we lack fundamental and educational information on what it all really means for us; and more importantly, how to *apply* ourselves.

Therefore, through various circumstances a multitude of information was made available in this publication. This knowledge was offered to allow the reader to have an opportunity to expand their understanding on the diverse subject of spiritual advancement, as well as a few other semi-interrelated topics, and particularly, of the importance behind the ongoing Spiritual Transmutation of Man as it concerns the *already* active Universal Changes.

As a follow-up point of interest:

Nearly one year after this book was originally finished I learned of an African American who was warmly accepted and taken in by the Native Americans who lived in the surrounding mountain area of Sierraville long ago. This particular man was later to become a spiritual teacher and medicine man.

He was known to many simply as: *Beckwourth*.

For this author, the odds of this piece of actual history being just a coincidence as it relates to the personage of Mr. Beckworth, is incalculable and further substantiates for me the significance of the material I am sharing.

CONTACT INFORMATION

If you would like to contact Thomas to share personal experiences, present information or questions, or to make a request to be added to a prayer list, you may do so through the publisher:

Quantum T.G., P.O. Box 12103, Reno, Nevada 89510-2103

Any *positive* thoughts or input you have to offer are important. All efforts will be taken to respond to any personalized letter so received.

Please allow for appropriate elapsed mailing and correspondence time, and if applicable, enclose a self addressed and stamped envelope (SASE) of business size (#10).

Additional copies of this book may be obtained from the publisher for $15/USA (money-order/cashiers check), which includes shipping. Also, should any reader discover a typographical error, a written notice to the publisher would be greatly appreciated. Thank You.

VISION

I've seen a vision and it beckons me,
It is what I have prayed so long to see;

A life in Light that shines so strong,
It is that sphere which has no wrong;

Even closer now, it's presence I can feel,
Soon to be here, we'll know that it's real;

For so many like me, this I can say,
It's difficult waiting to embrace that day.

WHAT I CAN DO

I Seek To Find God In All Things.

I Am Humble And Gentle In My Ways.

I Give Of Myself Whenever The Opportunity Exists.

I Generate Vibrations of Harmony Wherever I May Be.

I Live In Peace; With Myself, And Others.

I Allow Other's Their Right To BE, And Accept Their
Expression Of Those Rights.

I Find Love In All That I See. I Give Love Unconditionally.

I Hold And Project Only Kind And Peaceful Thoughts.

I Find Positive Meaning In All That I Do Or Experience.

I Display Compassion Freely.

I Place My Significance Ahead Of No-one.

I Seek Divine Realization, And Am All That I Can Be.

I Desire With All My Heart, A Relationship With My Source.

I Know That I Am Of God, And I Am Truly And Deeply Loved.

I AM MORE

When I AM sees GOD in all things;

When I AM knows of no boundaries or limitations;

When I AM feels compassion in all that it does;

When I AM can deny of no one;

When I AM focuses not on the Self, but on the whole;

When I AM precipitates harmony in each thought;

When I AM moves in accordance with all Cosmic Laws;

When I AM realizes that its' consciousness IS;

When I AM is controlled of no thing;

When I AM believes reality is manifest through desire;

When I AM is secured that there is no such thing as lack;

When I AM judges not, either wrong nor right;

When I AM visualizes that each path is walked only unto itself;

When I AM compares not itself with any other;

When I AM understands that it is of GOD;

When I AM awakens to why I AM,

I AM may wonder why this entity waited so long to be <u>more</u>...

THAT... I AM

ABOUT THE AUTHOR

"Thomas" has had multiple dozens of paranormal experiences beginning in the eighth year of this physical life, by his accounting. Born in the early 1950's, his experiences grew not only in significance, but quantity as the years have passed. Many of his childhood experiences were initially unquestioned and taken for granted, yet others in later years left deep questions within him as to the why's and how's. Experiences have ranged from simple precognition and extrasensory perception, to mental communication with animals, sensing other peoples thoughts over hundreds of miles, to extremely close encounters with ethereal and other entities, and nearby sightings of extraterrestrial spacecraft.

Beginning in 1969, he began reading all the metaphysical-type material he could get his hands on. Yet even with a multitude of experiences occurring yearly, he still didn't understand what was really behind it all. He now realizes the experiences were for his benefit... The special glimpses into unknown realms, the occasional activation of dormant energies and untapped gifts were the awakening signals for him to go 'within' and find his Higher Self and come to a more complete understanding of the true reality of his persona, existence and BEing.

Realizing that the unique encounters weren't occurring *to* him from outside random energies, but rather stemmed from some unidentified basis *within* himself, he joyfully admits he came into his 'own' in the year of 1989 after broadening his scope of what 'could be'. Having always had a very open mind, he feels this particular trait provided him with a good conduit for these special experiences to manifest. He continues steadfastly in his quest for subsequent enlightenment.

Further, he acknowledges that "Without hesitation or doubt, God does provide ALL blessings, and is the only true Source of power within us all." He gives total credit to our creator for his unique personal experiences relating to overself melding, participating in the special healing of others, the increased sensitivity of his hands for investigative and other work, the increased awareness of ethereal lights around people, and many other 'miracles'. On various occasions he believes he has been purposefully allowed to capture on 35mm film of various types and speeds what he believes is his immediate guide as a semi-circular formation of undulating white light. Tangible proof to him, of the intangible.

Thomas is frequently involved (at times with other spiritual associates) for the benefit of others in many fashions; from identifying discarnate energies, sending wayward spirits to the Light, working with emotional and physical aspects of a person's well-being, to providing spiritual counseling.